T0362205

ISLAM
AND ECONOMIC POLICY

ISLAM
AND ECONOMIC POLICY

• • •

RODNEY WILSON

EDINBURGH
University Press

© Rodney Wilson, 2015

Edinburgh University Press Ltd
The Tun – Holyrood Road
12 (2f) Jackson's Entry
Edinburgh EH8 8PJ
www.euppublishing.com

Typeset in 10/12.5pt Sabon by
Servis Filmsetting Ltd, Stockport, Cheshire,
and printed and bound in Great Britain by
CPI Group (UK) Ltd, Croydon CR0 4YY

A CIP record for this book is available from the British Library

ISBN 978 0 7486 8387 1 (hardback)
ISBN 978 0 7486 8388 8 (paperback)
ISBN 978 0 7486 8389 5 (webready PDF)
ISBN 978 0 7486 8391 8 (epub)

The right of Rodney Wilson to be identified as author of this work
has been asserted in accordance with the Copyright, Designs and
Patents Act 1988 and the Copyright and Related Rights
Regulations 2003 (SI No. 2498).

CONTENTS

TABLES

PART ONE

• • •

IDEAS, THEMES AND MEASURES

There is a growing literature on conceptual and theoretical issues in Islamic economics, but there has been no attempt to examine how far this might have relevance for economic policy in the Organisation of Islamic Cooperation (OIC) member states. This was partly because Islamist political parties were suppressed and excluded from government policy debates. The parties were more concerned about how they could attain power than how it would be used if they were ever able to participate in government. The Islamic revolution in Iran, the election of the Justice and Development Party in Turkey, and the coming to power of Islamists after the Arab Spring raised hopes of a change in the political landscape in the Middle East which could have had ramifications for the entire Muslim world.

Developments since the Arab Spring have revealed that the old order was more resilient than many believed. The Muslim Brotherhood failed to address the economic challenges in Egypt during their brief period in power, and paid a heavy price as the military once again took over and proceeded to suppress the Islamists. In Turkey, the Justice and Development Party continues to command much popular support, but the reluctance of Recep Tayyip Erdoğan to cede power and his increasingly autocratic tendencies threaten to undermine his undoubted success in managing the economy. In Iran, despite over four decades of Islamist rule, poor management brought the economy near to collapse, especially under Mahmoud Ahmadinejad, the controversial sixth president of the Islamic republic. The economic implications of these failures will be analysed in Part Two of this book, as they raise fundamental questions about how far Islam can be viewed as exceptional in terms of political economy, and whether being a Muslim majority state makes any difference to economic policy-making.

To understand how economic policy can be shaped by Islamic teaching it is necessary to appreciate what it involves. The first part of this study therefore provides a survey of the ideas, themes and concepts found in the literature on Islamic economics. Most aspects are covered from Islamic economic critiques of mainstream economics to alternative economic paradigms, notably the possibility to transform capitalism into a moral system informed by Islamic ideals. At the micro-economic level, the governance of business in a manner that is respectful to *Shari'ah* is explored, while at the macro-economic level consideration is given to the role of *zakat* and the extent to which it complements or partially replaces conventional fiscal policy. It is stressed that there is no single economic policy prescription which Islamists endorse. Rather, *Shari'ah* teaching provides general moral principles against which, for example, the merits of proportional versus progressive taxation can be considered, as well as the priority given to social expenditures rather than spending on security and defence.

In the first part of the book comparative country data is presented to demonstrate the economic diversity of OIC member states, the implication being that there can be no single policy fix for such contrasting economies. Data on the leading companies in the OIC is analysed in the chapter on micro-economic policy, while the discussion of macro-economic policy is backed up by data on government revenue and expenditure, as well as inflation and unemployment statistics. As the OIC states are classified as developing economies, there is a separate chapter on development policy, with the relationship between development and religion explored. Measures of development are discussed, including not only the widely used statistics on gross domestic product (GDP) per capita, but also the variables used by the New Economic Foundation such as life expectancy and well-being, which arguably have more relevance for the populations of OIC countries. Impediments to development are also quantified for OIC countries, including the lack of protection for property rights and corruption, matters of considerable concern for Islamic economists who condemn dishonest malpractices.

As paid-up members of many international economic organisations, Muslim majority countries have choices about which of these to prioritise in terms of budgetary and diplomatic support. Do Islamists favour the OIC and its affiliates such as the Islamic Development Bank (IDB) rather than, for example, an ethnic- and language-based organisation such as the Arab League? The OIC encompasses all eight countries whose economic policies are evaluated in this guide, as well as the members of the Gulf Cooperation Council (GCC). One issue is how far ideas on economic policy are transmitted between OIC states. Iran's policies are shown to have little influence on neighbouring states, whereas many regard Turkey as a more attractive example to follow. The ideas of the Islamist political parties associated with the Arab Spring were clearly influential across North Africa, at least in the short term. However, the banning of the Muslim Brotherhood in Egypt, and the financial support given by Saudi Arabia and the United Arab Emirates (UAE) to the subsequent military-backed regime has curtailed the transmission of the ideas associated with the revolutions to other countries in the Arab world and beyond.

The data in the chapter on international economic engagement reveals that while the economies of many OIC countries are quite open for trade and investment, economic links between OIC countries remain weak. Exports and imports are increasing rapidly, but most of this trade is with the fast growing economies of Asia, notably China and South Korea, which have small or negligible Muslim populations. Investment flows between OIC member states are increasing, but they are subject to the same constraints as flows from outside states, such as ease, or lack of ease, in doing business. A ranking of OIC countries according to the ease of doing business is provided.

Policies for the regulation of banking and monetary policy choices are discussed, which are constrained by *Shari'ah* teaching. As Islamic banking and finance is the most developed area of Islamic economics, where most research has been concentrated, it is appropriate to examine the policy issues in detail. The aim is not to provide a comprehensive account of Islamic banking and finance development, which is available in many other studies, but rather to focus on legal issues, with an examination of the laws pertaining to Islamic banking and finance in the UAE, Kuwait and Malaysia, three examples of good practice, but with quite distinctive approaches. Malaysia's efforts to promote Islamic finance have won widespread acclamation throughout the OIC and the country enjoys a much higher profile than Indonesia, its much more populous neighbour. Islamic economists from Pakistan have played a leading role in academic debates, but at the policy level most are critical of the economic policies pursued by successive governments in Islamabad.

ECONOMIC PHILOSOPHY FROM A *SHARI'AH* PERSPECTIVE

Shari'ah guidance on economic policy

The study of *fiqh*, or Islamic jurisprudence, involves the interpretation of the Quran and the hadith and its application to the issues that arise in everyday life, including economic policy. The *fuqaha* are the scholars, or jurists, who study *fiqh* to determine how it should be applied to contemporary issues, such as those that arise in the field of public policy. Their opinions, or rulings, are referred to as *fatwa*. The rulings of reputable scholars are usually respected, but they are not regarded as infallible, as the *fuqaha* may have different, and often conflicting, opinions reflecting their own particular interpretations of the Quran and the hadith. The teaching in the Quran and the hadith is eternal, but over time as circumstances change particular *fatwa* may become redundant.

In contemporary Islamic finance *Shari'ah* boards have been established to vet the contracts offered to Islamic bank and *takaful* (insurance) clients. In some cases, notably in Malaysia, these boards have also been established at national level to advise the Central Bank and the Securities Commission, the financial market regulator. There are no similar bodies to provide guidance on economic policy, however, and no demand for such boards from the *ulama*, the senior religious scholars.

There are several explanations for this different treatment of Islamic economics and Islamic finance issues. First, Islamic finance involves legal and contractual relations between clients and financial institutions which *Shari'ah* scholars are well placed to scrutinise given their eye for detail. In contrast, economic management involves policy choices, most of which are executive decisions rather than changes in the law. Economic management may be subject to political scrutiny, but it is less clear how an institutional framework can be created to ensure scrutiny from a religious perspective. Of course, religious scholars are usually free to give their opinions and can criticise policy, but this is not the same as having formal channels through which these opinions have to be taken into account by policy-makers.

Secondly, clients of Islamic financial institutions want and expect to have the contracts they are offered approved by a *Shari'ah* board. Without such vetting by religious scholars that they respect, it is unlikely that they would deal with the Islamic financial institution. The clients can conduct their financial affairs with a clear conscience in the knowledge that it is the scholars, and not themselves, who will be accountable to the Almighty in the event of the contracts having features that may contradict *Shari'ah*. As economic policy is determined and implemented at national level, however, there is no consensus that any *Shari'ah* input is needed. Apart from the concerns of non-Muslims about *Shari'ah* scholars influencing economic policy, even among Muslims there is scepticism that such scholars have anything useful to contribute to what is viewed as a secular area of debate. Many, perhaps the majority, are of the opinion that although the *Shari'ah* scholars are competent to pronounce on matters of religious observance, they usually have no education in economics or finance and no experience of policy-making in either government or the private sector.

Thirdly, the Quran is explicit about the prohibition of *riba*, the issue in contention being whether this applies to all interest receipts and payments, or if it is restricted to the condemnation of usury. There is, however, no explicit treatment of economic policy or endorsement of political systems. Most regard these as matters involving political choices, with those on the political left usually favouring more state intervention to protect the less affluent and redistributive tax and spending policies, while those on the right believe this could inhibit economic growth, an important priority being to ensure that markets function well and that business is freed from bureaucratic constraints imposed by governments. Both those on the political right and left may regard themselves as good Muslims, but this does not reduce the differences they have over economic policy issues and the best way forward.

Maqasid and the duties of the faithful

The term *maqasid* can be translated from Arabic to mean aims or objectives. Usually this is applied in a religious context and refers to the purposes of Islamic faith. For the individual this means acknowledging the Almighty as Creator of the universe and all that live in it, the duty of the believer being to seek spiritual guidance through prayer and the study of the Quran, the revealed word of God. The hadith, the sayings and deeds of the Prophet, as recorded in the *Sunnah*, are also regarded as a prime source for guidance, and these, together with the Quran itself, are the ultimate source of Islamic law, or *Shari'ah*, observance of which is a religious duty.

In terms of *Shari'ah*, there are five *maqasid*, foundational goals, for which the faithful should assume responsibility. These are the preservation of religion, life, lineage, intellect and property. The order of these goals is significant, and all five can be affected by economic policy, indeed, the aim of economic policy-making when viewed from a *Shari'ah* perspective is to serve these goals. How the *maqasid* are achieved may have very specific policy implications, but the faithful may have different opinions about what policies are best, while respecting all five goals.[1]

The preservation of religion, for example, can be helped by policies that ensure that mosques are adequately resourced. This could be by state subsidy, but this has dangers, as government may expect to exercise a degree of political control in return, perhaps even selecting the *imam* or *mufti*, and vetting what they preach during Friday prayers. An alternative way of encouraging funding is by giving the faithful tax exemptions in respect of donations they make to support their local mosques. This assumes, of course, that the state has a system of income taxation, as without this there would be no financial incentive to donate, although the spiritual incentive would remain. As a condition of receiving such funding, the mosque might have to produce audited accounts to show its income and expenditures, the purpose of this being to ensure that funds are being used in a reputable manner. This acts as assurance to the faithful donor, rather than being instigated to serve the interests of government. Ultimately, it is the believer who decides to donate, not the government, although there will, of course, be a cost to the state in terms of lower tax revenue.

The preservation of life, the second of the *maqasid*, has implications for economic policy-making with respect to health and social security expenditure. A policy that provides subsidised or even free health care for all will help the preservation of life. Such policies were originally adopted by affluent states in Europe with social democratic governments, but they have since spread to the United States and many Asian countries. Within the oil-rich Muslim states of the Gulf such provision applies to all local citizens, but in many poorer OIC countries governments have insufficient resources to fund free or heavily subsidised medical treatment for most of the population. High infant mortality rates provide evidence of government failure to achieve the second of *maqasid*. In some countries Islamic charities and Muslim voluntary organisations have attempted to organise basic health service provision to fulfil the needs that governments fail to meet.

Lineage or provision for progeny, the third *maqasid*, has important social and economic implications. These include a family law system to promote stable family arrangements to ensure the protection of children and the application of *Shari'ah* inheritance laws to provide materially for offspring when death occurs. *Shari'ah* courts play a major role in the protection of progeny in both Muslim majority countries and many Muslim minority countries, with public policy issues including the status of these courts under national laws, how the judges are appointed and the mechanisms for funding. In recent years the courts have dealt with rapidly increasing numbers of divorces with rising family breakdowns, with the divorce settlements and the custody of children often being highly emotive issues. The decisions of the courts have implications for state welfare policies, including levels of spending and their allocation.

The fourth *maqasid*, which concerns intellect, follows naturally from the third, as lineage is enhanced if offspring have access to good education which improves their life chances. High academic achievers can bring honour to their families. Public policies that provide for good quality education for both boys and girls can transform societies and strengthen economies. Although much traditional education provision was through madrassas that were associated with mosques, the curriculum always went beyond narrowly defined theology into writing and mathematics and wider scientific enquiry. For more than a century in most Muslim majority countries the state, rather than the religious authorities, has been the major education provider. A major public policy debate in recent years has been on the role of the state in education, how far the curriculum should be secular and whether there should be government control over the madrassas. Not surprisingly in view of the contentious nature of these issues, there is a wide spectrum of opinions among Islamists concerning the role of the state versus non-government organisations in education provision.

The protection of property is the fifth *maqasid*. It has particular relevance for economic systems, and has important implications for the role of governments and private sector enterprises. In many respects it sets the parameters for state economic policy-making. Ultimately, all property belongs to Allah, but during their lifetimes people can have ownership rights. These enable owners to manage property efficiently as exclusive access is necessary for effective control. Where property rights are unclear or contested there is inevitably a reluctance to invest funds in improvements. Ownership rights bring responsibilities, however, and property owners are ultimately accountable to their Creator for their decisions. In Islam, the concept of *khalifah* applies not just to the governance of an Islamic state, but also to corporate governance and even household management. Property owners are entitled to have their ownership rights respected and protected by the state provided the land or buildings they own are properly managed. The assumption is therefore that governments have duties to owners and that, therefore, policies of nationalisation and expropriation, common in many Marxist and socialist states, are not compatible with *Shari'ah*. However, there is still scope for policy debate as the issue of what constitutes proper management is debatable, as is the question of how far the state should limit the rights of owners through, for example, systems of planning permission.

Critique of utilitarianism as a driver of economic behaviour

Modern economics is based on utilitarian assumptions, the central premise of which is that human behaviour is conditioned by a striving for consumption satisfaction. The focus is on the accumulation of material wealth, with the promise of reward motivating people to work. Utilitarian doctrine is viewed as being hedonistic, the aim being the maximisation of happiness and the minimising of suffering. The proponents of utilitarianism, Jeremy Bentham and John Stewart Mill, were agnostic, and therefore viewed the world in material terms, their concern being with how human needs could be met without any reference to the spiritual dimension of life.

From a religious perspective, utilitarianism seems a very limited philosophy based on a narrow homocentric position.[2] It can be regarded as a rather superficial view of human nature even if this was not what Bentham and Mill intended. Resources are to serve human interests, but men are responsible to no one but themselves. For Mill, individuals are free to do as they wish provided they do not harm others. Individuals are assumed to be rational and capable of making decisions about their own well-being, including choosing whatever religion they want or no religion.

The views of Bentham and Mill may seem to alien to Islamic thinking with their stress on materialist rather than spiritual values, and individual freedom rather than social responsibility. The concept of utility can be extended beyond mere material satisfaction, however, to embrace spiritual comfort, although, admittedly, this is at best only one aspect of religious observance that involves unconditional submission to the will of the Almighty. Men can have contractual relations with each other and with legal entities, including states, but not with God who has absolute power. The benefits a believer gets from his faith in the Almighty are beyond measure, unlike utility which can be enumerated through proxies. An example of this is the price an individual is prepared to pay for a material good or a service, which assuming rationality will reflect the anticipated utility that the purchase will yield.

Even if much of utility theory is rejected on religious grounds there is much in Mill's writing that remains of value. He recognises that conflicts of interest inevitably arise between the decisions of free-thinking individuals and what is socially acceptable. Government intervention may therefore be needed to protect social interests, and this may result in restrictions on individual autonomy. In other words, Mill's writing helps to define the boundaries of what economic activities are best undertaken by the state and those that are best left to the individual.

Utilitarianism is often linked with positivism, a philosophy that suggests that human behaviour, including economic and financial choices, results from sensory experience. By studying this behaviour in detail, models can be derived that can be used to predict the outcomes of different policy choices. Modern experimental economics attempts to provide a detailed picture of the complexity of human decision by studying how people react to monetary incentives. Earlier models of public policy choices were built by making deductions from a set of *a priori* assumptions, such as, for example, whether demand for medications increases when prices decline or rises when prices increase. This may have implications for health service expenditure and resource management if demand for medications is not simply a result of need, but also of pricing factors.

There are no moral judgements in utilitarianism or positivism. In contrast, by accepting Islam or the other monotheistic religions, the faithful believe that they will ultimately be held to account for their behaviour by their Creator. This constrains human choice, arguably encouraging selfless rather than selfish behaviour. The faithful can seek guidance to ensure that their choices are *Shari'ah*-compliant, thus ensuring that there is an indirect religious input to public policy-making, even if there is no direct mechanism for *Shari'ah* guidance at national level. Syed Naqvi believes that economists should study the behaviour of individual Muslims and, through a process of inductive logic, examine how their needs can be served through public policy.[3]

The concept of a secular state making public policy choices in response to the demands of its citizens is far removed from traditional views on an Islamic state whose purpose was to serve the Almighty and enforce *Shari'ah* law. The doctrine of *tawhid* implied that the state was part of a unified harmonious whole, with national sovereignty exclusively belonging to the Almighty as Creator of the universe. This left no room for the evolution of nation-state ideas. According to Ozay Mehmet:

> Secularism, i.e., policies based on science and man-made rules rather than divine criteria, has been rejected as anti-Islamic. Traditionally, a Muslim is not a nationalist, or citizen of a nation-state; he has no political identity, only a religious membership in the *Umma*. For a traditional Muslim, Islam is the sole and sufficient identification tag and nationalism and nation-states are obstacles.[4]

Insofar as states are recognised by Islamists, their success is measured by primarily by their ability to implement *Shari'ah*, not by their delivery of economic policies serving earthly needs. These objectives are not necessarily in conflict as Mehmet suggests. The Almighty through *Shari'ah* teaching provides a code for good governance, and this can include the provision of high quality public services. As economically successful states can deliver better services than less successful economies, hence striving for development may serve Allah's purpose. In Islam there is no virtue in poverty or social exclusion, rather the doctrine of *tawhid* implies inclusion and social harmony. This means the contribution of all those who are able to work in economic activity, the fruits of which can be shared with the less well endowed.

Focus on spiritual fulfilment rather than material reward

For many religions the attainment of spiritual fulfilment is viewed as being in conflict with material reward. Those who crave the material may be seeking false gods, indeed, they may even worship their prized possessions. If people devote all their energy to work in order to accumulate material possessions, they may lack the time for worship, or even be distracted during prayers and fail to give them their full attention. In contrast, those who sacrifice material reward and focus their energy on spiritual fulfilment may be at peace with their Creator and enjoy greater respect from their fellow worshipers.

One tradition in Islam that focuses on the spiritual rather than the material is *tasawwuf*, usually referred to as Sufism, a type of mysticism. Although some Muslims reject Sufism, it should not be regarded as a sect, but rather as a way of approaching worship that many Sunni and Shi'a adherents find helpful. It was recognised by the great Muslim twelfth-century theologian and philosopher al-Ghazali,[5] and subsequently by the highly respected fourteenth-century Muslim scholar, philosopher and historian, Ibn Khaldun. In Islam the tradition of Sufism involves 'total dedication to Allah, disregard for the finery and ornament of the world, abstinence from the pleasure, wealth and prestige sought by most men and retiring from others to worship alone'.[6]

While Sufism has its place, however, if all the faithful devoted themselves to its practices all the time, economic activity would collapse. In Islam poverty is not regarded as a virtue and prosperity as a sin, the stress being on a balanced approach to life, where the material is necessary for daily sustenance, but this should not be at the expense of religious piety. Rather than there being a trade-off between religious duty and earning a living, the two are seen as complementary, as those without adequate food and shelter may be so distracted by their own poverty and that of their families that they cannot concentrate on prayer.

In the Quran the stress is on moderation, the avoidance of excess, but not on abstinence:

> O children of Adam, take your adornment at every *masjid*, and eat and drink, but be not excessive. Indeed, He likes not those who commit excess. (*Sura* 7:31)

In other words worship at a mosque (*masjid*) is an essential part of life, as is moderate eating and drinking, provided what is consumed is not harmful or *haram*.

As well as benefiting from material reward being viewed as just and natural from an Islamic perspective, materialism is not seen as being in conflict with spirituality. Rather, the material world is the creation of Allah, and therefore exploring the material world can lead us closer to knowing God through the splendour of His creation. Hence, the problem is not the material world, but human attitudes to their material circumstances. If humans value only the material, and are sceptical of the spiritual, they cannot be considered as Muslims. To be complete people crave, in full knowledge or unknowingly, for spirituality as this is built into their consciousness. The material will provide only partial and fleeting satisfaction; rather, what matters is aligning behaviour with the will of Allah as set out in the Quran and the hadith.

The costs of maximisation and moral market conduct

Neo-classical mainstream economics assumes maximisation and minimisation behaviour, with firms seeking to maximise profits and, in some circumstances, revenues, while they minimise costs. As workers seek to maximise wages and suppliers aim to maximise prices, this immediately results in conflict between the owners and managers of the firms, on the one hand, and the workers and suppliers, on the other. Marxist economists viewed such conflicts as class struggles, with the owners and managers depicted as exploiting the workers by extracting the surplus between the revenue generated in production and the low wages paid to workers. New institutional economists believe such conflicts can be reduced, if not resolved, by ensuring that firms have appropriate structures of corporate governance in place so that the interests of the different stake-holder groups – workers, suppliers, owners and managers – can be reconciled.

Islamic economists try to tackle such conflicts in three ways. First, although they see production efficiency as important, stakeholders should have a more holistic vision of the business enterprise that goes beyond maximising self-interest. Rather, stakeholders should build relationships and trust in the common good, rather than being adversarial and weakening the enterprise through internal conflict. The concept of *ijma*, consensus, is relevant as, although this is often seen as applying to a community of scholars such as the *Shari'ah* board of an Islamic bank, it can also be applied to the Muslims working together in an enterprise. Consensus does not imply weakness, as when stakeholders share common religious values and beliefs collective decisions are governed by the teachings of *Shari'ah*, through which all participants are given strength.

Secondly, there is the concept of *shura*, or consultation, usually applied to political consultation, but equally relevant for business consultations. Where employees have an input into business decision-making they feel valued in a way that goes beyond material remuneration. Short-term wage or salary maximisation becomes less important if employees believe that their long-term interests are being protected. It is important to stress that the opinions of the *shura* are advisory and not mandatory. In other words, the chief executive officer (CEO) of a business may consult with different stakeholder groups, but ultimately he or she has to take the decisions. If the decision turns out to be unwise or inappropriate, it is the CEO who should be held responsible and not the other stakeholders.

Thirdly, there is the concept of *amanah*, or trust. When the stakeholders in an enterprise trust each other there is less likely to be conflict and internal divisions. This strengthens the enterprise by reducing costs, which potentially results in greater competitiveness. Where trust is absent expensive contractual and internal performance evaluation measures may be needed, which in turn causes distraction from the major aim of the business and fosters resentment. It should be noted that trust does not imply guarantees, or *daman*. Employees may have confidence or trust in the CEO, who is expected to work for the greater good of the enterprise, but cannot guarantee success.

How a business is organised also influences behaviour, and the narrow view of the aims of a firm being simply profit maximisation and cost minimisation has been much criticised.[7] Investment strategies are constantly evolving, and most large businesses take a long-term view rather than focusing on adding shareholder value day by day or month by month. Much of the investment in listed companies is by institutions such as pension funds and life insurance companies, which have extremely long time horizons often stretching over decades. Since the late twentieth century there has been synergy between business historians, who seek to analyse changes in business behaviour, with specialists in corporate governance, who are, as already mentioned, concerned with how the interests of different stakeholder groups can be reconciled. This has resulted in a much richer understanding of corporate objectives than the limited models presented in micro-economic theory.

There is no objection from an Islamic perspective to firms being incorporated and listed on stock exchanges, even though potential conflicts of control and agency arise, notably between shareholders as owners and managers as employees. The concept of a limited liability firm was unknown in traditional Muslim jurisprudence, but it was also unknown in the Christian West until the early nineteenth century. Although such types of business organisation are very different to traditional Islamic partnerships, they are nevertheless accepted; indeed, they have become the dominant form of business model in virtually all Muslim majority countries.

The alternative Islamic form of business organisation is based on partnerships where the contractual arrangements aim to ensure that each partner is protected from the actions of others. How these partnership arrangements work in practice will be discussed in greater detail in the next chapter, but here it is sufficient to note that Islamic partnerships prevent internal maximising behaviour whereby one partner exploits another. The discretion of partners is limited by the agreement they sign when the partnership is established, the stress being on working together and collective action rather than partners seeking to further their own narrow self-interests. There are parallels between partnerships in Islamic law and those found in medieval Europe, in particular the practices in the Ottoman Empire.[8]

The bounty of Allah, notions of scarcity and resource allocation

Economics has been defined as the study of the allocation of limited means among competing ends, with the assumption being that resources are scarce.[9] This view contradicts Islamic teaching, which stresses that Allah has provided abundant resources for the needs of man. Therefore, mankind should not be pessimistic about the future, but rather keep the faith and trust in the Almighty, who will take care of his followers.

The notion of the scarcity of resources in economics comes from the later classical economists, notably Malthus who saw population growth rising exponentially while the food supply at best increased arithmetically.[10] Hence, famine and mass starvation would result, causing the human population to fall until it was in line with what the world could produce. This alarming prognosis resulted in economics being viewed as the dismal science, as the future was seen as being a period of doom and gloom. As Malthus was a clergyman these views were all the more surprising, especially as he appeared to have no hope that God would be able to save mankind from its plight.

The empirical evidence of the last two centuries has dramatically demonstrated how wrong Malthus' predictions were. The population of the planet has risen more than tenfold, but the food supply has managed to keep pace. There has, of course, been localised famine and starvation, but this was the result of inefficient systems of distribution not from global food shortages. Those who took a Malthusian approach to natural resource depletion have also been proved wrong. It was predicted that coal would run out, but in the end most coal will never be mined as other fuels have proved to be cheaper to exploit. The same gloomy predictions have been made for oil and gas resources, on which, arguably, too many Muslim majority countries are dependent for their export earnings and government revenue. However, it looks less likely that oil and gas reserves will be depleted, rather it is more likely that other fuels will be used increasingly, including renewable energy, and that the demand for energy will fall as new technologies reduce consumption needs.

It is evident that rather than considering resource production, use and allocation from a static perspective a more dynamic approach is needed. The notion that Allah will provide may work through human agency, and mankind has demonstrated ingenuity in tackling constraints and in ensuring that needs are fulfilled. The poor and malnourished are a declining proportion of the population, even in underdeveloped countries, though the numbers in absolute poverty have increased somewhat. In the Muslim world, as elsewhere, development has resulted in an expanding middle class; the challenge being for the poor to be upwardly mobile so that they can join its ranks. In terms of short-term strategy to alleviate poverty, the issue is not the supply of food, but rather the channels for its distribution. Markets usually work well for the middle classes and others with the purchasing power to obtain the supplies their families need, but those without resources are dependent on the state, which is often inefficient, or variable and uncertain charitable donations.

The concept of *khalifah*, or stewardship, is central to Islamic teaching on resource management. *Khalifah* can be applied to the governor of a state, the *caliphate*, but in Islamic economics it usually refers to the guardianship over resources that Allah has provided in abundance. Those who use resources, such as land as owners or tenants, are accountable to the Almighty for their actions. Their governorship is temporary, but during their lifetimes they have a responsibility to ensure that resources are used in a sustainable manner so that they can be passed on to the next generation in a fit state for use. More will be said about *khalifah* in the next chapter when the theory of the firm is discussed from an Islamic perspective, but the concept is mentioned here as resources do not manage themselves. The notions of accountability have resonance in the contemporary corporate governance literature, especially in the recognition that governance practices are influenced by behaviour,[11] which in turn are a reflection of moral and ethical values.[12]

Perfect and imperfect competition and fair pricing

In Islam markets are seen as a natural way of conducting business; indeed, the spread of Islam in its early years was accompanied by the growth of trade and commerce. The great cities of the Islamic world such as Mecca, Cairo, Damascus and Isfahan owed their existence to trade, and when Islam spread to southeast Asia, it was through Malacca, a strategic trading port. Market transactions and trade are viewed in a favourable light, as they stimulate economic activity, create employment and bring prosperity. Furthermore, conversion to Islam often followed trade, possibly because of the role model provided by Muslim merchants, but also because shared religious beliefs facilitated trade with greater trust, which lowered transaction costs.[13]

In neo-classical economics, the determination of market prices is analysed in terms of supply and demand. Competitive markets are viewed as efficient in contrast to less competitive markets where monopoly power prevails, which can distort prices and result in surpluses accruing to suppliers at the expense of consumers. The focus is on price competition rather than on quality of service or output, hence the assumption is made that products are homogeneous or standardised. Such competition is described as perfect or pure, whereas competition involving differentiated products is classed as imperfect or impure.

This terminology of perfect and imperfect could be translated into Islamic parlance as *halal* or *haram*, but this would be mistaken. There is no particular virtue in standardised commodities, indeed, it reduces consumer choice and narrows the market excessively. Hence, imperfect competition may be preferable to perfect competition, although when competition involves more variables, and not just price, it is more complicated to compare what is on offer.

Trust between buyers and sellers increases in importance and, as already indicated, trust is more likely when the parties to a transaction share a common religion and culture.

Islam recognises that markets can be abused and that the market price is not always a just price. Merchants who seek to raise prices in times of shortage are seen as being unfair to their customers, especially if the cost of production is unchanged but the profits from distribution are increased.[14] The renowned Muslim scholar Ibn Taymiyyah wrote extensively on the concept of a just price.[15] For him pricing was a moral issue with social consequences, as, although the better off could afford to pay more, the poorest were especially vulnerable to the actions of monopolists and price fixers who sought to manipulate the market for their own selfish gains. Such exploitation should not be blamed on the market system, which Ibn Taymiyyah supported, as trading was viewed as a normal business activity. Rather, the issue was the behaviour of traders. Most traders were seen as honest and fair in their dealings, especially if their religious faith was translated into their business lives. However, there were always the unscrupulous, without moral principles, whose activities needed to be controlled in the interests of the wider social good. Without control there would be widespread social discontent that would ultimately lead to disorder.[16]

Nevertheless, Ibn Taymiyyah recognised that price rises could result from supply shortages, and no moral blame should be assigned for this, as supply fluctuations in prices for agricultural products might simply reflect poor harvests and climatic conditions. Rises in demand could also result in price increases, but purchasers should not be criticised for this. In other words, price fluctuations did not necessarily mean that there should be general intervention by government in the market to stabilise prices. Rather, intervention should be selective and aimed at curbing the actions of monopolists and others intent on speculative behaviour for their own selfish interests.

Ibn Taymiyyah favoured the establishment of an institution, the *hisba*, to regulate markets and to ensure fair trading and honest dealings, including with weights and measures.[17] This policy was also supported by his student and follower Ibn Al Qayyim.[18] The contemporary analogy is a trading standards authority which serves to ensure that buyers are not mislead and have accurate information on the supplies they hope to purchase. In particular, the *hisba* is a regulatory authority which can intervene in the case of misconduct, but it does not have the resources to pay subsidies or the power to impose taxes on supplies. Its remit is to tackle economic crime and not to serve as an agent of the government in controlling prices through its own buying and selling activity.

Although the *hisba* does not exist today in any Muslim majority country, it played a significant role in Ottoman trade and commerce until the early twentieth century, seven hundred years after the writing of Ibn Taymiyyah.[19] Whether the institution can be revived remains to be seen, but the history of its workings reveals much about the application of Islamic teaching on markets and pricing, which can be summarised as selective intervention with the aim of enhancing the operation of markets rather than destroying them, as was too often the case in the twentieth-century Arab revolutionary states that arose after colonial domination.

Notes

1. Murat Cizakca, 'Democracy, development and *maqasid al-Shari'ah*', *Review of Islamic Economics*, 2(1) (2007): 101–18.
2. M. Umer Chapra, *Islam and the Economic Challenge* (Leicester: Islamic Foundation, 1992), pp. 25–7.
3. Syed Nawab Haider Naqvi, 'The Dimensions of an Islamic Economic Model', *Islamic Economic Studies*, 4(2) (May 1997): 1–23.
4. Ozay Mehmet, *Islamic Identity and Development: Studies of the Islamic Periphery* (London: Routledge, 1991), p. 57.
5. Jules Janssens, 'Al-Gazali between philosophy *(falsafa)* and Sufism *(tasawwuf)*: his complex attitude in the *Marvels of the Heart (Ajaib al-Qalb) of the Ihya Ulum al-Din*', *Muslim World*, 101(4) (October 2011): 614–32.
6. Ibn Khaldun, *al-Muqaddima* (reprinted Dar al-Baz, Mecca, 1978 (1397)), p. 467.
7. William Lazonick, *Business Organisation and the Myth of Market Behaviour* (Cambridge: Cambridge University Press, 2011), pp. 1–55.
8. Murat Cizakca, *A Comparative Evolution of Business Partnerships: The Islamic World and Europe, with Special Reference to the Ottoman Archives* (Leiden: Brill Academic Publishing, 1996), vol. 8.
9. Lionel Robbins, *An Essay on the Nature and Significance of Economics Science* (London: Macmillan, 1932), pp. 12–15.
10. Thomas Malthus, *An Essay on the Principle of Population* (London: J. Johnson, 1798), pp. 6–11.
11. Morten Huse, 'Accountability and creating accountability: a framework for exploring behavioural perspectives of corporate governance', *British Journal of Management*, 15 (suppl.) (March 2005): S65–S79.
12. Christine A. Hemingway and Patrick W. Maclagan, 'Managers' personal values as drivers of corporate social responsibility', *Journal of Business Ethics*, 50 (2004): 33–44.
13. Jean Ensminger, 'Transaction costs and Islam: explaining conversion in Africa', *Journal of Institutional and Theoretical Economics*, 153(1) (March 1997): 4–29.
14. Raymond de Roover, 'The concept of the just price: theory and economic policy', *Journal of Economic History*, 18(4) (December 1958): 418–34.
15. M. Yassine Essid, 'Islamic economic thought', in S. Todd Lowry (ed.), *Pre-Classical Economic Thought: From the Greeks to the Scottish Enlightenment*, Recent Economic Thought Series (Rotterdam: Springer Netherlands, 1987), vol. 10, pp. 77–102.

16. Boaz Shoshan, 'Grain riots and the "moral economy": Cairo, 1350–1517', *Journal of Interdisciplinary History*, 10(3) (1980): 459–78.

17. Ibn Taymiyyah, *Public Duties in Islam: The Institution of Hisba*, trans. from original fourteenth-century text by Muhtar Holland (Leicester: Islamic Foundation, 1982), pp. 1–45.

18. Abdul Azim Islahi, *Economic Thought of Ibn al-Qayyim* (Jeddah: International Centre for Research in Islamic Economics, 1984), pp. 13–14.

19. Serif Mardin, 'Power, civil society and culture in the Ottoman Empire', *Comparative Studies in Society and History*, 11(3) (1969): 258–81.

2

MICRO-ECONOMIC MORALITY: A THEORY OF THE FIRM ENLIGHTENED BY ISLAMIC VALUES

Corporate organisation and business freedom

The choice of models of business organisation depends partly on the nature of the activity, the markets in which the businesses compete and their access to finance. Religion does not at first sight seem to have much relevance for business organisation, although in the case of Islam the favoured financing methods may have some influence. Business activity has, of course, to be *halal*, which precludes a wide range of industry from *riba*-based banking to alcohol and pork production and distribution, but this will not affect the scale of individual businesses or their corporate structures. The markets of the time of Ibn Taymiyyah involved individual or family traders rather than large companies, but that has not ruled out the subsequent rise of joint stock companies and even multinational enterprises in many majority Muslim economies in recent years.[1]

In Islam there is freedom to make decisions on all business activities unless such activities are explicitly forbidden. In other words, the working assumption is that the owners of the business are unconstrained in choosing both tactics and strategy, their freedom of action being limited only where it conflicts with *Shari'ah* teaching. Such conflicts are likely to arise only where business decisions have adverse social implications, especially for those who are disadvantaged and in need of support. Of course, if excessive constraints on business activity undermine profitability, businesses will be less able to engage in charitable giving. Hence, it is arguably not in the interests of the socially disadvantaged to impose impediments to business as there may be opportunity costs or even losses for all. Worthy objectives such as the alleviation of poverty are more easily attained in vibrant economies where businesses prosper rather than in stagnant state-dominated economies where resources are misallocated.

Khalifah and contemporary corporate governance

The concept of *khalifah* is usually applied to the ruler of a Muslim state who is ultimately accountable to the Almighty for his or her actions. The social contract between the ruled and the ruler is based on the understanding that there will be such accountability and that the actions of the ruler will be guided, indeed bound by, *Shari'ah* teaching. In other words, the ruler cannot act in an arbitrary manner, serving his or her own interests, but rather should govern in the wider interests of society. Furthermore, although most Muslim rulers were not democrats in the modern sense of representing the winning political party in a contested system, there was a process of *shura*, or consultation, through which they were obliged to consult with those that they ruled over before making policy decisions. The aim, if possible, was to achieve a social consensus on the way forward, while not binding the ruler by constraining his or her powers of decision-making. The stress was on responsible government, and as far as possible accountable government, while recognising that not all the ruled shared the same views on policy and some would inevitably be disappointed by the decisions of the ruler, or indeed completely opposed to the actions taken.

The guardianship of resources is described as *khilafah*, or vicegerency, invested with or characterised by delegated authority from God. The CEO of a business enterprise can be regarded as the *khalifah* who has responsibilities to the Almighty for his or her actions, there being parallels with the Christian concept of stewardship.[2] Ultimately, all wealth is owned by God, but that does not undermine the control of resources through private property rights, as it is through the exercise of these rights that a just economy can be created for the benefit of society as a whole. It is only if responsibilities to God are ignored that corruption and wrongdoing will ensue, to the detriment of society. In other words, the CEO has a moral and spiritual as well as a social responsibility.

The concepts of *khalifah* and *shura* can also be applied to corporate governance with the CEO acting as *khalifah*, and the *shura* referring to the mechanisms for consultation with the stakeholders. In a listed company this process of *shura* will be formalised through the annual general meeting, which all shareholders as owners have the right to attend and question the management. The company statutes will usually have provision for the convening of extraordinary general meetings where consent is required for major changes such as takeovers or mergers involving the business.

Applying the concepts of *khalifah* and *shura* to contemporary corporate governance is not simply a matter of renaming in Arabic. In Arabic *khalifah* simply means the person who replaces someone else, and *shura* means consultation. Both concepts have, however, higher religious implications and are informed by *Shari'ah* teaching. In particular, as the *khalifah* of a business will ultimately be accountable to the Almighty for his or her actions, his or her decisions will be subjected to moral judgement. They have, of course, freedom of action and may even make unsound decisions, but these are not without consequences for themselves as well as for those who they manage. There is an understanding that the *khalifah* is the viceroy to Allah, who should seek divine guidance through prayer and the observance of *Shari'ah*. *Shura* implies that the *khalifah* should not act without constraint in social isolation, the emphasis being on social inclusion rather than exclusion.

If the CEO is the *khalifah*, but decision-making is consensual, this clearly restricts the freedom of action of the CEO. There may be differences of opinion among board members and shareholders about how much latitude the CEO should have. The power of the CEO may ultimately reflect personality factors and management style even where the framework for decision-making is bounded by the corporate governance structure. The question arises that if the concept of *khalifah* is applied to a CEO, does this imply greater freedom of manoeuvre? If consultation through *shura* is necessary, does this reduce discretion? In other words, does the corporate governance of a self-designated Islamic business, such as an Islamic bank, or *takaful* operation or *Shari'ah*-compliant investment company differ from its secular counterpart?

Outside the fields of banking and finance there are, of course, companies that employ Muslims or are managed by Muslims, but they do not claim to be Islamic businesses. Their corporate governance and issues such as the relationship between shareholders as owners and the management is the same as that of other businesses, and religion, or indeed secularism, has no effect on how firms are organised. Normally a company's articles of association will determine the authority of decision-makers, usually comprising the company board. The articles will also determine how decisions by the CEO and board are ratified, whether by a simple majority of voters at the annual general meeting or by some type of qualified majority voting. Changes to the articles of association may, for example, require a two-thirds majority for approval.

It is only in the financial sector where there are formal systems to ensure *Shari'ah* compliance, and these are built into the corporate governance arrangements. This will usually imply the establishment of a *Shari'ah* board to provide oversight, with its main responsibilities being to ensure that contracts do not contain any element of *gharar* or *riba*, and that the activities being financed are *halal*. In many Muslim majority countries there are laws that provide for formal systems of *Shari'ah* compliance, as with the Malaysian Islamic Banking and Takaful legislation of 1983 and 1984, respectively, which have now been superseded by the Islamic Financial Services Act of 2013.[3] Although the new legislation is comprehensive, it does not apply beyond the financial sector to ordinary companies.

Islamic business organisation and corporate governance

The lack of formal governance structures to ensure *Shari'ah* compliance does not mean that non-financial businesses should be considered as non-Islamic. Their activities may be *halal*, and their leveraging below the one-third debt to asset ratio that many Islamic scholars accept as being *Shari'ah*-compliant. Beyond these formalistic requirements, however, there are wider ethical issues that arguably need to be taken on board by businesses if they are to be regarded as respectable investments. Employment issues and health and safety for employees at work can be regarded as ethical concerns.

Business structures in the Muslim world are determined by both economic conditions and opportunities, as well as by the values and beliefs of those involved in managing the enterprises. The slow emergence of joint stock companies compared with the West, and the limited development of equity markets partly reflects the strength of family and kinship bonds, and the reluctance to see control of family businesses moving to external shareholders. It was also a reflection of a preference for partnership structures between fellow believers, the traditional Muslim business enterprise being based on the concepts of *shirkah*, or partnership, which also implies fellowship beyond the realm of business into common worship.[4]

Furthermore, profits are to be shared among the partners under an operating structure referred to as *musharakah*; one debate in Islamic jurisprudence being whether the sharing should be equal regardless of the amount invested or if the profit distributions should be made in relation to funds committed. The latter approach has been favoured in recent years, largely on the pragmatic grounds that altruism and business dealings should be separated if investors are to be attracted to *musharakah* undertakings.

Musharakah investment is often equated with private equity placement, or even venture capital, although the structures can be quite flexible. With traditional *musharakah* the partnership is set up in perpetuity, but every partner has the right to terminate the contract after giving due notice to the other partners, and if one of the partners dies their heirs can succeed.[5] Where a partner decides to terminate their participation in the *musharakah* the other partners may buy their share on mutually agreed terms and continue the business. In recent years *musharakah* have been established for a fixed period of time, after which one of the partners usually agrees to return the capital that the others initially contributed. Diminishing *musharakah* contracts are also possible, where one of the partners buys out the others' share over a period of years and increases their ownership stake in the business.[6]

There are three possible types of *musharakah* arrangement: a finance partnership (*shirkah mal*), a labour partnership (*shirkah a'mal*) and a credit partnership (*shirkah wujuh*). In the case of Islamic banks it is always the former that is used. Islamic banks and Muslim investors not unnaturally prefer limited liability arrangements, with the *'inan* form of partnership being the most usual rather than the *mufawada*, where the partners are both agents and guarantors for their colleagues.[7] There is mutual agency in *'inan* partnership but not mutual surety, and hence the individual partner is not liable for the debts of the other partners. This is still different to the limited liability of a western joint stock company, however, where the company itself is a legal entity, and in the event of bankruptcy the equity holders lose their investments, but have no further personal liability. With an *'inan* partnership there is personal liability, as this is seen as just, but only with respect to personal obligations and not those of the business partners.

There has been much debate among *Shari'ah* scholars about the merits of limited liability, as obligations were viewed as irreducible and indestructible without the agreed release or forgiveness of the creditor.[8] Those to whom money is owed are nevertheless expected to show leniency towards debtors, as the teaching in the Quran makes clear:

> If the debtor is in difficulty, grant him time till it is easy for him to repay. If ye remit by way of charity that is best for you if ye only knew. (*Sura* 2:280)

In practice, a distinction is drawn between the inability to pay because of circumstances beyond the debtor's control and an unwillingness to honour commitments that the debtor has the ability to pay, the latter being a deliberate breach of contract. The principle of limited liability has become accepted in recent years, provided all parties from the outset are clear on their exact obligations and rights under such a company structure.

In the Quran the importance of certainty in contracts is stressed, and arguably through *ijtihad*, or interpretation,[9] this can be applied to the articles of association of companies as well as to personal obligations:

> When you deal with each other in transactions involving future obligations reduce them to writing. Let him who incurs the liability dictate, but let him fear his Lord God and not diminish aught of what he owes. (*Sura* 2:282)

In Islamic law there is specific provision for a partnership involving a financier (*rabb-ul-mal*) and an entrepreneur (*mudarib*), where the former provides the capital and the latter the labour or effort. This more restricted, but historically significant, form of partnership is referred to as a *mudarabah* contract.[10] In this case, the *rabb-ul-mal* is a sleeping partner who does not get actively involved in the business, this having the advantage of giving more autonomy to the *mudarib*. As with *musharakah*, profits are shared according to previously agreed proportions, the remuneration of the *mudarib* being a profit share rather than a fixed salary, but in the event of losses only the *rabb-ul-mal* is liable. Furthermore, the *rabb-ul-mal* cannot be considered an equity investor as, although the profit share can be regarded as a dividend, the financier does not benefit from any capital gains from the value of the business, because at the end of the contract period they normally only receive the return of their initial capital. It is the *mudarib* who benefits from any rise in the value of the business if they decide to sell, but this is seen as fair as it is they who have put in the effort and taken the most risks, whereas for the financier the funds invested in a particular *mudarabah* contract may only be part of a wider asset portfolio. Modern Islamic banks have provided relatively little *mudarabah* financing largely because of potential problems of moral hazard, as there is asymmetric information with the *mudarib* knowing much more about the running of the business and the bank has to trust that the financial disclosure is honest.[11]

Islamic business ethics

The Quran provides a realistic view of human motivation, as Man's love of wealth and his propensity for greed and selfishness is recognised:

> To whom I granted resources in abundance and sons to be by his side! To whom I made life smooth and comfortable! Yet he is greedy that I should add yet more. (*Sura* 74:12–15)

As business has to be conducted in a social context, there clearly have to be rules governing behaviour, and *Shari'ah* law provides a divinely inspired code for devout Muslims to follow.[12] As Muslims are accountable to God for all their actions, business success should not simply be viewed in material terms, but rather judged by the degree to which the believer has been able to realise the goals of Islam, *maqasid al Shari'ah*.[13] The key principle governing business philosophy is that of the unity of God, His universe and His people, *tawhid*. God is the sole Creator of the universe, and his people should cooperate in carrying out His will.[14] In business this implies honesty and trust, and a relationship between employers and employees that reflects the fact that they are part of the same brotherhood or sisterhood and spiritually equal before God, even if not materially equal on earth.[15]

In Islam faith, or *iman*, is the basic motivating factor for believers, and it is this that determines conscience. Hence, business decisions are guided by *iman*, which in practice means following *Shari'ah* law, and engaging in what is *halal* or permitted and avoiding that which is *haram* or forbidden.[16] The business decision-maker has free choice, but religious principles provide a framework for the appropriate exercise of that choice.[17] Human psychological development for the Muslim has to be seen in terms of gaining experience in carrying out God's will, and through that gaining a deeper understanding of His intent in the sphere of business.[18] The term *jihad*, or struggle, is all too often equated with Islamic war or even terrorist activities because of a distorted interpretation of Islam by some politically motivated fringe groups, but its application to business life is much more positive. It should be interpreted as a striving with oneself and the struggle for self-improvement by believers so that they can carry out God's will more effectively.[19]

Central to God's will is the concept of *adalah*, or justice, that has obvious application in business activity. Injustice involves exploitation of employees by the management of a company, abusing market power to short-change suppliers or using a monopoly to over-charge consumers. Although it might be premature to speak of an Islamic human resource management model, it is clear that religious principles have applicability in this field.[20] One premise is that employees are responsible for their own actions, and cannot simply blame the management for their shortcomings. In the Quran it is stressed that:

> No bearer of burdens can bear the burden of another; that man can have nothing but what he strives for. (*Sura* 53:38–9)

It is widely recognised that national cultures have important implications for employee–management relations, and Islam certainly has an effect, even though it is difficult to isolate its influence empirically from that of other factors.[21]

Modern systems for consumer protection are in their infancy in most of the Muslim world, although Islam does provide a comprehensive framework for protecting the rights of purchasers.[22] Traditionally, as mentioned in Chapter 1, markets were regulated through the institution of the *hisba*, which provided for fair weights and measures and functioned as a type of trading standards authority to which consumers could take their complaints if they felt they were being exploited.[23] The Quran is explicit on the penalties for market abuse:

> Woe to those that deal in fraud, those who, when they have to receive by measure from men exact full measure, but when they have to give by measure or weight to men give less than due. Do they not think that they will be called to account? (*Sura* 83:1–4)

The market regulator is known as the *muhtasib*, the traditional view being that this should be a state appointment, but that the criteria for the person appointed should be that they are conversant with both *Shari'ah* law and the practicalities of market operations and are viewed by all as impartial and just. Although a servant of the state, the *muhtasib* does not represent state interests, but rather has to be seen as an independent arbitrator.

Islamic ethics imply that accurate product information should not only be provided when a good is sold, but also in marketing literature and in advertising. Although there has been relatively little work on marketing from an

Islamic perspective, it has been suggested that a value maximisation approach should be adopted, stressing the value of the products offered from a social perspective and not merely in terms of value for money for the purchaser.[24] Advertisements should not offend Islamic values, and the use of scantily clad women for product promotion would certainly be regarded as unacceptable. Television commercials in Muslim countries often depict consumers in a respectable family environment.

In Islam, as in the other monotheistic religions, there are ethical concerns over income and wealth distribution, and a recognition that material wealth can be corrupting and distract believers from the achievement of *falah* that implies a state of spiritual as well as material well-being.[25] Islam is not against family wealth accumulation, and indeed sees socioeconomic inequalities as inevitable, but those that are entrusted with abundant resources have a duty to God to manage them well for the benefit of society as a whole. The Prophet himself is reported to have said in a frequently quoted hadith that:

> There is no harm in opulence for the one who fears God. And for the God-fearing health is better than wealth and happiness is also wealth.[26]

The plight of the poor should not be ignored, and the Quran stresses the virtue of altruism:

> And those in whose wealth is a recognised right for the needy who asks and him who is prevented for some reason from asking. (*Sura* 70:24–5)

It is narrated that Ali, a follower of the Prophet, cited Him as saying:

> Allah has levied upon the rich among Muslims, in their wealth, an amount that would suffice for the poor amongst them. If the poor starve or go unclad it is because of what the rich are doing.[27]

Provision for the poor and needy comes through *zakat*, a self-assessed tax on wealth whose proceeds are earmarked for social expenditures.[28] This can be regarded as a form of alms-giving, with the liability calculated annually as one-fortieth of the value of financial assets such as money in bank accounts. It does not apply to immovable property such as an owner-occupied house, and there has been much debate by Islamic scholars over the assets that should be subject to *zakat*, as the Quran provides general guidance rather than precise advice.[29] It is recognised that the proceeds from *zakat* may be insufficient to alleviate poverty, and that it is a complement to rather than a substitute for social commitment.[30] Certainly *zakat* should not be used as an excuse for Muslim governments not to introduce other redistributive taxes, as has been the case in Saudi Arabia and the Gulf.[31]

Wealth gets broken down through the Islamic inheritance system that ensures all the children receive an immediate entitlement on the death of a parent, rather than all the estate passing to the spouse, as is the case with most inheritance provision in the West, where children can suffer if there is remarriage. The Quran is explicit on how an estate should be redistributed, with a wife receiving one-sixth of the estate on the death of her husband on the understanding that the children will also take care of their mother, but if the widow is childless then she will receive one-third of the estate, the remainder going to the husband's relatives.[32] In any case, the widow is entitled to reside in the family home for at least a year, and to have a year's maintenance allowance.[33] Of course, inheritance primarily brings about redistribution of wealth within families rather than more widely, but bequests to the poor in wills are praised, and beneficiaries of wills may wish to help those less fortunate than themselves.[34]

Towards an Islamic mode of capitalism

The collapse of communism and the lack of success of socialist movements in many Muslim countries resulted in self-designated Islamic economists proposing a *Shari'ah*-compliant system as the only suitable alternative to western capitalism. It was clear in any case that western forms of capitalism had not found fertile ground in the Muslim world, although the extent to which development failures could be ascribed to the suggested incompatibility of Islam with capitalist values must be open to question. Western authors such as Maxime Rodinson, who made a careful study of the historical evidence, have not found Islam to be a handicap to the development of capitalism; the endurance of feudalism in many parts of the Muslim world reflecting economic structures rather than religious values.[35] Rodinson did not see the prohibition of *riba*, or interest, as a barrier to capitalist development, as he demonstrates how it was circumvented in the Ottoman Empire. He denied that there was, or could be, a distinctive Islamic mode of capitalism.

Modern Islamic economic writers have taken a different approach, however, notably Mohammad Baqir al-Sadr, Umer Chapra and Syed Naqvi, who question the excesses of western capitalism and see these as needing to be curbed in Muslim societies. Al-Sadr is critical of those who see capitalism as a natural economic system, as economic laws are, he believes, always related to human choices, and humans can be motivated and inspired by divine guidance.[36] This is not to deny, however, that resources are limited, and that there are laws of increasing and decreasing returns to scale in production that are determined by the technology available.[37] Al-Sadr supports the concept of private property, but if land is not utilised effectively, then he believes that the state has the right to confiscate it and to redistribute the property to those with the capability to use it for the public good.[38] Similarly, what al-Sadr describes as capitalistic freedom can be abused, unless those who exercise the freedom are subject to moral restraint and seek spiritual help. In a free market, where the participants are amoral, inequalities will inevitably increase, and some will abuse their market power to drive their competitors out of business and create monopolies that they can exploit. Such behaviour is not likely to meet with God's approval, and will certainly not create a just society.

Umer Chapra sees capitalism as bringing about joyless affluence for the few, but insecurity and poverty for the many.[39] Social Darwinism is condemned, and he believes that capitalism is unable to resolve the conflict between private and public interests. Priorities become distorted by material imperatives, and spiritual needs are neglected as society becomes increasingly driven by a narrow, short-term utilitarian ethic that ultimately brings no meaningful satisfaction. However, Chapra is under no illusions that Muslim countries are any better than their western capitalist counterparts. He sees formerly socialism and now Islam as being abused by many governments in the Muslim world, as the principle of *shura*, or consultation, has been ignored or manipulated by autocratic and frequently corrupt state administrations.[40] The religious leadership, the *ulama*, have too often failed their followers, and they have become preoccupied with trivial legal matters, rather than trying to apply Islamic principles to contemporary economies.[41] The stagnation of *fiqh*, Islamic jurisprudence, is identified as a prime cause of Muslim decline, but Chapra sees hope in the revival of *ijtihad*, the reinterpretation of Islamic law so that it can provide a moral filter for determining the appropriate path to follow for believers in a changing world.

Syed Naqvi is as equally critical of capitalism as Umer Chapra, but he believes Islamic economies have to be rebuilt from the bottom up rather than from the top down. His focus is at the micro- rather than the macro-level, and he is more concerned with the decision-taking behaviour of individual Muslims than seeking, perhaps in vain, to bringing about a better Islamic society through political means. Muslim man can exercise free will (*ikhtiyar*) in making business decisions, but it is a moral imperative for the faithful to exercise responsibility (*fardh*), both to those they deal with, and ultimately to God by being His representative on earth.[42] By becoming closer to God, believers do not lose their individuality, but they do become less selfish and more motivated to serve the wider public good. Syed Naqvi acknowledges that western capitalist society also fosters a sense of social responsibility, as capitalists are often altruistic rather than being the brutal exploiters depicted by Marx, but in Islam social obligations are a central focus.

Islam and the multinational corporation

Traditional Islamic business partnerships are arguably more applicable to small businesses than multinational corporations where the companies are usually listed and their stock traded. The main objective of most multinational corporations is the enhancement of shareholder value, and although they may also have social responsibility policies, these are more a matter of corporate image and public relations rather than being what the business is primarily about. Multinational corporations are not usually associated with any particular religious faith, indeed, any discrimination on the grounds of religion with regard to employment policy, suppliers used or the award of contracts would be regarded as inappropriate, if not totally wrong, and in many jurisdictions may actually be illegal. While few multinational corporations would designate themselves as specifically secular, and many of their employees may be regular worshipers, religious faith is kept strictly separate from business considerations.

The largest businesses in the Islamic world are listed in Table 2.1. Of the FT Global 500 listed companies, only fourteen are based in the Islamic world, eight of which are banks.[43] The Saudi Basic Industries Corporation (SABIC), a world leader in petrochemical production and the largest listed company in the Islamic world, can be considered a multinational enterprise, as it has a wholly owned subsidiary in the Netherlands and is actively considering further international diversification. Astra, the second largest, in contrast, is mainly a domestic assembler of vehicles for its home market in Indonesia.

Although the majority of employees of these large businesses are Muslim, they do not designate themselves as Islamic, their major adaptation being to provide prayer facilities for their employees that are well used. The only specifically Islamic designated business is the Al Rajhi Banking and Investment Corporation, the largest Islamic bank in the world, which is ranked 358 in

Table 2.1 Largest listed companies in the Islamic world

Company	Country	FT 500 rank	Market cap.	Sector	Income	Assets
SABIC	Saudi Arabia	83	77.6	Chemicals	6.6	90.2
Astra	Indonesia	270	32.9	Vehicles	1.9	18.8
Bank Central Asia	Indonesia	326	28.6	Bank	1.2	46.0
Industries Qatar	Qatar	355	26.7	Industrial	2.3	11.0
Al Rajhi Bank	Saudi Arabia	358	26.6	Bank	2.1	71.3
Qatar National Bank	Qatar	371	25.8	Bank	2.3	100.8
Maybank	Malaysia	375	25.6	Bank	1.9	161.4
Bank Mardiri	Indonesia	407	23.8	Bank	1.6	65.7
Telekomunikasi	Indonesia	425	22.8	Telecoms	1.3	11.6
Turkiye Is Bankasi	Turkey	434	22.3	Bank	1.9	99.2
Bank Rakyat	Indonesia	443	22.0	Bank	1.9	57.1
Akbank	Turkey	460	21.0	Bank	1.9	91.6
Etisalat	UAE	461	21.0	Telecoms	1.8	21.7
Saudi Telecom	Saudi Arabia	462	21.0	Telecoms	1.9	31.2

Source: FT Global 500, *Financial Times*, London, March 2013.

the FT Global 500 companies. It has the largest retail banking network in Saudi Arabia and has offices in several European cities, including Istanbul, Zurich and London, plus a substantial retail banking subsidiary in Malaysia. Al Rajhi stresses that all its operations are in compliance with *Shari'ah* law;[44] as it avoids interest-based transactions its depositors hold either current accounts or *mudarabah* profit-sharing accounts, while much of its financing is through leasing (*ijara*) and mark-up trade finance (*murabahah*). The Islamic designation is clearly important for Al Rajhi, as it aims to appeal to Muslim clients who wish to manage their financial affairs in a manner that is *Shari'ah*-compliant, and this is its principal distinguishing feature from other banks in Saudi Arabia, which mainly offer conventional financing, although most offer some Islamic financial products.

Apart from banking, the other field in which Islamic values have an influence on multinational business is satellite television, especially in the Middle East, where the major channels are Saudi-owned, but mostly based in Lebanon or other Gulf states.[45] Although there is no effective state censorship, the entertainment programmes of channels such as the Lebanese Broadcasting Corporation (LBC), the Middle East Broadcasting Centre (MBC), Arab Radio and Television (ART) and Orbit are designed for Muslim family viewers, and do not include the type of content that western channels provide that would cause great offence. Nevertheless, LBC and MBC, despite having very pious owners, have often carried risqué material, including an Arabic version of 'Big Brother' until it was withdrawn following objections from viewers in Riyadh.

There is substantial overseas investment by Muslims resident in the Gulf, estimated to amount to almost US$1.2 trillion in 2001.[46] Overall outward investment from the Islamic world was worth US$400 billion in 2012, of which US$230 billion was accounted for by the Middle East and North Africa region, mainly the Gulf countries, and US$134 billion was accounted for by southeast Asian countries, mainly Indonesia and Malaysia.[47] Although most of individuals of high net worth who are placing this investment are practising Muslims, their agenda has been primarily financial, and they have made little attempt to influence the recipient businesses through exercising their power as shareholders. Prince Waleed, the richest member of the House of Saud, has not tried, for example, to change the policies of Citicorp or the French hotel chain Accor in which he owns substantial stakes.[48]

There are nevertheless many investors in the Gulf and Malaysia who wish to invest in a manner that is specifically *Shari'ah*-compliant, with companies vetted according to both sector and financial screening. For example, companies whose main business is the production and distribution of alcohol, or pork products or gambling are excluded, as are companies that are heavily reliant on debt financing.[49] There is even a service provided by the Dow Jones Islamic Indices that provides outsourced screening for Islamic investors placing funds in stock markets around the world.[50] Furthermore, for Muslims wanting fixed income investments for whom interest-yielding bonds are unacceptable, Islamic sovereign and corporate *sukuk* securities have been developed that provide a non-interest return that is related to the returns on the real underlying assets.[51]

In the past much of the opposition to foreign direct investment by multinational corporations in the Muslim world was because of local nationalisms rather than due to religious objections to western business penetration.[52] The opposition was largely a product of the post-colonial world. There was also a preference for smaller enterprises, which, arguably, could contribute more to employment than larger enterprises, an important consideration given the unemployment and under-employment in many Muslim countries.[53] Some writers also preferred cooperative businesses organised locally rather than multinational corporations where decision-making and power was often remote from Muslim countries, but the limitations of such cooperative ventures was recognised, although this was a matter of regret.[54]

Some Muslim countries have been much more successful in adapting to globalisation than others; most notably Malaysia, which has welcomed multinational companies and been transformed from an economy largely dependent on palm oil and rubber to a modern industrial nation exporting high-technology goods.[55] In the Middle East it is the traditional monarchies that have adapted most successfully to globalisation, while the so-called reformist governments of the Arab republics have adopted a bunker mentality, and have failed to attract significant foreign direct investment and the technology that accompanies it.[56] More radically, there are a number of Muslim writers who see the supposedly painful choice between modernisation and Islam as no longer relevant. Masoud Kavoossi asserts that to be a Muslim is to be modern, and there is therefore no need to contemplate post-Islamic secularist societies in Muslim lands.[57] Multinational corporations, even those based in the West, should, he believes, be welcomed in the Muslim world provided that they can adapt their operations so that their Muslim clients, employees and suppliers are comfortable with their business practices. In other words, multinational corporations should embrace multiculturalism, and not simply transmit and impose the dominant culture of the country in which they are based.[58]

The conditions for multinational corporations and Islamic finance to flourish in the Muslim world are similar. First and foremost, the governments of Muslim countries should give businesses and pious businessmen and women space to pursue their plans and ambitions rather than thwarting them by mistakenly equating so-called 'Islamic' terrorism with Muslim business.[59] It is preferable to have a dialogue with those who wish to see *Shari'ah* law applied to commerce and finance rather than trying to oppress Muslim businesses and Islamic finance. Political pluralism is likely to be helpful to Islamic commerce, while autocracy hinders its development. The power of religion can be put to constructive use, rather than viewing it as destructive.

Notes

1. Ibn Taymiyyah, *Public Duties in Islam: The Institution of Hisba*, trans. from original fourteenth-century text by Muhtar Holland (Leicester: Islamic Foundation, 1982), p. 9.
2. Rodney Wilson, *Economics, Ethics and Religion: Jewish, Christian and Muslim Economic Thought* (London: Macmillan, 1997), pp. 74–6 and pp. 208–9.
3. Laws of Malaysia, Islamic Financial Services Act, No. 759, Kuala Lumpur, 2013.
4. Muhammad Nejatullah Siddiqi, *Partnership and Profit Sharing in Islamic Law* (Leicester: Islamic Foundation, 1985), pp. 11–18.
5. Muhammad Taqi Usmani, *An Introduction to Islamic Finance* (The Hague: Kluwer Law International, 2002), p. 11.
6. Mohammad Mohsin, *Economics of Small Business in Islam*, Visiting Scholar Research Series, No. 2 (Jeddah: Islamic Research and Training Institute, Islamic Investment Bank, 1995), p. 41.
7. Nabil A. Saleh, *Unlawful Gain and Legitimate Profit in Islamic Law* (Cambridge: Cambridge University Press, 1986), pp. 92–3.
8. Frank E. Vogel and Samuel L. Hayes, *Islamic Law and Finance: Religion, Risk and Return* (The Hague: Kluwer Law International, 1998), pp. 168–9.
9. The effort of a qualified *fiqh* (Islamic legal) scholar to determine the true meaning of divine law.
10. Usmani, *An Introduction to Islamic Finance*, pp. 12–13.
11. Habib Ahmed, 'Incentive-compatible profit sharing contracts: a theoretical treatment', in Munawar Iqbal and David T. Llewlan (eds), *Islamic Banking and Finance: New Perspectives on Profit Sharing and Risk* (Cheltenham: Edward Elgar, 2002), pp. 40–54.
12. Nik Mohamed Affandi Bin Nik Yusoff, *Islam and Business* (Selangor, Malaysia: Pelanduk, 2002), pp. 1–12.
13. M. Umer Chapra, *Islam and the Economic Challenge* (Leicester: Islamic Foundation), pp. 6–9.
14. Gillian Rice, 'Islamic ethics and the implications for business', *Journal of Business Ethics*, 18 (1999): 345–58.
15. M. Cherif Bassiouni, 'Business ethics in Islam;, in Paul M. Minus (ed.), *The Ethics of Business in a Global Economy* (Dordrecht: Kluwer Academic Publishers, 1993), pp. 117–22.
16. Shafiq Falah Alawneh, 'Human motivation: an Islamic perspective', *American Journal of Islamic Social Sciences*, 15(4) (Winter 1998): 19–39.
17. Ali J. Abbas and Manton Gibbs, 'Foundations of business ethics in contemporary religious thought: the ten commandment perspective', *International Journal of Social Economics*, 25(9/10) (1998): 1552–64.
18. Salisu Shehu, 'Towards an Islamic perspective of developmental psychology', *American Journal of Islamic Social Sciences*, 15(4) (Winter 1998): 41–70.

19. Abbas J. Ali, Manton Gibbs and Robert C. Camp, 'Jihad in monotheistic religions: implications for business and management', *International Journal of Sociology and Social Policy*, 23(12) (2003): 19–46.

20. Daniel J. Koys, 'Integrating religious principles and human resource management activities', *Teaching Business Ethics*, 5(2) (2001): 121–39.

21. Monir Tayeb, 'Islamic revival in Asia and human resource management', *Employee Relations*, 19(4) (1997): 352.

22. Kishwar Khan and Sarwat Aftab, 'Consumer protection in Islam: the case of Pakistan', Australian Economic Papers, 39(4) (2000): 483–503.

23. Ibn Taymiyyah, *Public Duties in Islam*, pp. 29–33.

24. Mohammad Saeed, Zafar U. Ahmed and Syeda-Masooda Mukhtar, 'International marketing ethics from an Islamic perspective: a value maximisation approach', *Journal of Business Ethics*, 32(2) (2001): 127–42.

25. Rafik Issa Beekun, *Islam and Business Ethics* (Herndon, VA: International Institute of Islamic Thought, 1996), p. 1.

26. Ibn Maja, K., 'al-Tijarat, Chapter Al-Haththt ala al-Makasib', cited in S. M. Hasanuzzaman, *Islam and Business Ethics* (London: Institute of Islamic Banking and Insurance, 2003), p. 12.

27. Muhammad Nejatullah Siddiqi, 'The guarantee of a minimum level of living in an Islamic state', in Munawar Iqbal (ed.), *Distributive Justice and Need Fulfilment in an Islamic Economy* (Leicester: The Islamic Foundation, 1988), p. 255.

28. Ataul Huq Pramanik, *Development and Distribution in Islam* (Petaling Jaya, Selangor, Malaysia: Pelanduk Publications, 1993), pp. 11–27.

29. Yusuf al-Qardawi, *Fiqh az-Zakat: A Comparative Study* (London: Dar Al Taqwa Publishing, 1999), pp. 65–100.

30. Ismail Sirageldin, 'The elimination of poverty: challenges and Islamic strategies', in Munawar Iqbal (ed.), *Islamic Economic Institutions and the Elimination of Poverty* (Leicester: The Islamic Foundation, 2002), pp. 43–4.

31. Syed Nawab Haider Naqvi, *Perspectives on Morality and Human Well-Being: A Contribution to Islamic Economics* (Leicester: The Islamic Foundation, 2003), p. 212.

32. *Sura* 4:11–12.

33. *Sura* 2:240.

34. *Sura* 4:8–9.

35. Maxime Rodinson, *Islam and Capitalism* (Harmondsworth: Penguin Books, 1977), pp. 137–57 and 185–94 (originally published by Éditions du Seuil, Paris, 1966).

36. Muhammad Baqir al-Sadr, *Our Economics: Iqtisaduna*, trans., commentary and ed. Kadom Jawad Shubber (London: Books Extra, 2000), pp. 182–3.

37. Rodney Wilson, 'The contribution of Muhammad Bäqir al-Sadr to contemporary Islamic economic thought;, *Journal of Islamic Studies*, 9(1) (1998): 48.

38. Mohamed Aslam Haneef, *Contemporary Islamic Economic Thought: A Selected Comparative Analysis* (Kuala Lumpur: Ikraq Books, 1995), p. 124.

39. Chapra, *Islam and the Economic Challenge*, pp. 17–69.

40. M. Umer Chapra, *The Future of Economics: An Islamic Perspective* (Leicester: The Islamic Foundation, 2000), pp. 74–6.
41. M. Umer Chapra, *Islam and Economic Development* (Islamabad: International Institute of Islamic Thought, 1993), p. 122.
42. Syed Nawab Haider Naqvi, *Islam Economics and Society* (London: Kegan Paul International, 1994), pp. 29–34.
43. FT Global 500, *Financial Times*, London, March 2013.
44. www.alrajhibank.com.sa.
45. Naomi Sakr, *Satellite Realms: Transnational Television, Globalisation and the Middle East* (London: I. B. Tauris, 2001), pp. 27–65.
46. Brad Borland, 'Outward flows, inward investment needs in the GCC', *Arab Banker*, 16(2) (2001): 49–51.
47. UNCTAD data for IDB member states, Geneva, 2013.
48. Sharaf Sabri, *The House of Saud in Commerce: A Study of Royal Entrepreneurship in Saudi Arabia* (New Delhi: I. S. Publications, 2001), pp. 120–3.
49. Mohamed A. Elgari, 'Islamic equity investment', in Simon Archer and Rifaat Ahmed Abdel Karim (eds), *Islamic Finance: Innovation and Growth* (London: Euromoney Books, 2002), pp. 151–9.
50. Rodney Wilson, 'Screening criteria for Islamic equity funds', in Sohail Jaffer (ed.), *Islamic Asset Management: Forming the Future for Shariah-Compliant Investment Strategies* (London: Euromoney Books, 2004), pp. 35–45.
51. Nathif J. Adam and Abdulkader Thomas, *Islamic Bonds: Your Guide to Issuing, Structuring and Investing in Sukuk* (London: Euromoney Books, 2004), pp. 81–146.
52. Riad A. Ajami, 'The multinationals and Arab economic development: a new paradigm', in Robert A. Kilmarx and Yonah Alexander (eds), *Business and the Middle East: Threats and Prospects* (Oxford: Pergamon Press, 1982), pp. 178–99.
53. Mohsin, *Economics of Small Business in Islam*, pp. 17–20.
54. Dmenico Mario Nuti, *The Economics of Participation*, Eminent Scholar Lecture Series, No. 11 (Jeddah: Islamic Research and Training Institute, Islamic Development Bank, 1995), pp. 59–64.
55. Rodney Wilson, 'Islam and Malaysia's economic development', *Journal of Islamic Studies*, 9(2) (1998): 259–76.
56. Clement M. Henry and Robert Springborg, *Globalisation and the Politics of Development in the Middle East* (Cambridge: Cambridge University Press, 2001), pp. 99–133 and 168–93.
57. Masoud Kavoossi, *The Globalisation of Business and the Middle East* (London: Quorum Books, 2000), pp. ix–x.
58. Felix Pomeranz, 'Ethics: towards globalisation', *Managerial Auditing Journal*, 19(1) (2004): 8–14.
59. Clement M. Henry and Rodney Wilson (eds), *The Politics of Islamic Finance* (Edinburgh: Edinburgh University Press, 2004), pp. 286–95.

FISCAL POLICY CHOICES TO PROMOTE SOCIAL JUSTICE

Political discourse

Fiscal policy concerns include the extent of public sector involvement in an economy; the level and sources of taxation; and the amount of government spending and how it should be prioritised. These issues can be highly divisive and subject to contentious political discourse between socialist parties, which generally favour more government spending and higher taxes, and conservative or populist parties, which urge less government involvement in an economy with lower spending and taxes. Although the outcomes of the discourse have profound implications for income and wealth distribution and the living standards of the poor, the political debate usually takes place in a secular context with no reference to religious teaching. Politicians prefer the clergy not to get involved in this discourse, even though they may have much to contribute given their knowledge of religious teaching on social justice.

Politicians can argue that they have greater legitimacy than the clergy if they are democratically elected, whereas the religious leadership is self-selected. Of course, the clergy can stand for election, but most choose to stay out of politics; a stance encouraged by politicians not only in the West, but in most of the Muslim world. Although most Muslim countries acknowledge Islam in their constitutions, this is meaningless in terms of domestic political debate over economic policy choices. Of course, the faithful can get involved in politics, either by joining secular political parties and trying to influence their agendas or by forming Islamist parties.

The latter course of action has proved to be less successful in Muslim countries, where Islamist parties have a long history of being banned as they are perceived as a threat to existing centres of entrenched power. The sectarian values that some Islamist parties propagate are also viewed as socially divisive, especially given the fault lines between Sunni and Shi'a adherents in most of the Islamic world and beyond. Joining existing political parties, as in the United Kingdom, has brought concrete benefits, such as provision in financial legislation to ensure Islamic banks are not at a competitive disadvantage because of the tax regime. Allowing Muslim schools to be classified as charitable institutions has also brought tax benefits, but in return the schools must implement the national curriculum and be subject to state inspections.

Economic policy implications of Muslim moral concerns

The relationship between economic efficiency and distributional justice is a core concern that has clear moral dimensions for economic policy-makers. Economic policy issues include decisions over the level and nature of taxation and government spending priorities. There is no specific Islamic teaching on fiscal policy, however, and no consensus among Islamic economists. Fiscal policy choices are to a large extent determined by political preferences, and Islamists disagree among themselves about the role of the state in economic affairs, some favouring a substantial direct role for government in economic activity while others favour a freer market economy.[1]

Although there are disagreements over economic policy, an equitable distribution of income and wealth as well as fair access to resources are viewed as moral imperatives.[2] An equitable distribution does not mean an equal distribution, which would be inefficient and detrimental to the interests of society as a whole as people's ability to manage assets varies according to their intellect, knowledge, experience and honesty. Those with command over more resources have greater accountability to their Creator, with equity defined in terms of the balance between rights and responsibilities. The latter involves ensuring resources are used for the benefit of the wider community and not simply for personal consumption and gratification. Nevertheless, consumers should not feel guilty, and having attractive and valuable possessions should not be seen as immoral or unethical provided that it is not as the result of the exploitation of others. Rather, this can be viewed as part of the bounty of Allah for which the faithful should be thankful, indeed, the faithful should not worry about their needs as Allah will take care of those who submit to His will. This certainty is liberating for believers and ensures that they are not distracted by concerns about how they will live in the future. Rather, they can focus on serving others instead of worrying about themselves.

There were four major forms of taxation levied in Muslim societies in the past, *kharaj*, land taxation; *jizya*, a head tax; *fai*, a tax on war booty; and *zakat*, a form of wealth tax. Land taxation is obviously important in traditional rural societies, and it can provide an incentive for agricultural production as if land is left fallow the owner will incur the same tax liability as the more productive farmer. There is also an equitable and redistributive dimension to *kharaj*, as those owning more land will pay more. Applying *jizya* is arguably more controversial from a moral perspective, as a head tax where everyone pays the same amount is arguably regressive and inequitable. The justification is that if everyone benefits from the resultant expenditure, as with street lighting for example, then this demands an equal contribution. The poor are, however, usually exempted from *jizya*, as are women and children.

The notion of individuals gaining from war booty is repugnant in most modern societies, but in traditional societies this was regarded as normal. The application of *fai* in Islamic societies served to reduce individual gains and meant that a proportion of the booty would accrue to the state, which would arguably be appropriate if the war was serving a just cause.

The writings of Islamic economists stress the importance of *zakat* and *waqf* in facilitating wealth redistribution and creating a fairer and more equitable society. *Zakat* charitable donations are the third of the five pillars of Islam, it being incumbent on every Muslim to pay an annual sum equivalent to one-fortieth of their financial assets. *Waqf* involves the establishment of charitable foundations, with the more affluent donating a portion of their wealth to these foundations whose beneficiaries include the poor and those in need. Needless to say, the achievement of the worthy objectives of *zakat* and *waqf* depends on how they are administered and by whom. There is a long history of debate on these matters, and whether *zakat* and *waqf* can be viable alternatives to taxes collected by governments to fund state expenditure. Controversially, many governments in the Islamic world have established ministries to control *zakat* and *waqf*, effectively politicising these institutions. Needless to say, many Islamic clerics have condemned this state interference with the nationalisation of hitherto private voluntary organisations.

The role of *zakat*

Translated from the Arabic *zakat* means to purify or, in other words, to recognise the social obligations involved in the accumulation of wealth. Payment of *zakat* is obligatory for Muslims, apart from those with little or no wealth. As with modern direct taxes, there is a threshold and it is only wealth in excess of that amount, referred to as the *nisab*, that incurs a *zakat* obligation. The threshold amount was traditionally defined in terms of gold and silver, which were widely used for payments in most Muslim countries. However, as the prices of gold and silver are very volatile, today the threshold for the *nisab* is calculated in national currencies, the amount in the United Kingdom being £3,500. Muslims with wealth below that amount are exempt from *zakat*.

Zakat is viewed as more central to Islamic taxation, as none of the other traditional taxes are any longer applied in contemporary Muslim states, and, most importantly, *zakat* is one of the five pillars of Islam and an obligation for all the faithful. *Zakat* is levied annually, the amount collected being, as already indicated, one-fortieth of the value of assets of each Muslim believer. As the value of the assets is related to the amount of the payment, *zakat* can be viewed as equitable. It is proportionate as the ratio is a constant 2.5 per cent, rather than being levied at a higher rate for those with more assets, which would result in it being classified as a progressive tax. *Zakat* payments are due on 15th of Rajab in the lunar year, which is, of course, shorter than the Gregorian year used in the West, meaning that the amount payable in the Gregorian year exceeds 2.5 per cent.

There is much debate over *zakat* issues, including to which assets it applies, how it should be collected, the use of the proceeds and whether it should be a substitute for secular taxes such as income or value added tax (VAT) or an additional levy.[3] Usually *zakat* is regarded as applying to financial assets such as funds in bank accounts and securities such as bonds or their Islamic equivalent, *sukuk*. Whether it applies to other financial assets such as shares in listed companies is more doubtful, as investors might face difficulties if they were obliged to sell their holdings to meet *zakat* obligations. Modern forms of capital gains taxation may be seen as preferable, as these are borne by those who can afford to pay, rather than by those suffering from losses in the value of their equity holdings. *Zakat* is not levied on owner-occupied property, but it can be debated whether it should be applied to private rented property or commercial real estate, which might also have to be sold to meet *zakat* obligations. If immovable property and equity investment is exempted from *zakat*, this may encourage holdings of these types of assets and discourage excessive monetary holdings in bank accounts and debt instruments.[4]

In most Muslim countries a government ministry is responsible for *zakat* collection and disbursement. In Saudi Arabia, for example, there is a Department of Zakat and Income Tax, and in Indonesia, where *zakat* collection used to be decentralised, there is now a national *zakat* agency.[5] In the UAE a state Zakat Fund was established under Federal Law 4 of 2003 as a separate agency independent from the Ministry of Justice, Islamic Affairs and Endowments. A similar position already existed in Malaysia, where a Zakat Collection Centre (*Pusat Pungutan Zakat*) was established in 1991,[6] and in Pakistan where the Ministry of Religious Affairs has exercised responsibility for the organisation of *zakat* collection and distribution since independence.[7] In the United Kingdom, there is no government involvement in *zakat* collection, but there are several voluntary agencies administrating *zakat* which are registered charities. These include *Jam'iat Ihyaa Minhaaj Al Sunnah* (JIMAS), the Association to Revive the Way of the Messenger, and the Malay Community Association of the United Kingdom. The Zakat Foundation of America has played a similar role in the United States since 2001. All these organisations have websites.[8]

Whether *zakat* collection and disbursement should be nationalised or undertaken by voluntary organisations is a debatable matter. Provided the ministries or agencies of national governments are honestly managed and maintain detailed records of receipts and payments, preferably independently audited, there is a strong case for them to be involved in *zakat* administration. Democratic legitimacy is not necessarily a prerequisite, but transparency and good governance of *zakat* funds are important, as is effective management. Where *zakat* collection and disbursement is independently undertaken by voluntary organisations, it may be preferable for them to be registered charities rather than profit-making commercial organisations. If professional asset management is required, this can be outsourced to financial institutions, but the charities should maintain overall control and responsibility to *zakat* payers. In most jurisdictions registered charities have to submit annual independently audited accounts to a state regulator so that they can benefit from tax advantages, such as claiming back the income tax that *zakat* payers will have already had deducted from their salaries.

Zakat revenue must be used for social expenditure for the benefit of the poor and needy, and it cannot be used for general government expenditure on investments in infrastructure or defence. Defining who qualifies as poor and needy is a debatable issue, however, as poverty is relative and a poor person in the UAE or Qatar may have a much higher income than a poor person in Afghanistan or Bangladesh. There is also the issue in countries with large expatriate populations, such as those in the Gulf, regarding whether *zakat* should be disbursed only to local nationals or to foreign workers, who are generally poorer. In the UAE, the needy are defined as those with little income, orphans, widows, divorcees, the elderly, those who are ill or incapacitated, students, the unemployed and families of prisoners and missing people. Inevitably, the same sort of questions arise with *zakat* disbursements as with other social security spending, notably whether it should be used to support broken families, who arguably have some responsibility for their own predicament, and whether these payments produce a dependency culture.

Organisations such as JIMAS confine *zakat* disbursements to within the United Kingdom, although they help asylum seekers who have already arrived, as well as those with unaffordable debts, the homeless, single parent families and Muslim students having problems in paying tuition fees. The Zakat Foundation of America focuses on emergency relief, as well as long-term sustainable development through the funding of water wells, education and skill training, access to health care and micro-finance for those who cannot obtain bank funding due to not having collateral or a regular income.

As *zakat* is designated for social security expenditure, it should not be regarded as a substitute for secular income or expenditure taxes. Indeed, there is the issue of whether it should be regarded as a tax, but rather as a form of alms-giving, which benefits not only the recipient but also the donor, as their wealth is purified through such charitable donation. In some countries, notably Malaysia, *zakat* donors are given a receipt that can be used to offset income tax payments. In the Gulf, there is no income tax as most government receipts come from oil revenue, but companies as well as individuals are liable for *zakat* on their financial assets.

As *zakat* is fixed it cannot be used as a tool of fiscal policy as is the case with expenditure taxes such as VAT or income tax. These can be raised to curtail aggregate demand in an economy to restrain inflation or lowered in a recession to provide an economic stimulus. *Zakat* income is pro-cyclical, rising in a boom and falling in a recession, although it is during recessionary times that more *zakat* disbursement may be required. This highlights the need to maintain reserves in *zakat* funds rather than simply balancing current receipts with current expenditure during a boom. *Zakat* funds should be cautiously managed, and they should not fall into deficit, as payment for borrowing from financial institutions would not constitute a legitimate use of *zakat*.

Waqf charitable trusts

Another important Islamic institution with a strong moral purpose is *waqf*, charitable trusts that are usually created through bequests in wills on death. Islam prescribes a fair and equitable distribution of inheritance that recognises the rights and obligations of each of the beneficiaries of an estate, but each person has discretion over how one-third of their estate can be distributed. It is usually from this portion that *waqfs* are established, but they can also be created through a lifetime donation. Once funds are designated for *waqf*, the donor has no recourse, and it is no longer their property. *Waqf* are often used to fund the building of mosques and madrassas, the educational establishments attached to mosques designated for Islamic studies.

In addition to their role in providing facilities for worship and education, *waqf* can also generate income that can be used for charitable purposes. Unlike *zakat*, where although there are reserves, most expenditure is financed from current income, *waqf* represent endowments where the initial donation can generate income which can continue in perpetuity. Although cash *waqf* can be established, which invest in *Shari'ah*-compliant securities yielding dividends and capital gains, the majority of *waqf* involve real estate, the major source of income being rent. Where *waqf* are situated in prime urban locations, such as Singapore or central Kuala Lumpur, even though some of the land may be occupied by a mosque, the remainder can be leased for commercial or residential use. The land cannot be sold, but property developers who have an opportunity to acquire a leasehold site for ninety-nine years have been willing to invest and develop these sites at no cost to the *waqf* fund. Indeed, the developers are often prepared to pay a substantial up-front sum to acquire the leasehold, with the subsequent rental income shared between the developer and the *waqf*. Such arrangements unleash the income-generating potential of *waqf* and increase the funds that can be paid to charitable causes.

As with *zakat* administration, who governs *waqf* and the system of governance has been the subject of much debate. Historically, most *waqf* were private endowments associated with particular individuals or families, but in many countries of the Muslim world, especially those that pursued socialistic policies in their post-independence periods, *waqf* endowments were taken under the control of the state with special ministries established for their administration.[9] Such policies were pursued in Syria, Egypt and Turkey, although in the latter new legislation was passed in 2005 allowing greater autonomy for *waqf* and indeed provided tax incentives for the foundation of new *waqf*. Not unnaturally many Islamists resented the interference of the state in *waqf* affairs, although there were precedents in the Ottoman Empire where a register was maintained of *waqf* property and state courts dealt with disputes. Many of the issues debated today concerning *waqf* have preoccupied those involved with *waqf* in previous centuries, as a detailed study of *waqf* in Ottoman Algeria illustrates.[10]

The establishment of *waqf* can have implications for taxation and government spending. If *waqf* are established to help fund social expenditures by the voluntary sector, this may lower government spending on welfare.[11] Often charities are more efficient at disbursing welfare funding than government, as those who work for voluntary organisations are highly motivated, especially where charities have a religious ethic.[12] Charities being bottom up rather than top down institutions may be in a better position to ascertain society's needs than governments, which are all too often distrusted and seen as excessively bureaucratic and inflexible. Government welfare payments often result in the creation of a dependency culture and end up being non-sustainable. Naturally, when the inevitable cutbacks come, recipients are resentful of their former paymasters as their expectations of continuing support are disappointed. Charities are usually more targeted in their support, with many Islamic charities focused on helping with education funding through scholarships that enable the beneficiaries and their families to escape from dependency as their economic prospects are enhanced.

In many jurisdictions the founders and administrators of *waqf* seek charitable status for the foundation which brings tax advantages. In the United Kingdom, for example, when a *waqf* obtains charitable status donations can be offset against income tax, which enables the *waqf* administrators to reclaim a sum equivalent to the tax paid by the donor.[13] The *waqf* must be non-profit-making and submit its articles of association and annual, independently audited, financial statements of income and expenditure to the Charities Commission. Failure to submit the accounts by the deadline can result in the loss of charitable status. Where the *waqf* supports an Islamic school or college, teaching must conform to the national curriculum and be subject to government inspections to ensure the education provision is of an acceptable quality.[14] This will also make the school eligible for state funding, although with such support it will forgo the benefits of being independent, which apply to schools free of local authority control, but still subject to national inspection.

Government revenues and expenditures

Although *zakat* receipts and the value of *waqf* are more substantial than they have ever been, reflecting the increasing Muslim population worldwide and rising levels of wealth, they are not a substitute for government revenue and expenditures. The Islamic charitable sector has expanded rapidly in most Muslim countries, but the role of governments has grown even faster. There are, however, no accurate estimates of the value of *zakat* and *waqf* at state level, given the diversity of sources and the competing organisations involved. Most government expenditure cannot in any case be regarded as charitable, whether it is on infrastructure, or defence expenditure or, indeed, general administrative spending by government ministries with their many employees. In all Muslim countries taxation and government expenditure are largely secular, and even though many states profess a role for Islam in their constitutions in practice there is no clerical input into fiscal decision-making.

The level of government expenditure and revenues varies considerably in relation to gross domestic product (GDP) in the leading twenty Muslim majority economies, as Table 3.1 shows. As major oil exporting nations with relatively small populations, Libya and Kuwait received more revenue than any other Muslim countries, while resource-poor states such as Bangladesh and Pakistan received least. Iran's oil revenues in 2012 were adversely affected by sanctions, but Iraq's remained relatively buoyant in spite of an internal security situation that remained challenging. Saudi Arabia remained the world's largest oil exporting nation in 2012, and in absolute terms enjoyed the highest government revenue in the Islamic world.

The government of Libya spent more in relation to GDP than any other Muslim country, but some of the expenditure in 2012 may have been exceptional given the need for reconstruction and to pacify the militias following the revolution and the overthrow of the Gaddafi regime. Most oil exporting countries had a higher proportion of government spending than resource poor countries, but they managed to maintain surpluses without the need to resort to borrowing. The exceptions were Algeria and Iran, who, despite being oil and gas exporting states, had unsustainable levels of government spending. An easing of sanctions could improve Iran's revenues, however, and turn the deficit into a surplus. Despite domestic economic mismanagement in recent years, Iran is fortunate in having a relatively modest amount of government debt.

Egypt is by far the largest debtor nation in the Islamic world, with government expenditure being well in excess of revenues for many decades. The situation worsened considerably after the overthrow of Mubarak and the subsequent insecurity that crippled the tourist industry and much local manu-

Table 3.1 Government revenues, expenditure, borrowing and debt

Country	Government revenue	Government expenditure	Government borrowing	Government debt
Algeria	39.5	44.6	−5.1	10.5
Azerbaijan	40.0	37.0	3.0	11.6
Bangladesh	12.9	16.3	−3.4	N/A
Egypt	22.6	33.4	−10.7	80.6
Indonesia	18.0	19.7	−1.7	24.5
Iran	16.5	19.0	−2.5	9.5
Iraq	49.4	44.1	4.0	34.1
Kazakhstan	27.0	22.5	4.5	12.4
Kuwait	70.0	36.0	34.0	6.4
Libya	72.3	52.9	19.3	0
Malaysia	25.2	29.8	−4.5	55.5
Morocco	28.1	35.7	−7.6	60.4
Nigeria	25.5	27.3	−1.7	18.3
Pakistan	13.1	21.5	−8.4	63.8
Qatar	39.2	31.1	8.1	35.8
Saudi Arabia	51.8	36.8	15.0	3.7
Sudan	10.0	13.8	−3.8	N/A
Tunisia	30.6	35.4	−4.9	44.0
Turkey	34.8	36.4	−1.6	36.2
UAE	35.1	21.8	13.3	16.5

Note: All data as % of GDP for 2012.

Source: World Economic Outlook Database, IMF, Washington DC, 2013.

facturing. Pakistan also has high levels of debt and unsustainable government finances despite expenditure levels being relatively modest in relation to GDP.

Indirect taxes, notably VAT and generalised sales tax (GST), have become the major source of government revenue for the resource-poor Muslim countries.[15] These sales taxes are levied in Egypt, Turkey, Morocco, Tunisia, Pakistan, Kazakhstan, Malaysia and Indonesia. In the long run these taxes will also be applied in oil and gas exporting countries as resource revenues fail to cover expenditure commitments, but for the moment these states are reluctant to introduce VAT or GST because of popular resistance despite International Monetary Fund (IMF) encouragement. From an Islamic perspective sales taxes, although not mentioned in traditional *fiqh*, can be accepted on the ground of necessity. There has been no discussion by contemporary Islamic clerics about the distributional consequences of sales taxes. They are usually classified as being neutral as they are proportionate to spending, with the poor who spend less paying minimal amounts. In countries such as Egypt, where higher rates apply on imported luxury vehicles purchased by the more affluent, the tax could be regarded as progressive insofar as the revenue is used for spending, which benefits the poor.

Income tax is deducted from the salaries of government employees with higher earnings and those in the state sector, but as salary levels are low, the tax base is restricted. Collecting income tax from those in the private sector and the self-employed is problematic, as tax enforcement is patchy and evasion widespread. Income tax is usually more progressive than sales taxes, with higher earners being liable for increased rates of tax. There has been little discussion of these issues by Muslim clerics, their main concern being that *zakat* payments can be offset against income tax liabilities. However, moral issues inevitably arise with income taxes, not least as to whether they should be applied to individuals or families and whether families with more children should pay lower rates. The opinions of contemporary Muslim clerics on such issues would be interesting, and indeed more relevant to modern fiscal policy choices than simply arguing that given *zakat* obligations income tax is unnecessary. This is not a practical or realistic position.

Inflation and unemployment concerns

The decision on what are the most appropriate economic policies depends on the objectives of the policy-makers. Unfortunately, objectives may conflict as, for example, most governments aim at low targets for inflation, but this may be at the expense of employment, as measures to reduce inflation by curtailing demand by government spending cuts may result in rising unemployment. If government spending exceeds revenues, the scope for looser monetary policy is also reduced, and the higher interest rates needed to curb inflation will also cause unemployment to rise as the greater costs of credit result in companies deferring investment plans.

Islamic economists highlight the social injustices arising from inflation as the poor are much less able to protect themselves than the more affluent. Unscrupulous traders are blamed for inflation as suppliers hoard stocks in the expectation of getting a higher price later. Subsidies are recommended as a means of helping the poor to cope. However, there is a failure to recognise that the anti-social behaviour of some traders is a symptom of a deeper malaise due to inappropriate macro-economic policies being pursued that fail to tackle fiscal deficits.[16] Populist measures such as increasing subsidies only worsen the problem and are unsustainable in the long run. There is little acknowledgement of trade-offs, such as the negative relationship between inflation and unemployment. Should Islamist political parties give priority to reducing unemployment, especially the youth employment so prevalent in the Muslim world, or to tackling inflation because of the distortions it causes in the banking system and capital markets?

Egypt, Iran and Sudan appear to have the worst records on inflation with double digit rates most years over the period from 2010 to 2014, as Table 3.2 shows. In contrast, Malaysia, Morocco and the UAE appear to have inflation

Table 3.2 Inflation in consumer prices and broad money (%)

Country	2010	2011	2012	2013	2014	M2/GDP
Algeria	2.7	5.2	9.0	8.2	4.5	61.0
Azerbaijan	7.9	5.5	−0.3	6.0	6.5	31.1
Bangladesh	8.3	10.6	7.7	6.9	6.5	69.7
Egypt	10.7	11.8	7.2	9.7	10.4	74.1
Indonesia	6.9	3.8	4.3	9.5	6.0	40.1
Iran	20.0	21.8	41.2	35.0	25.0	N/A
Iraq	3.3	6.0	3.6	4.0	5.5	31.5
Kazakhstan	7.8	7.4	6.0	6.0	6.2	34.7
Kuwait	4.5	4.9	3.2	3.0	3.5	N/A
Libya	3.3	26.6	−3.7	10.0	9.0	N/A
Malaysia	2.1	3.0	1.7	2.0	2.6	141.2
Morocco	2.2	0.9	2.6	2.3	2.5	113.9
Nigeria	11.7	10.3	12.0	9.7	7.0	36.5
Pakistan	11.8	13.3	11.3	5.8	10.0	39.9
Qatar	0.4	1.9	1.8	3.7	3.9	54.4
Saudi Arabia	5.8	3.6	3.7	3.8	3.5	54.1
Sudan	15.3	18.9	44.4	19.8	30.2	27.9
Tunisia	4.1	4.2	5.9	5.3	5.0	66.7
Turkey	6.4	10.4	6.2	8.0	6.0	55.4
UAE	0.9	0.7	1.1	2.0	2.5	61.2

Source: World Economic Outlook Database, IMF, Washington DC, 2014.

well under control, as 2 per cent inflation annually represents zero inflation in reality due to continuous improvements in the quality of the goods included in the index. Historically, Turkey had high rates of inflation, but a combination of policies to increase the supply capacity of the private sector and to pursue more responsible government spending has resulted in inflation falling, although it remains high by European standards.[17] This is of concern given the extent of Turkey's trade with the European Union (EU).

Unemployment is wasteful as if people are not engaged in economic activity they cannot realise their God-given potential by contributing to society. From an Islamic perspective unemployment can be regarded as immoral, and much of the debate about unemployment centres on who is responsible, governments or the unemployed themselves, or indeed both. Contributors to the Islamic economics literature stress the social obligation to help the poor, but does this extend to a responsibility to provide employment for everyone, something which no society anywhere has been able to achieve. The discussion over responsibility for unemployment is part of the wider debate between the religiously orthodox, who adopt a communitarian perspective viewing individuals as subsumed by the larger community of believers, and modernists, who stress individual moral decisions.[18] For the latter, individuals who drop out of school or college without making much effort to learn or who are unreliable employees bear responsibility for their own unemployment.

Unemployment, especially youth unemployment, is prevalent throughout the Muslim world, and is probably higher than the global average. The rate is particularly high in Sudan, Tunisia, Iran and Egypt, as Table 3.3 shows, but lower in resource-rich countries and in the more successful southeast Asian economies, notably Malaysia and Indonesia. Youth unemployment was regarded by many as a significant cause of the Arab Spring, although the subsequent political instability has aggravated matters further.[19] The accuracy of unemployment statistics must, of course, be questioned in Muslim majority countries with no unemployment benefit systems. People are less likely to classify themselves as unemployed if there are no state hand-outs, but rather to work casually in the informal sector simply to survive.[20]

In low population, resource-rich countries such as Kuwait unemployment is low largely because governments employ most local citizens, and the employees in the private sector are mostly foreign nationals on short-term contracts. Any economic downturn results in the contracts not being extended and the workers returning to their home countries, rather than remaining in countries such as Kuwait and being unemployed. Resource-rich countries with larger populations are, however, struggling to provide employment for local citizens as in the case of Saudi Arabia.[21] The situation has worsened since the Arab Spring as the substantial salary increases given to local nationals by governments trying to buy off discontent have made them internationally uncompetitive and resulted in a wage bill that is not sustainable, especially if oil and gas prices drop.

Table 3.3 Unemployment rates (%)

Country	2010	2011	2012	2013	2014
Algeria	10.0	10.0	10.0	10.0	9.8
Azerbaijan	6.0	6.0	6.0	6.0	6.0
Egypt	9.2	12.1	12.3	13.0	12.8
Indonesia	7.1	6.6	6.1	5.9	5.8
Iran	13.5	12.3	12.2	13.2	14.5
Kazakhstan	5.8	5.4	5.3	5.3	5.3
Kuwait	2.1	2.1	2.1	2.1	2.1
Malaysia	3.3	3.0	3.0	3.1	3.0
Morocco	9.0	8.9	9.0	8.9	8.8
Nigeria	21.1	23.9	N/A	N/A	N/A
Pakistan	5.5	5.9	6.4	6.7	6.9
Saudi Arabia	5.5	5.8	5.5	N/A	N/A
Sudan	17.5	17.5	18.0	19.0	20.0
Tunisia	13.0	18.3	17.6	16.7	16.0
Turkey	11.9	9.8	9.2	9.4	9.5

Source: World Economic Outlook Database, IMF, Washington DC, 2014.

Misallocation of government spending

Military spending has been a priority in many Muslim countries, usually not to defend nations against the threat from *infidels*, but rather as a result of perceived threats internally or from other Muslim countries. The sectarian split between Sunni and Shi'a has long fermented conflict, and the divisions seem to have increased in recent years. Evidence for this is apparent from the civil war in Syria, the divisions in Lebanon, and the violence in Iraq since the Sunni leadership under Saddam Hussein was overthrown and replaced by Shi'a majority leaders.

The high levels of military expenditures in Saudi Arabia and the UAE shown in Table 3.4 reflect the perceived threat from Shi'a Iran and not worries about Israel and the failures of the peace process between Israel and the Palestinians. Military expenditures in Egypt and Turkey would be much higher were it not for domestic budgetary constraints, as these countries lack the oil incomes of the Gulf states who can afford to spend more. Military spending fell as a percentage of GDP in Saudi Arabia and UAE between 2000 and 2008, but it is now rising again in both countries, and the contracts that have already been signed for highly sophisticated and expensive military equipment means spending is likely to rise further over the next ten years, even if the Iranians agree to an inspection system for their nuclear facilities to verify

Table 3.4 Military expenditures (% GDP)

Country	2000	2004	2008	2012
Saudi Arabia	10.6	8.4	8.0	8.9
UAE	8.3	4.6	3.7	5.4
Algeria	3.4	3.3	3.0	4.5
Morocco	2.3	3.4	3.3	3.5
Kuwait	7.2	5.8	3.0	3.3
Libya	3.1	1.9	1.2	3.2
Pakistan	3.7	3.6	2.8	2.7
Iraq	N/A	1.7	2.2	2.7
Turkey	3.7	2.8	2.3	2.3
Egypt	3.2	3.0	2.3	1.7
Tunisia	1.8	1.6	1.3	1.6
Malaysia	1.6	2.3	1.9	1.5
Kazakhstan	0.8	1.0	1.1	1.2
Bangladesh	1.3	1.1	1.0	1.1
Nigeria	0.8	0.7	0.8	1.0
Indonesia	0.5	0.9	0.6	0.8
Iran	3.8	3.1	2.1	N/A
Sudan	4.5	4.7	N/A	N/A

Source: Stockholm International Peace Research Institute, 2013.

that they have been installed for peaceful purposes. Elsewhere in the Muslim world, military spending remains much more modest, with Pakistan's military focused on combating internal dissent rather than the historical threat from India. Indonesia, the most populous Muslim country, spends relatively little on defence. Malaysia spends more, partly reflecting the large amounts of territory it has to defend in North Borneo.

Far from being a bellicose religion as has been suggested by some during the post-9/11 period, Islamic teaching stresses the value of peace.[22] Apart from in Saudi Arabia and the Gulf states, there is no evidence that Muslim majority countries allocate more spending to the military than Christian or Buddhist countries or those where other religions predominate. In Saudi Arabia and the Gulf states, military spending reflects oil wealth, not religion, and, given this wealth, spending decisions are not constrained by military imperatives. Elsewhere in the Islamic world, it is even more difficult to assert that religion is distorting spending with detrimental effects on economic activity. Indeed, given the size of the army and the extent of the military establishment in countries such as Egypt, which includes schools and hospitals, much of the military spending can be classified as social spending rather than expenditure on weapons. The manpower bill accounts for much of the spending, fuelling demand for goods and services in the wider economy; hence, not all of the military spending should be regarded as unproductive.

Notes

1. Charles Tripp, *Islam and the Moral Economy: The Challenge of Capitalism* (Cambridge: Cambridge University Press, 2006), pp. 77–102.

2. Syed Nawab Haider Naqvi, *Perspectives on Morality and Human Well-Being: A Contribution to Islamic Economics* (Leicester: Islamic Foundation, 2003), pp. 143–83.

3. Timur Kuran, *Islam and Mammon: The Economic Predicaments of Islamism* (Princeton: Princeton University Press, 2004), p. 105.

4. Rodney Wilson, 'Economy', in Amyn B. Sajoo (ed.) *A Companion to Muslim Ethics* (London: I. B. Tauris, 2010), pp. 141–3.

5. Arskal Salim, *The Shift in Zakat Practice in Indonesia: From Piety to a Socio-Politico-Economic System* (Bangkok: Silkworm Books, 2008), pp. 17–60.

6. Mohamad Idham Md Razak, Roaimah Omar Maymunah Ismail, Afzan Sahilla Amir Hamzah and Mohd Adnan Hashim, 'Overview of zakat collection in Malaysia: regional analysis', *American International Journal of Contemporary Research*, 3(8) (2013): 140–8.

7. http://www.zakat.gop.pk.

8. http://www.jimas.org; http://www.zakat.org.

9. Gabriel Baer, 'The *waqf* as a prop for the social system (sixteenth–twentieth centuries)', *Islamic Law and Society*, 4(3) (1997): 264–97.

10. Miriam Hoxter, *Endowments, Rulers and Community: Waqf al-Haramayn in Ottoman Algiers*, Studies in Islamic Law and Society (Leiden: E. J. Brill, 1998).

11. Timur Kuran, 'The provision of public goods under Islamic law: origins, impact and limitations of the waqf system', *Law and Society Review*, 35(4) (2001): 841–98.

12. Razak, Mohamad Idham Md, Roaimah Omar Maymunah Ismail, Afzan Sahilla Amir Hamzah and Abul Hasan M. Sadeq, '*Waqf*, perpetual charity and poverty alleviation', *International Journal of Social Economics*, 29(1) (2002): 135–51.

13. Zia Akhtar, 'Charitable trusts and *waqf*: their parallels, registration process and tax reliefs in the United Kingdom', *Statute Law Review*, 34(3) (2013): 281–95.

14. Marie Parker-Jenkins, 'Equal access to state funding: the case of Muslim schools in Britain', *Race, Ethnicity and Education*, 5(3) (2002): 273–89.

15. For rates, see Ernst and Young, *Worldwide VAT, GST and Sales Tax Guide*, 2013.

16. Timur Kuran, 'Further reflections on the behavioural norms of Islamic economics', *Journal of Economic Behaviour and Organization*, 27 (1995): 159–63.

17. Sabri Sayari, 'Turkey's Islamist challenge', *Middle Eastern Quarterly*, 3(3) (1996): 35–43.

18. Nancy J. Davis and Robert V. Robinson, 'The egalitarian face of Islamic orthodoxy: support for Islamic law and economic justice in seven Muslim majority nations', *American Sociological Review*, 71(2) (2006): 167–90.

19. Filipe R. Campante and Davin Chor, 'Why was the Arab world poised for revolution: schooling, economic opportunities and the Arab Spring', *Journal of Economic Perspectives*, 26(2) (2012): 167–88.

20. Stanislaw Wellisz, 'Dual economies, disguised unemployment and the unlimited supply of labour;, *Economica*, 35(137) (1968): 22–51.

21. Mohamed Bosbait and Rodney Wilson, 'Education, school to work transitions and unemployment in Saudi Arabia;, *Middle Eastern Studies*, 41(4) (2005): 533–45.

22. M. A. Muqtedar Khan, 'Islam and peace', *American Journal of Islamic Social Sciences*, 15(1) (1998): 158–62.

DEVELOPMENT POLICY

Secular and Islamic determinants of development morality

In secular societies morality can be socially determined, with what is right and what is wrong being assessed with regard to what is socially acceptable or, indeed, what is politically correct. This inevitably changes over time as society evolves, with what is morally unacceptable during one historical period perhaps becoming acceptable at a later stage. For example, in the financial sphere paying and receiving interest has become widely accepted, although not by advocates of Islamic finance who equate interest with *riba*. Nevertheless, even those who do not accept the arguments for prohibiting interest voice much criticism of credit card providers that levy high charges. Their distain extends to money lenders and pawn brokers whose practices are viewed by many as exploitative, especially when they target the poor and misinformed, and encourage them to borrow amounts that they are unlikely to be able to repay. The unscrupulous selling of excessive mortgages by many banks prior to the global financial crisis of 2008 has also been widely criticised and has resulted in the social status of bankers being diminished. Since the global financial crisis many of those in financial difficulties have turned to payday lenders as they cannot obtain bank loans. However, the payday lenders exploit their clients with usurious interest charged by the day and employ heavy-handed treatment of debtors if they fail to make payments on time.

Religious teaching guides the morality of believers, and in the case of the monotheistic religions, Judaism, Christianity and Islam, the holy books are regarded as the revealed word of God. In the case of Islam, it is the Quran that provides guidance, together with the hadith, the sayings and deeds of the Prophet. This guidance is eternal and unchanging, but over time as societies and economies evolve, the interpretation and application of Islamic teaching may change. It is Islamic scholars versed in *fiqh*, Islamic jurisprudence, whose views on how the teaching should be applied are sought. Through a process known as *ijtihad*, or moral reasoning, they attempt to ascertain how Islamic teaching should apply in circumstances that are very different to those prevailing at the time of the Prophet. They provide opinions, or *fatwa*, on how believers should conduct their affairs, including commercial and financial dealings.

For example, there were no stock markets or listed limited liability companies fourteen hundred years ago. Are such markets useful, and is limited liability possible under Islamic law, the *Shari'ah*? The answer is that such markets facilitate corporate finance and economic activity, which can benefit society, and that limited liability is an acceptable concept. However, if the companies are engaged in morally dubious activity, or if market traders are aiming for speculative gains at the expense of others, then this is seen as being incompatible with religious teaching. The faithful should therefore refrain from any involvement.

An economic analysis of religion

There are three major lines of inquiry regarding the relationship of economics to religion.[1] The first interprets religious behaviour from an economic perspective, focusing on both individual and group behaviour by, for example, investigating the utility or satisfaction that individuals or households gain from the time they spend on religious pursuits and devotion, as well as the positive externalities that believers can derive from being part of a group of worshipers or members of sects. The second is concerned with the economic consequences of religion, which is not only whether religious belief can result in greater economic justice, but whether it can actually contribute to economic efficiency; the hypothesis being that believers are more motivated than non-believers. The third approach, which is adopted in this book, is concerned with the implications of religious belief for economic policy-making and whether the choices are governed by the moral values of the faithful.

If individual denominations function as religious firms, then collectively they constitute a religious market, competing for the membership of potential adherents. Most people are, of course, born into a particular faith rather than converting. Competition, however, comes when people change denomination, as from Catholicism to Protestant evangelising groups such as Jehovah Witnesses or Mormons in Latin America, or when former, lapsed, Christians or Muslims decide to return to worship in churches or mosques.

Although some may object to religious devotion being analysed in this way, the outcomes from this research are positive and encouraging for believers. One conclusion is that contrary to the twentieth-century experience of a small group of countries in western Europe, economic development and rising income are not associated with secularisation, but with stability or even increasing religious adherence. Believers are more likely to be successful in business than non-believers, partly because good morality is good business. Business and financial malpractice can bring short-term material reward, but only longer-term pain and misery, not least from the worry about being caught out.

Being a member of a faith group brings networking opportunities. The strong bonds between fellow believers can build trust that can be translated into long-term productive business relations. The success of MÜSİAD members, the independent association of Muslim businessmen in Turkey, is an example of this.[2] Those that are secure in their religious beliefs may be better equipped to manage risk in their business dealings as they become highly focused, while at the same time they know that their fellow believers will stand by them and offer comfort if misfortune results.

One controversial theme in examining the economic consequences of religious belief has been to ascribe business success to particular religious groups, as with Weber's thesis on *The Protestant Ethic and the Spirit of Capitalism*[3] and its development by Tawney.[4] A detailed examination of the evidence casts doubt on this thesis, not least that from Europe where industrialisation in the largely Catholic Rhineland was more rapid than in Protestant Prussia. Although not surprisingly a western style of capitalism has failed to develop in most non-Christian countries, those who have examined the experiences of the Muslim world have not found any inherent contradictions between Islam and capitalism.[5] Indeed, far from being an exclusively western phenomenon, it is now possible to identify Chinese, Russian, possibly Indian and Islamic forms of capitalism, consistent with the views of the Catholic theologian, Michael Novak, who saw capitalism as being capable of accommodating any religious faith.[6]

Much of the literature by self-designated Islamic and Christian economists is an analysis of economic policy from a religious perspective. The aim has often been to provide a radical critique of the workings of market economies, fiscal and government spending priorities, income distribution, interest-based banking, business exploitation of suppliers or employees and the power of multinational corporations. Leading contemporary Christian writers have included John Atherton,[7] Donald Hay,[8] John Sleeman[9] and Philip Wogman,[10] and their Muslim counterparts include Umer Chapra,[11] Masood Waqar Khan,[12] Timur Kuran[13] and Syed Nawab Haider Naqvi.[14] Similar Hindu,[15] Buddhist[16] and Confucian[17] literature exists, although it has been subject to much less attention in the West.[18]

Development, income distribution and social responsibility

The relationship between economic efficiency and distributional justice is a core concern for economic policy-makers that has clear moral dimensions.

Economic policy issues include decisions over the level and nature of taxation and government spending priorities. As discussed in Chapter 3, there is no specific Islamic teaching on fiscal policy and no consensus among Islamic economists. Fiscal policy choices are to a large extent determined by political preferences, and Islamists disagree among themselves about the role of the state in economic affairs, some favouring a substantial direct role for government in economic activity, while others favour a freer market economy.[19]

Although there are disagreements over economic policy, an equitable distribution of income and wealth as well as fair access to resources are viewed as moral imperatives.[20] An equitable distribution does not mean an equal distribution, which would be inefficient and detrimental to the interests of society as a whole as people's ability to manage assets varies according to their intellect, knowledge, experience and honesty. Those with command over more resources have greater accountability to their Creator, with equity defined in terms of the balance between rights and responsibilities. The latter involves ensuring resources are used for the benefit of the wider community and not simply for personal consumption and gratification. Nevertheless, consumers should not feel guilty, and having attractive and valuable possessions should not be seen as immoral or unethical provided it is not the result of the exploitation of others. Rather, this can be viewed as part of the bounty of Allah for which the faithful should be thankful, indeed, the faithful should not worry about their needs as Allah will take care of those who submit to His will. This certainty is liberating for believers and ensures that they are not distracted by concerns of how they will live in the future. Rather, they can focus on serving others rather than worrying about themselves.

Measuring economic development

Most countries with predominately Muslim populations are categorised as developing nations, a categorisation that is entirely defined by material indicators such as GDP per capita, the extent of industrialisation or the number of consumer items, such as vehicles or telephones per thousand people. On such measures some Muslim countries, such as Bangladesh, fare very badly, while others, such as the oil-rich Gulf nations, appear to be among the most affluent in the world, although in the Gulf states GDP per capita varies enormously according to whether only local citizens are counted or the entire population, most of whom are migrant workers. While Islam is not opposed to material production and consumption, merely measuring development in terms of such indicators is viewed as rather meaningless, although the relationship between national economic wealth and political power and influence is understood and accepted.

A GDP ranking for Muslim majority countries is provided in Table 4.1, with Indonesia ranked first despite its low per capita GDP figure as

Table 4.1 GDP and population for leading OIC economies

Country	GDP 2012 (US$ billion)	Per capita GDP (US$)	Population (million)	Muslims (%)
Indonesia	1,212	3,660	246.8	87.2
Turkey	1,125	10,457	74.0	98.0
Iran	1,006	6,356	76.4	99.0
Saudi Arabia	740	22,823	28.3	93.0
Egypt	538	3,109	80.7	94.9
Pakistan	514	1,288	179.2	96.4
Malaysia	492	10,578	29.2	63.7
Nigeria	450	1,654	168.8	48.8
Bangladesh	305	791	154.7	89.8
Iraq	283	3,882	32.6	99.0
Algeria	274	5,660	38.4	97.9
Kazakhstan	232	12,021	16.8	70.4
UAE	271	65,377	9.2	76.9
Qatar	189	100,377	2.0	67.7
Morocco	171	2,988	32.5	99.0
Kuwait	166	46,142	3.2	74.1
Tunisia	104	4,152	10.7	99.0
Azerbaijan	98	7,726	9.3	96.9
Libya	88	12,879	6.1	96.6
Sudan	80	1,539	37.1	90.7

Sources: IMF, October 2012; United Nations, 2013.

it is by far the most populous country. Turkey, with its diversified middle income economy, is ranked second, and Iran third. Indonesia, Turkey and Saudi Arabia are members of the G20, the forum that includes the world's leading twenty economies. Iran is excluded because of sanctions, and even if these are lifted it would be politically controversial to expel Saudi Arabia and replace it with Iran. The GDP figures are estimated in purchasing power parity terms. This tends to boost the estimate for Iran. Qatar and the UAE have very high levels of GDP per capita, much higher than western countries, indeed, Qatar boasts the highest figure in the world. This reflects its very small population, numbering only 2 million. Indeed, if only local citizens were counted, the figure would be eight times larger, as there are just 250,000 Qataris

More appealing measures from an Islamic perspective include human development indicators, such as the degree of literacy or education levels more generally. Traditional Islamic education focused on religious studies, with the madrassas attached to mosques being the major institutions for learning, but during the twentieth century there was a huge expansion in state education in nearly all Muslim countries resulting in virtually universal primary education and high levels of literacy and numeracy. Primary school completion rates reached 100 per cent in Indonesia in 2013, the world's most populous Muslim country, while the comparable figures were 95 per cent for Egypt, 93 per cent for Turkey and 93 per cent for Saudi Arabia, with virtually no gender gap remaining.[21] A majority also benefited from secondary education and university education became accessible to many, although academic standards varied considerably, being arguably highest in countries such as Turkey, but lower in many Arab countries. Most modern Islamic scholars appreciate the empowering effect of education, with higher education not viewed in any way as a threat to religious piety, but rather as a way of ensuring that there will be better informed believers.

Islam is concerned with fulfilment rather than happiness, but the former can result in the latter. In the *Happy Planet Index* measures of life satisfaction and carbon footprints in predominately Muslim countries are ranked much higher than those of most western, so-called, developed economies.[22] Bangladesh is ranked eleventh in the world and Indonesia fourteenth. This largely reflects their low carbon footprints, which means that they contribute to environmental conservation rather than development with adverse ecological implications.

Life expectation and years of healthy living are relatively low in Bangladesh, Pakistan and Nigeria, as Table 4.2 shows. In contrast, in

Table 4.2 *Happy Planet Index*

Country	HPI rank	Life expectancy	Happy life years	Well-being	Footprint
Bangladesh	11	68.9	42.2	5.0	0.7
Indonesia	14	69.4	45.0	5.5	1.1
Pakistan	16	65.4	41.5	5.3	0.8
Algeria	26	73.1	46.2	5.2	1.6
Iraq	36	69.0	42.4	5.0	1.4
Tunisia	39	74.5	43.9	4.7	1.8
Morocco	42	72.2	40.8	4.4	1.3
Turkey	44	74.0	48.2	5.5	2.6
Saudi Arabia	56	73.9	55.2	6.7	4.0
Iran	77	73.0	43.5	4.8	2.7
Azerbaijan	80	70.7	39.1	4.2	2.0
Libya	81	74.8	45.4	4.9	3.2
Malaysia	84	74.2	48.8	5.6	3.9
Egypt	91	73.2	38.5	3.9	2.1
Sudan	101	61.5	34.8	4.4	1.6
Kazakhstan	119	67.0	43.8	5.5	4.1
Nigeria	125	51.9	30.9	4.8	1.4
UAE	130	76.5	59.9	7.2	8.9
Kuwait	143	74.8	54.9	6.6	9.7
Qatar	149	78.4	57.7	6.6	11.7

Source: New Economics Foundation, London, 2014.

oil-rich UAE and Qatar life expectancy and years of healthy living are among the highest in the world. This reflects increased dietary awareness and excellent health facilities, which result in very low rates of infant mortality. There are much fewer family breakdowns in most Muslim societies than in the West and high levels of social capital, which in the case of poorer Muslim countries more than compensates for the lack of physical capital. Unfortunately, however, divorce rates are rising in many Muslim countries, especially in the most affluent states, and whether social harmony can be preserved is an open question. Class differences are increasing rather than reducing, and although the expanding middle class is helpful for social stability, many of the 'have-nots' resent the growing inequalities, especially for those with no access to employment opportunities or at best limited access at very low wages.

Islamic perspectives on development

As most Muslim economies are classified as developing, there has been considerable interest in development issues by economists who are searching for Islamic solutions to the problems of poverty and the lack of economic empowerment of the poor. There is great stress on the concept of *tawhid*, divine unity under the one and only God, which in social terms implies solidarity or brotherhood.[23] There is no virtue in poverty in Islam, and there is no equivalent to the monks in Buddhism or Christianity who not only forgo material aspirations for a life of prayer, but expect to be supported materially by their fellow believers who work and earn income. In Islam opting out of worldly pursuits is seen as trying to escape reality; rather, believers should contribute to society through their work, as they have been endowed with the capacity of work by their Creator.

These premises also apply at the level of the nation-state or the Muslim community within a nation-state. Although the ultimate purpose of life is to serve the Almighty and not personal or social material enrichment, successful Muslim states have advanced economically and are seen as better role models than those that are stagnant or face economic decline. During the early centuries of Islam, when this new religion spread rapidly from its Arabian heartland as far as the Atlantic and to central Asia, the adoption of Islam was associated with increasing commerce as barriers to trade and movement of people within the new Muslim territories were reduced or eliminated, a process that resulted in greater prosperity for the new converts. Great trading centres emerged, such as Istanbul, Damascus, Cairo and Isfahan, and eventually Islam was to spread to south Asia and across the Indian Ocean to Malaysia and Indonesia. That this spread came through commerce was not surprising given that Mecca and Medina themselves were significant trading centres, and that in the Quran the virtues of honest trade are stressed and contrasted to the evils of usury, which is viewed as exploitative.[24]

The stress on the benefits of trade in Islamic economic literature has parallels in the work of Adam Smith, who saw free trade as an engine for creating the wealth of nations. Smith, however, saw little need for intervention in markets, as the so-called 'invisible hand' would ensure efficient outcomes. Islamic writers, however, are not only concerned with efficiency, but also with justice, their preoccupations being similar to those of the advocates of 'fair' trade today.[25] There is concern over the treatment of market suppliers, and with ensuring that farmers and manufacturers get a fair price for their produce and that workers are not exploited. In other words, the morality of markets is as important as their functioning. There is also concern that consumers should get a fair deal, and traditionally this was the responsibility of the Islamic institution that regulated markets, the *hisba*. Its mandate was comprehensive, including selling practices, with a prohibition on monopoly behaviour which could result in consumers being exploited. There was also concern with the information supplied to consumers with, for example, the enforcement of accurate weights and measures through inspection of the scales for weighing. The remit of the *hisba* also covered food safety and hygiene, and in this there are parallels with contemporary trading standards authorities.[26]

Markets are regarded as the normal mechanism for transactions by Islamic economists, rather than the state playing the major role in resource allocation. For markets to function effectively property rights must be respected, and Islamic economists regard private property as justifiable with the proviso already mentioned that private ownership implies responsibility to the Almighty for the resources exclusively managed. The legal protection of property rights varies widely in the Islamic world, however, as Table 4.3 shows, with a high degree of enforcement in the economies of the Gulf, notably in Qatar, UAE and Saudi Arabia, but a poor degree of protection in Algeria, Pakistan, Bangladesh, Libya and Egypt. Property rights are better protected in Malaysia than in Indonesia, with effective dispute settlement procedures and higher standards of business ethics. Judicial independence can ensure less state interference with property rights as in the Gulf, but elsewhere the degree of judicial independence is problematic, with the gap between Pakistan and Bangladesh being especially notable.[27] Usually there is a positive relationship between the protection of property rights and the other variables, but there are exceptions, such as Indonesia's higher than expected score on dispute settlements. It is important to note that the World Economic Forum numbers are based on perceptions, which may be mistaken or biased by cultural factors. Approval levels for institutions may be higher in small homogeneous states, such as Qatar, than in divided societies with a history of suspicion and mistrust, such as Algeria, Bangladesh or Libya.

Table 4.3 Protection of property rights

Country	Property rights	Judicial independence	Dispute settlement	Business ethics
Qatar	6.0	6.1	5.4	6.0
UAE	5.4	5.5	4.9	5.7
Saudi Arabia	5.3	5.3	4.5	5.1
Malaysia	5.2	4.5	5.1	5.0
Kuwait	5.0	5.0	3.8	3.0
Morocco	4.8	3.4	3.7	4.0
Turkey	4.7	3.4	3.9	4.2
Iran	4.3	3.7	3.4	3.8
Kazakhstan	4.3	3.4	3.9	4.1
Indonesia	4.1	3.7	4.1	4.0
Azerbaijan	4.0	3.3	3.8	4.0
Egypt	3.7	3.5	3.2	4.1
Libya	3.4	3.2	2.9	3.6
Bangladesh	3.4	2.4	3.1	2.8
Pakistan	3.3	4.1	3.1	3.5
Algeria	3.2	3.2	3.1	3.1

Note: 1–7 scale, 1 extremely weak; 7 excellent.

Source: World Economic Forum, *Global Competitiveness Report*, Geneva, 2013–14.

Honesty and development

The relationship between development and corruption is complex and there has been much debate over the direction of causality.[28] On the one hand, corrupt practices can increase transaction costs and result in a sub-optimum allocation of resources, but, on the other hand, the insider knowledge associated with crony capitalism may actually enhance development by increasing the stakes for the key decision-makers driven by both greed and fear. Furthermore, as more rapid development tends to be destabilising, this increases the opportunities for corruption. From an Islamic perspective corrupt practices are, of course, condemned, with greed and fear depicted as negative emotions indicative of sinful behaviour. While recognising that faster development can have negative consequences in the short term, Islamic economists are not opposed to development which can result in more prosperous and just societies in the longer term.

While Islamic teaching abhors corruption, it applauds honesty and morality in business transactions. Bribery especially is singled out for particular condemnation and is contrasted to reward for honest work. Those predominately Muslim states where corruption is rampant are either failed states, where there is no social order, or countries ruled by leaders who are widely condemned because of their immoral cronyism and nepotism. One of the appeals of Islamist political parties is the perceived honesty of their members despite

Table 4.4 The consequences of malpractice

Country	Diversion of public funds	Public trust in politicians	Wastefulness of government spending	Business costs of terrorism
Qatar	6.3	6.1	6.0	6.7
UAE	5.8	5.9	5.8	6.3
Saudi Arabia	4.9	5.3	5.1	5.8
Malaysia	4.2	4.3	4.3	5.3
Morocco	3.8	3.1	3.5	5.3
Turkey	3.6	3.6	4.1	4.1
Kuwait	3.5	3.2	2.8	5.7
Indonesia	3.4	3.2	3.8	4.6
Kazakhstan	3.3	3.8	3.8	5.5
Iran	3.2	3.3	3.2	4.6
Azerbaijan	3.1	3.4	3.7	5.8
Bangladesh	2.7	1.9	2.9	4.6
Pakistan	2.7	2.2	2.5	2.7
Egypt	2.5	2.8	2.1	2.6
Libya	2.4	3.1	2.8	4.1
Algeria	2.3	2.3	2.8	3.7

Note: 1–7 scale, 1 serious corruption, low public trust and high security threat; 7 no diversion or waste, high public trust and no terrorist threat.

Source: World Economic Forum, *Global Competitiveness Report*, Geneva, 2013–14.

living in societies where corruption is rampant. However, as with other states, there appears to be an inverse relationship between the degree of corruption and the level of development of Muslim countries, which may be because high levels of corruption impede development. The notion that material advance encourages corruption is certainly not borne out by the data on Muslim countries from the World Economic Forum and Transparency International, as the most developed are the least corrupt.

Table 4.4 provides data on perceptions of malpractices in Muslim countries, with the rankings similar to those for the protection of property rights. Public trust in politicians is highest in the Gulf, despite the lack of democracy in countries such as Qatar, UAE and Saudi Arabia. In contrast, in Kuwait, which has a democratically elected parliament, public trust in politicians is significantly lower, as are perceptions that public funds are being diverted or wastefully spent. Terrorism is viewed as having a negative effect on business for much of the Islamic world, the effects being greatest in those countries where there has been a breakdown in law and order such as Pakistan and Egypt. In the Gulf, where security is much more effective, the threat from terrorism has been much reduced.

While Tables 4.3 and 4.4 provide a snapshot of perceptions of property rights and maladministration, Table 4.5, using historical data from Transparency

Table 4.5 Corruption perception rankings

Country	Rank 2013	Rank 2007	Rank 2001	2013 score	2012 score
UAE	26	34	N/A	69	68
Qatar	28	32	N/A	68	68
Turkey	53	64	54	50	49
Malaysia	53	43	36	50	49
Saudi Arabia	63	79	N/A	46	44
Kuwait	69	60	N/A	43	44
Tunisia	77	61	31	41	41
Algeria	94	99	N/A	36	34
Morocco	91	72	N/A	37	37
Egypt	114	105	54	32	32
Indonesia	114	143	88	32	32
Azerbaijan	127	150	84	28	27
Pakistan	127	138	79	28	27
Bangladesh	136	162	91	27	26
Kazakhstan	140	150	71	26	28
Iran	144	131	N/A	25	28
Nigeria	144	147	90	25	28
Iraq	171	178	N/A	16	18
Libya	172	131	N/A	15	21
Sudan	174	172	N/A	11	13

Source: Transparency International, Berlin, 2014.

International, reveals how perceptions are changing over time. Corruption is seen as becoming less in UAE, Qatar, Turkey and Saudi Arabia, with improving rankings and stable scores. In contrast, in Tunisia and Egypt corruption increased significantly over period from 2001 to 2013. Not surprisingly, Sudan, Libya and Iraq were viewed as the most corrupt states, although no data were available for 2001 which would have helped show longer-term trends. For countries such as Indonesia, Pakistan, Bangladesh and Kazakhstan the position deteriorated over the period from 2001 until 2007, but has subsequently improved.

A moral framework for development policy

Islamic teaching and the rich traditions of *fiqh muamalet*, the area of Islamic jurisprudence concerned with everyday living, provides a moral framework for decision-making on development policy. Although there is no consensus view among *Shari'ah* scholars on development priorities, there is agreement that the objective should be equity and distributional justice. Islam provides public and private mechanisms to help achieve these goals, notably *zakat* and *waqf* as discussed in Chapter 3, but these are not substitutes for fiscal and government expenditure policies.

Much of this chapter has been devoted to developmental issues, a particular concern of Islamic economists given the developing classification of much of the Muslim world. Islamic teaching has much to say on the morality of development, yet it is evident from the data presented here and empirical observation that there is much that needs rectifying in the Islamic world. The Jasmine Revolution and the Arab Spring have been inevitable reactions to the perceived injustices, and it is to be hoped that the new leaderships adopt better governance practices and policies than their predecessors, although at the time of writing it is difficult to be hopeful. The great Muslim philosopher of history Ibn Khaldun stressed the importance of morally just rule for successful economic activity.[29] Even today – indeed, more than ever today – there is much that can be learnt from his writing.

Notes

1. Laurence R. Iannaccone, 'Introduction to the economics of religion', *Journal of Economic Literature*, 36 (September 1998): 1465–96.
2. Filiz Baskan, 'The political economy of Islamic finance in Turkey: the role of Fethullah Gülen and Asya Finans', in Clement Henry and Rodney Wilson (eds), *The Politics of Islamic Finance* (Edinburgh: Edinburgh University Press, 2004), pp. 216–39.
3. Max Weber, *The Protestant Ethic and the Spirit of Capitalism*, English translation (London: Allen, Unwin & Scribners, [1905] 1930).
4. R. H. Tawney, *Religion and the Rise of Capitalism* (New York: John Murray and Harcourt Brace, 1926, republished by Penguin Books, London, 1938).
5. Maxime Rodinson, *Islam and Capitalism* (Harmondsworth: Penguin Books, 1977) (originally published by Éditions du Seuil, Paris, 1966).
6. Michael Novak, *The Spirit of Democratic Capitalism* (Lanham, MD and London: Madison Books and Institute of Economic Affairs, 1982).
7. John Atherton, *Christianity and the Market: Christian Social Thought for Our Times* (London: SPCK, 1992).
8. Donald Hay, *Economics Today: A Christian Critique* (Leicester: Inter-Varsity Press, 1989).
9. John Sleeman, *Economic Crisis: A Christian Perspective* (London: SCM Press, 1976).
10. Philip Wogman, *Economics and Ethics: A Christian Enquiry* (London: SCM Press, 1986).
11. M. Umer Chapra, *The Future of Economics: An Islamic Perspective* (Leicester: Islamic Foundation, 2000).
12. Masood Waqar Khan, *Towards an Islamic Interest Free Economic System* (Leicester: Islamic Foundation, 1985).
13. Timur Kuran, 'Islam and underdevelopment: an old puzzle revisited', *Journal of Institutional and Theoretical Economics*, 153(1) (1997): 41–71.

14. Syed Nawab Haider Naqvi, *Perspectives on Mortality and Human Well-Being: A Contribution to Islamic Economics* (Leicester: Islamic Foundation, 2003).

15. J. Barkley Rosser and Marina V. Rosser, *The Transition between the Old and New Traditional Economics of India*, unpublished paper, March 2004, available at: http//cob.jmu.edu/rosserjb/oldnewtransindia.doc

16. Ven P. A. Payutto, *Buddhist Economics: A Middle Way for the Market Place* (Dhammavijaya, 1992), available at: www.buddhistinformation.com/buddhist_ economics.htm.

17. Chen Huan-Chang, *The Economic Principles of Confucius and his School* (Ganesha Publishing, 1911, reprinted by University of Chicago Press, 2002).

18. Max Stackhouse, Dennis McCann and Shirley Roels (eds), *On Moral Business: Classical and Contemporary Resources for Ethics in Economic Life* (Grand Rapids, MI: Eerdmans, 1995), pp. 370–411.

19. Charles Tripp, *Islam and the Moral Economy: The Challenge of Capitalism* (Cambridge: Cambridge University Press, 2006), pp. 77–102.

20. Naqvi, *Perspectives on Morality and Human Well-Being*, pp. 143–83.

21. World Bank Database, accessed July 2014.

22. *Happy Planet Index*, New Economic Foundation, 2014, available at: www. happyplanetindex.org.

23. M. Umer Chapra, *Islam and the Economic Challenge* (Leicester: Islamic Foundation, 1992), pp. 199–212.

24. Patricia Crone, *Meccan Trade and the Rise of Islam* (Piscataway, NJ: Gorgias Press, 2004).

25. The Fair Trade Foundation, London, 2014, see at: www.fairtrade.org.uk.

26. Yaron Klein, 'Between public and private: an examination of *hisba* literature', *Harvard Middle Eastern and Islamic Review*, 7 (2006): 41–62.

27. Lars P. Feld and Stefan Voigt, 'Economic growth and judicial independence: cross-country evidence using a new set of indicators', *European Journal of Political Economy*, 19(3) (2003): 497–527.

28. Leslie Palmier, 'Corruption and development', *Institute for Development Studies Bulletin*, 9(3) (1978): 30–2.

29. Ibn Khaldun, *The Muqaddimah: An Introduction to History*, trans. Franz Rosenthal, ed. and abridged N. J. Dawood, Bollingen Series, 9th edn (Princeton: Princeton University Press, 1989), pp. 297–332.

INTERNATIONAL ECONOMIC ENGAGEMENT

Trade and shared religious values

To what extent does having a common religion facilitate trade and investment between countries, or is belief irrelevant for commerce? Was trade a
prerequisite for the spread of religion, or was the causality the reverse with the
work of missionaries in encouraging religious conversion preceding trade and
financial exchanges? Shared religious beliefs and values potentially increase
trust between traders and investors, reducing transactions costs. Less monitoring and guarantees may be required if those involved are expected to honour
their commitments to their fellow believers.[1] Even where there are religious
differences, if those involved in transactions understand and respect the beliefs
and values of their counterparties this may help economic and financial relationships. If, however, the parties fail to appreciate the religious convictions
of each other and there is hostility and contempt, this cannot be the basis for
lasting relationships, as they may quickly deteriorate with the business challenges that inevitably arise.

The hypothesis that religious belief has an influence on trade has a long
history dating back thousands of years to the states of the ancient classical
world of Greek and Roman civilisation.[2] Dutch overseas commercial expansion into North America with the founding of the colony of New Amsterdam,
later renamed by the English as New York, was at least partly motivated
by religion.[3] Protestant piety in the sixteenth and seventeenth centuries also
seemed to be a driver for English commercial expansion, the aim being less to
convert those in the colonies to Anglicanism, but rather to boost the economic
underpinnings of the Church of England and give it an edge over Roman
Catholicism.[4] In the modern western world religion and commerce are often
treated as two separate realms with no connection, yet this secularisation of

commerce often belies the conscious or unconscious effect of religious traditions on economic decisions in practice.[5] In North America historically religion
played a major role in shaping commerce, an influence that perhaps remains
more significant than in the more secularist countries of northern Europe.[6]

As pointed out in Chapter 4, the spread of Islam has always been associated
with the growth of commerce in Muslim lands,[7] possibly aided by the fact that
the Hijaz heartland of Mecca and Medina were important trading centres.[8]
Indeed, there is evidence that the influence of Islamic teaching on the virtues
of trade spread beyond the Muslim world into medieval Europe.[9] Trade was
viewed as a productive activity and contrasted to lending money for interest,
which was seen as barren and exploitative.[10] Trade was also associated with
the relatively free movement of people and the exchange of ideas in the Muslim
world, with the great empires such as that of the Ottomans having porous
borders in contrast to the visa and work permit restrictions found in most
Muslim majority countries today. There were few restrictions on the camel
caravans crossing Arab lands or the dhows sailing across the Indian Ocean,
unlike the protectionist policies driven by narrow nationalisms with the division of the caliph.

The economic openness of Muslim majority countries

Trade continues to be a leading driver of development in the Muslim world
today, not only in the resource-rich oil and gas exporting countries, but also for
countries exporting a wide range of manufactured goods, such as Indonesia,
Turkey and Malaysia. Other countries with large populations, such as Egypt,
are important import markets, with inflows of foreign investment and politically motivated budgetary assistance meaning that they can run substantial
trade deficits without becoming insolvent. Movement of people is larger than
ever, especially to the economies of the Gulf, despite immigration and work
permit restrictions.

The overall value of the OIC economies exports amounted to US$1,680
billion, and imports amounted to US$1,501 billion in 2010.[11] The share of
trade between Muslim countries was only 18.5 per cent, however, with most of
their exports being to east Asian economies, the EU and North America. These
regions are also major sources for imports, notable country suppliers being
China, Japan, South Korea and Germany, all of which have small or negligible
Muslim populations. In contrast, much of the trade in the early years of Islam
was across Muslim lands.

Today there has been a proliferation of organisations to promote pan-OIC
economic links, notably the Jeddah-based International Islamic Trade
Finance Corporation,[12] the Islamic Corporation for the Insurance of Investment
and Export Credit,[13] and the Islamic Chamber of Commerce and Industry.[14]
However, their budgets are modest, reflecting the limited support by govern-

ments of Muslim majority economies for the promotion of trade based on religious affiliation. Sectarian divisions in the Muslim world are unhelpful, as Saudi Arabia provides much of the funding for institutional support, but though Shi'a Iran participates actively in the IDB, its support for the more specialist affiliates of the bank is limited. Furthermore, many republican Arab countries define their identity in terms of language and culture, preferring to support pan-Arab organisations such as the Cairo-based Arab League rather than those based on Islam.

Although there have been discussions concerning an Islamic free trade pact, a customs union and even a common market, such proposals have made little progress given the heterogeneity of the Muslim economies and their widely differing trade regimes, some of which are highly controlled and protectionist.[15] A customs union for the Islamic world would imply a common tariff, which is unlikely to be agreed as the lower income countries need the tariff revenues while the more affluent countries have fewer levies on imports, preferring to use VAT or GST. A common market would be even more difficult to agree, as this would involve free movement of capital as well as people. Although the governments of the Gulf states have no controls on capital movements, poorer countries in the Muslim world, fearing capital flight, mostly have stringent controls. Free labour movement is even more problematic, as the economies of the Gulf states would have to abandon immigration controls and work permits, policies that would be very unwelcome by most local citizens, especially those who are unemployed, but unwilling to work at immigrant wages.

Economic openness can be measured by the size of trade and investment flows in proportion to GDP. Table 5.1 shows the data for major Muslim majority trading nations, with Malaysia having the highest exports to GDP ratio followed by the UAE. In the case of the latter, the figure includes goods destined for re-export from Dubai, which is the most important transhipment centre in the Muslim world. It is also a major centre for retail sales to international visitors, as it has the largest shopping mall in the world plus fifteen other major malls. Kuala Lumpur has similar malls, but is less significant for transhipment. However, with the development of Johor in the south adjacent to Singapore, which has little spare capacity, Malaysia hopes to become a major re-exporter.

The UAE and Malaysia also recorded the highest export to GDP ratios, the level for the former partly accounted for by oil and gas exports from Abu Dhabi. Low income economies with limited natural resources, such as Sudan, Pakistan and Egypt, appear to have the lowest ratio of exports to GDP. The ratios therefore largely reflect country size, with smaller countries having more open economies, and level of development, with the more developed being more open.

Table 5.1 also shows foreign investment flows outward and inward as a percentage of GDP. Inward investment in Azerbaijan and Kazakhstan is largely in the oil industry, the figure being lower for Saudi Arabia as most of

Table 5.1 Economic openness (% GDP)

Country	Imports	Exports	FDI inward	FDI outward
Algeria	27.7	37.2	0.8	0.0
Azerbaijan	25.6	53.7	7.9	6.7
Bangladesh	32.1	23.2	1.0	0.0
Egypt	25.8	17.4	1.1	0.1
Indonesia	25.8	24.3	2.2	0.6
Kazakhstan	30.3	47.6	7.4	1.3
Malaysia	75.3	87.1	3.2	5.5
Morocco	50.4	36.2	3.0	0.4
Nigeria	22.8	55.4	2.7	0.6
Pakistan	20.3	12.3	0.4	0.0
Saudi Arabia	30.3	56.2	1.7	0.6
Sudan	17.8	6.3	4.2	0.0
Tunisia	58.6	48.0	3.4	0.0
Turkey	31.6	26.4	1.6	0.5
UAE	74.5	95.2	N/A	N/A

Source: World Bank Database, Washington DC, 2014.

the investment is financed internally. Pakistan attracts the least foreign direct investment, partly reflecting the terrorist challenges the country faces and the style of politics, which is often corrupt. Only Azerbaijan and Malaysia have high ratios of outward foreign investment, and, as the latter's economy is much larger, it is the dominant foreign direct investor. Much of the activity is accounted for by Malaysian-based multinational companies, including Petronas,[16] an oil exploration and production company, Sime Darby, a plantation company that has diversified into industry and property development,[17] Air Asia, the world's largest low-cost airline,[18] and Astro, the leading consumer media and entertainment group in southeast Asia.[19]

Analysis of trade data

The trading relations of OIC countries have changed remarkably over the last century, with the economies of the Gulf and southeast Asia becoming ever more integrated into the global economy, while countries such as Egypt and Pakistan have suffered from serious decline and are in many respects economically isolated. The twentieth century witnessed the rise of the Muslim world as a major supplier of energy exports, especially oil and gas from Saudi Arabia and the economies of the Gulf, as well as Iran, Iraq, Algeria and the Muslim economies of central Asia that were to arise following the collapse of the Soviet Union. Even relatively minor oil and gas suppliers such as Egypt and Sudan had their exports dominated by hydrocarbons, while traditional exports of cotton went into serious decline.

Table 5.2 Exports of Muslim economies (US$ million)

Country	2000	2004	2008	2012
Saudi Arabia	77,583	125,997	313,462	388,370
UAE	49,835	90,997	239,213	350,000
Malaysia	98,229	126,511	199,516	227,388
Indonesia	65,403	70,767	139,606	188,496
Turkey	27,775	63,167	132,027	152,489
Qatar	11,594	18,684	67,307	132,968
Kuwait	19,436	28,599	87,457	118,546
Nigeria	20,975	38,631	86,274	116,000
Iran	28,739	41,697	113,668	104,000
Iraq	20,603	17,810	61,273	94,400
Kazakhstan	8,812	20,093	71,172	92,286
Algeria	22,031	31,304	79,298	71,866
Libya	13,380	20,410	62,100	62,216
Azerbaijan	1,742	3,615	30,586	32,634
Egypt	5,276	9,661	26,224	29,385
Bangladesh	6,389	8,305	15,370	25,113
Pakistan	9,028	13,379	20,323	24,567
Morocco	7,432	9,925	20,345	21,417
Tunisia	5,850	9,685	19,320	17,008
Sudan	1,807	3,778	11,671	3,368

Source: World Trade Organization, Geneva, 2014.

In the twenty-first century, the composition and direction of trade is chang-ing radically, with inevitable gainers and losers in the Muslim world. It is no longer sufficient to export crude oil and unprocessed agricultural products, rather, to be economically successful countries have to move up the value chain with product diversification. Saudi Arabia remains the leading exporter in the Muslim world, as Table 5.2 shows, but an increasing proportion of its exports are accounted for by petrochemicals, including polymers, innovative plastics and paints. These diversified products are supplied by the Saudi Basic Industries Corporation (SABIC), which is the largest manufacturing business in the OIC.[20] Its operations are not only in Saudi Arabia, but in Europe and Asia, where its subsidiary petrochemical plants provide a captive market for Saudi oil, resulting in a vertically integrated business that is better able to withstand the volatility of crude oil prices. SABIC has diversified into energy-intensive businesses, notably steel fabrication and fertilisers, taking advantage of low Saudi feedstock prices to give it an international competitive advantage.

The growth of UAE exports of energy, goods and commercial services over the period from 2000 has been dramatic, with a sevenfold increase in current dollar terms. Increased prices for oil and gas exports from Abu Dhabi accounts for some of the rise, but a more important factor was Dubai's rise as a transhipment hub, as already mentioned. The growth of UAE-based multinational companies has also been significant, with Dubai-based Emaar[21] and Nakheel Properties[22] involved in commercial and residential real estate developments throughout the Islamic world and beyond. Jumeirah, the Dubai-based hotel group, manages properties around the world and is a global leader in the luxury hospitality business.[23] The airline Emirates has become the world's leading international carrier, with by far the largest fleet of Airbus A380 aircraft. It contributes around 10 per cent to the Dubai economy.[24]

At the other end of the spectrum, exports from Sudan, Tunisia, Morocco, Pakistan, Bangladesh and Egypt have fared badly, although Bangladesh has overtaken Pakistan as a result of its textile and clothing exports based on low-cost female labour. Turkey's exports have fared well, especially industrial exports as its economy has become more diversified. Tariff-free access to the EU has helped,[25] but Turkish companies such as the conglomerate Koç Holdings have also built strong relations with Turkic-speaking central Asia,[26] the economies of the Gulf and North Africa.[27] Vestel, a consumer appliance manufacturer, has become the leading television supplier in Europe.[28] ENKA, a leading construction and engineering company, has undertaken projects in many neighbouring countries as well as in the Russian Federation.[29]

Turkey is the largest import market in the Muslim world, as Table 5.3

Table 5.3 Imports of Muslim economies (US$ million)

Country	2000	2004	2008	2012
Turkey	54,503	97,540	201,964	236,545
UAE	35,009	72,082	177,000	230,000
Malaysia	81,963	105,283	156,896	196,615
Indonesia	43,595	54,877	127,538	190,383
Saudi Arabia	30,238	47,376	115,134	155,593
Egypt	14,578	15,950	48,382	69,254
Iran	13,898	31,976	57,401	57,092
Iraq	13,384	21,302	33,000	57,000
Nigeria	8,721	14,164	49,951	51,000
Algeria	9,171	18,169	39,479	47,490
Morocco	11,534	17,822	42,366	44,776
Kazakhstan	5,040	12,781	37,889	44,539
Pakistan	10,864	17,949	42,329	44,157
Qatar	3,252	6,005	27,900	34,200
Bangladesh	8,883	12,036	23,860	34,131
Kuwait	7,157	12,631	24,840	25,880
Tunisia	8,567	12,818	24,638	24,447
Libya	3,732	6,326	9,150	23,000
Azerbaijan	1,172	3,516	7,574	10,417
Sudan	1,553	4,075	9,352	9,475

Source: World Trade Organization, Geneva, 2014.

shows. This reflects its status as a middle income country with sufficient foreign exchange to pay for imports, as although Turkey has a substantial trade deficit earnings from commercial services and tourism help to cover the gap. Most imports are destined for the local market, which is substantial given the country's population of over 74 million. As well as local residents being purchasers, Turkey attracted 35.7 million tourists in 2012, making it the sixth most popular destination in the world. Malaysia is the only other Muslim majority country that is a major destination for tourists, attracting 25 million visitors making it tenth in the world. Tourist spending helps not only to generate business for the hotel sector, but also results in very favourable multiplier effects as visitors frequent the shopping malls, and in the case of Istanbul, its historic bazaars. Saudi Arabia is the third most popular country for visitors in the Islamic world, with 17.4 million arriving annually for the *hajj* and *umrah* pilgrimages.[30] Egypt's tourist industry has declined substantially since the Arab Spring, with European and Gulf tourists visiting Morocco instead where the security situation is much better.

The UAE accounts for the second highest level of imports in the Islamic world, some of which are transhipped to adjacent countries, including Iran. Retail spending by Dubai's 10 million visitors also accounts for a significant proportion of imports; the annual shopping festival being especially successful in attracting high spenders from Africa, south Asia and Europe.[31] In Malaysia and Indonesia some of the imports are consumer goods for the retail market, but there are also substantial amounts of imports of capital goods as both countries have substantial manufacturing capacity which relies on imported specialist equipment and materials. This also applies in the case of Turkey, where much of the increase in imports was related to investment by private listed companies and public infrastructure expenditure. The low level of imports into Sudan not only reflects the limited retail market in a country with very low income levels, but also a chronic lack of investment due to political uncertainty and mismanagement.

Openness to investment and financial inflows

All the OIC economies are open to foreign direct investment (FDI), but the incentives that can be offered to foreign companies varies widely. In practice, it is the oil and gas exporting states that have an advantage as international energy companies are interested in exploiting their resources and are more prepared to make long-term investment commitments. The establishment of national oil companies and curbs on the activities of major multinational companies from the mid-twentieth century was more the result of nationalism and leftist ideology rather than religious guidance as, with the exception of Mohammed Baqir Al Sadr who favoured state ownership, few clergy took a position on oil and gas issues.[32] There has never been a debate, for example, about whether oil companies based in the Muslim world, such as Petronas of Malaysia, should be favoured over western companies. Nor has there been any suggestion that Turkish companies should enjoy positive discrimination in the award of contracts in the Gulf, North Africa or central Asia because they are based in a Muslim majority country. Infrastructure and construction contracts have been awarded on grounds of cost competitiveness and the perceived ability of the bid winners to complete contracts on time and to the specifications required.

In value terms it is Saudi Arabia that has attracted the most FDI in the Muslim world, worth US$12.2 billion in 2012, with most coming from the West and China.[33] Much of the FDI is energy-related, although the growing consumer market in the kingdom has also attracted foreign companies. There has been no criticism from the clergy of such investment; indeed, many regard it as inevitable given increasing economic globalisation. In any case, the investment can always be justified in Islam on the grounds of necessity as there may not be companies based in the Muslim world to undertake complex and often highly technical projects. With the shift of economic power to east Asia, Muslim clergy no longer equate globalisation with Americanisation, although the situation of the Muslim minority in western China is a cause for concern. However, these concerns are not sufficient to prevent the award of contracts to Chinese companies.

Foreign direct investment represents long-term investment, with the investments being inherently illiquid, but from the investor perspective there is a level of control through having an ownership stake that can ensure some influence over outcomes. The ease of doing business in the Muslim world varies considerably from country to country, as Table 5.4 shows, with Malaysia ranked sixth in the entire world, and first in Islamic world. Start-ups are ranked sixteenth and construction permits forty-third, but it is the number one ranking for credit access that results in the low overall score of 6. The UAE and Saudi Arabia are highly ranked, especially for construction permits and company registration, the major weakness being the insolvency regimes, as in the UAE many debtors are imprisoned. Though this may have a deterrent effect in encouraging businessmen to meet their contractual obligations, it is expensive to keep debtors in prison where they cannot earn money to discharge their debts.

Most Muslim majority countries have low ranks in the ease of doing business index, which may partly explain their low levels of FDI. Libya is among the worst in the world on most counts, and in Algeria, Iran and Iraq businesses are stifled by excessive, unhelpful bureaucracy. In the case of Iran, the position has been made worse by international sanctions. Credit access is poor in Kuwait, which is perhaps surprising given the size of its banks and their relative sophistication. Pakistan ranks ahead of Bangladesh on most counts, but business start-ups are faster in the latter country. Egypt also fares relatively

Table 5.4 Ease of doing business (rankings)

Country	Rank	Start-up	Construction permits	Registration	Credit access	Insolvency regime
Malaysia	6	16	43	35	1	42
UAE	23	37	5	4	86	101
Saudi Arabia	26	84	17	14	55	106
Qatar	48	112	23	43	130	36
Kazakhstan	50	30	145	18	86	54
Tunisia	51	70	122	72	109	39
Turkey	69	93	148	50	86	139
Azerbaijan	70	10	180	13	55	86
Morocco	87	39	83	156	109	69
Kuwait	104	152	133	90	130	94
Pakistan	110	105	109	125	73	71
Indonesia	120	175	88	101	86	144
Egypt	128	50	149	105	86	146
Bangladesh	130	74	93	177	86	119
Nigeria	147	122	151	185	13	107
Sudan	149	131	167	41	170	89
Iraq	151	169	20	108	180	189
Iran	152	107	169	168	86	129
Algeria	153	164	147	176	130	60
Libya	187	171	189	189	186	189

Source: International Finance Corporation, Washington DC, 2013.

well on the start-up rankings, but its other scores are disappointing, with the difficulty in obtaining construction permits and the insolvency regime being especially problematic.

The amount of international flows of portfolio investment has increased enormously in recent years despite the global financial crisis of 2008. The aim of portfolio investors is to make capital gains and receive income, with much of the investment in companies listed on stock markets. As shares are traded, portfolio investment is therefore much more liquid than FDI.[34] The amount of inward portfolio investment in the Muslim world is very limited, however, largely reflecting the lack of development of capital markets. The largest market, in absolute terms, is that of Malaysia, followed by Saudi Arabia; however, the latter market is not open to foreign investors, but only to Saudis and other Gulf nationals and residents. The Turkish market is the only other exchange of significance. The Malaysian stock market accounts for 0.88 per cent of total global stock market capitalisation, the Saudi Arabia exchange for 0.68 per cent and the Istanbul bourse for 0.59 per cent.[35] In aggregate the Islamic world accounts for less than 2.5 per cent of global stock market capitalisation.

Not only are portfolio investment inflows into the Islamic world minimal, but so too are flows between Muslim majority countries. Outward flows to

Table 5.5 Capital market development (% GDP)

Country	Stock listed	Turnover
Saudi Arabia	72.3	144.4
Turkey	44.2	136.5
Malaysia	40.8	28.6
Bangladesh	10.8	61.2
Indonesia	10.4	23.3
Egypt	7.7	37.8
Pakistan	5.3	31.3
Morocco	3.6	6.2
Tunisia	2.7	13.5
Nigeria	1.6	8.8
Kazakhstan	0.5	3.3
Iran	N/A	17.8
Kuwait	N/A	23.2
Qatar	N/A	12.2
UAE	N/A	25.3

Source: World Bank Database, Washington DC, 2014.

western countries and Asian markets such as Hong Kong and Singapore are much more significant. The Kuala Lumpur market attracts some portfolio investment from the Gulf, and the Malaysian government has done much to promote the country as an international centre for Islamic finance.[36] However, the introduction of capital controls following the Asia crisis of 1997 undermined foreign investor confidence. Although this was a long time ago and most of the capital controls have been subsequently lifted, Gulf investors have long memories. The sovereign wealth funds of Kuwait, Abu Dhabi and Qatar have a global investment remit which focuses on the financial performance of different markets and not on investment allocation according to religious preferences.[37]

The influence of Muslim majority states on the global economic agenda

Countries that are developed have the power to influence global economic decision-making. Throughout the twentieth century, it was largely non-Muslim states that were in the ascendancy and determined the international economic agenda, but with the defeat of fascism in the Second World War, the collapse of the Soviet Union and the limitations of the subsequent global hegemony of the United States increasingly apparent, economic and political power is becoming more diffuse. In particular, the group of twenty industrialised nations (G20), which accounts for 80 per cent of global economic activity, has become the major forum for international economic decision-making, including over development issues.[38] Three Muslim countries are represented on the G20, Saudi Arabia, Turkey and Indonesia, the first time Muslim states have had a say over the direction of international economic policy since the demise of the Ottoman Empire. Although so far these three Muslim states have not advocated an Islamic economic agenda, they can represent the interests of Islamic banks and other *Shari'ah*-compliant institutions in the debates on global economic reform.

The presence of three Muslim nations in the G20 increases awareness of global issues in the Islamic world, which is likely to result in a widened agenda for *ijtihad*, the process of applying *Shari'ah* teaching to changing circumstances. Islamic economists have already given much attention to the analysis of the global financial crisis of 2008 and its implications for *Shari'ah*-based finance. There is also concern over climate change and its implications for the Muslim world. All these issues raise moral concerns with, for example, the concept of *khilafah*, or responsibility to the Creator for the management of resources, having direct implications for the climate change debate and the notion of a just financial system based on Islamic teaching. Such a system can be contrasted to the greed and capitalistic excesses associated with the period leading up to the 2008 global financial crisis.[39]

Although political differences between Saudi Arabia, Turkey and Indonesia prevent them working as a coherent bloc in international forums such as the G20, they are all keen participants in international Islamic institutions such as the OIC and its economic affiliates. All three countries are regular hosts to OIC gatherings, and although Saudi Arabia is an Arab country it prefers politically to support pan-Muslim world organisations rather than the Arab League, the members of which include many of its adversaries. Relations between Saudi Arabia and Iran have always been problematic, but the differences have never been as great as those currently with Syria and Iraq, or in the past with Nasser's Egypt and Gaddafi's Libya. The OIC serves as a forum for debates where external issues such as the situation in Palestine are discussed, but relations between OIC members are never on the formal agenda, and Saudi Arabia, Turkey and Indonesia are content to maintain this focus.

Saudi Arabia is the largest subscriber to the IDB, which from its inception in 1974 has been based in Jeddah. Its original aim was to provide financial assistance to Muslim resource-poor countries to help to pay for imported oil, but it soon took on a broader development agenda involving longer-term trade project funding rather than short-term trade financing.[40] In May 2013, the IDB tripled its authorised capital to US$150 billion. Originally most capital came from member's subscriptions, with Saudi Arabia owning 26.5 per cent of the equity, Iran, the third largest subscriber, 9.3 per cent, Turkey 8.4 per cent and Indonesia 2.9 per cent. The oil- and gas-rich economies of the Gulf have been generous shareholders, with the UAE and Kuwait both subscribing over 7 per cent of the capital. The subscriptions reflect ability to pay, with the oil-rich states paying more relative to poorer developing members such as Bangladesh or Yemen. Increasing the IDB has leveraged its subscribers' equity finance by raising further funds through *sukuk* issuances.

The IDB collaborates extensively with the World Bank and the Asian and African Development Banks. It co-funds projects with these organisations and exchanges information on project appraisals in these instances.[41] Through such cooperation, the IDB influences the development funding agendas of its partners for infrastructure, education and health provision in Muslim countries. This practical cooperative approach is much more effective than confrontation, as the IDB utilises the skills and know-how of existing international development institutions. The IDB is engaged in quiet international economic diplomacy, and its work is both respected and highly regarded by the global development assistance community.

This approach of engaging with established international institutions rather than seeking a utopian new Islamic order has worked well. The Kuala Lumpur-based Islamic Financial Services Board (IFSB), which provides guidelines for regulators on Islamic banking and insurance, collaborates with the IMF and the Bank for International Settlements. It has been supportive of the new Basel standards introduced in response to the global financial crisis, even though the crisis was caused by the irresponsible behaviour of international investment banks promoting interest-based financial products, which had already been much criticised by the Islamic finance community. The activities of the IFSB will be examined in Chapter 6, which deals with regulatory issues and monetary policy decisions.

Notes

1. Joshua J. Lewer and Hendrik Van den Berg, 'Religion and international trade: does the sharing of a religious culture facilitate the formation of trade networks?', *American Journal of Economics and Sociology*, 66(4) (2007): 765–94.

2. Nicholas K. Rauh, *The Sacred Bonds of Commerce: Religion, Economy, and Trade Society at Hellenistic Roman Delos, 166–87 BC*, ed. Thomas Hocker (Amsterdam: J. C. Gieben, 1993).

3. George Leslie Smith, *Religion and Trade in New Netherland: Dutch Origins and American Development* (Ithaca, NY: Cornell University Press, 1973).

4. Louis Booker Wright, *Religion and Empire: The Alliance between Piety and Commerce in English Expansion, 1558–1625* (Chapel Hill, NC: University of North Carolina Press, 1943).

5. Linda M. Scott, 'Religion and commerce', *Advertising and Society Review*, 10(4) (2009): 1–3.

6. Mark Valeri, *Heavenly Merchandize: How Religion Shaped Commerce in Puritan America* (Princeton, NJ: Princeton University Press, 2010).

7. Kirti N. Chaudhuri, *Trade and Civilisation in the Indian Ocean: An Economic*

History from the Rise of Islam to 1750 (Cambridge: Cambridge University Press, 1985).

8. Patricia Crone, *Meccan Trade and the Rise of Islam* (Piscataway, NJ: Gorgias Press, 2004).

9. William Montgomery Watt, *The Influence of Islam on Medieval Europe* (Edinburgh: Edinburgh University Press, 1972).

10. A. S. Khalifa, 'The multidimensional nature and purpose of business in Islam, accounting, commerce and finance', *Islamic Perspective Journal*, 7(1/2) (2003): 1–25.

11. Islamic Centre for the Development of Trade (ICDT), *Annual Report*, Casablanca, 2013, p. 19.

12. See at: http://www.itfc-idb.org.

13. See at: http://www.iciec.com.

14. See at: http://www.iccionline.net.

15. Ruzita Mohd Amin and Zarinah Hamid, 'Towards an Islamic common market: are OIC countries heading the right direction?', *IIUM Journal of Economics and Management*, 17(1) (2009): 133–76; Tariq Mohammad Yasir and Aihu Wang, 'Is the Organisation of Islamic Cooperation promoting trade among members?', *Pakistan Journal of Statistics*, 30(1) (2014): 113–28.

16. See at: http://www.petronas.com.my/Pages/default.aspx.

17. See at: http://www.simedarby.com/Core_Businesses.aspx.

18. See at: http://www.airasia.com/ot/en/home.page.

19. See at: http://www.astro.com.my/portal/about-astro/index.html.

20. See at: http://www.sabic.com/corporate/en/ourcompany.

21. See at: http://www.emaar.com/index.aspx?page=about.

22. See at: http://www.nakheel.com.

23. See at: http://www.jumeirah.com/en.

24. See at: http://www.emirates.com.

25. Bilin Neyaptıa, Fatma Taşkına and Murat Üngörb, 'Has European Customs Union Agreement really affected Turkey's trade?', *Applied Economics*, 39(16) (2007): 2121–32.

26. Gareth Winrow, 'Turkey and the newly independent states of Central Asia and the Transcaucasus', *Middle East Review of International Affairs*, 2 (1997): 30–45.

27. See at: http://www.koc.com.tr/en-us.

28. See at: http://www.vestel.com/homepage.

29. See at: http://www.enka.com.

30. Hamira Zamani-Farahani and Joan C. Henderson, 'Islamic tourism and managing tourism development in Islamic societies: the cases of Iran and Saudi Arabia', *International Journal of Tourism Research*, 12(1) (2010): 79–89.

31. Syed Aziz Anwar and M. Sadiq Sohail, 'Festival tourism in the United Arab Emirates: first-time versus repeat visitor perceptions', *Journal of Vacation Marketing*, 10(2) (2004): 161–70.

32. Rodney Wilson, 'The contribution of Muhammad Bäqir al-Sadr to contemporary Islamic economic thought', *Journal of Islamic Studies*, 9(1) (1998): 46–59.
33. Arab Investment and Export Credit Guarantee Corporation (AIECGC), Kuwait, 23 June 2013.
34. John S. Ahlquist, 'Economic policy, institutions, and capital flows: portfolio and direct investment flows in developing countries', *International Studies Quarterly*, 50(3) (2006): 681–704.
35. Greenwich Asset Management, *Global Stock Market Listings*, Connecticut, 2013.
36. See at: http://www.mifc.com.
37. Jean-François Seznec, 'The Gulf sovereign wealth funds: myths and reality', *Middle East Policy*, 15(2) (2008): 97–111.
38. See at: www.g20.org.
39. Habib Ahmed, Mehmet Asutay and Rodney Wilson, *Islamic Banking and Financial Crisis: Reputation, Stability and Risks* (Edinburgh: Edinburgh University Press, 2014), pp. 1–14.
40. Saeed Ahmed Meenai, *The Islamic Development Bank: A Case Study of Islamic Co-operation* (London: Kegan Paul, 1989).
41. Islamic Development Bank, *Annual Report 1433* (2012), Jeddah, pp. 31–2.

6

BANKING REGULATION, MONETARY POLICY AND ISLAMIC FINANCE

Challenges of Islamic finance for economic policy-makers

Progress in implementing an Islamic finance agenda has advanced much more in the last half century than have debates about how an ideal Islamic economy might function and the practical measures required to achieve this. There is no economy that can be described as Islamic, whereas Islamic banking and finance are flourishing with assets in excess of US$1.5 trillion worldwide by 2014. However, providing a legal and regulatory framework for the existing Islamic banks and *takaful* operators, and the issuance and trading in *Shari'ah*-compliant financial instruments is itself a challenge for policy-makers. It is these issues that are addressed in this chapter, where the policy choices involving legislative provision for Islamic finance in the UAE, Kuwait and Malaysia are compared and contrasted. The experiences of these three countries highlight best practices, but there is no one ideal model. In addition, Islamic perspectives on monetary policy are examined, as this also is a major responsibility of central banks. Though there have been proposals for an Islamic monetary policy, these have yet to evolve into a workable system for tackling inflation without excessive monetary tightening that can severely damage emergent economies.

Early initiatives in the UAE

Islamic banking in its modern form first emerged with the launch of Dubai Islamic Bank in 1975. The government of Dubai was a shareholder in the new bank as a gesture of support, but there were no moves to provide new legislation to cover its activities. Banking laws and regulations are federal matters in the UAE, and the absence of laws may have simply reflected the lack of coordination between Dubai and Abu Dhabi. There was in any case no system of bank regulation until December 1980 when Union Law No. 10 was enacted establishing a Central Bank.[1] Hitherto the UAE had a currency board, but it was only concerned with dirham issuance, not with bank regulation.

Following the enactment of the Union Law, the Dubai Islamic Bank was brought under the Central Bank's regulatory umbrella, but in practice the regulation was light-touch, with the Dubai Islamic Bank essentially left to its own devises. However, in 1985, a federal law was finally passed on Islamic banking providing for a higher *Shari'ah* authority attached to the Ministry of Justice and Islamic Affairs.[2] Arguably, it would have been better to have the higher *Shari'ah* authority attached to the UAE Central Bank as in Malaysia, rather than under the Ministry of Justice, as its effectiveness involves two institutions that have little experience of cooperation. Each Islamic bank was to appoint a *Shari'ah* board with at least three *fiqh* scholars to ensure its operations were in conducted accordance with Islamic teaching. Subsequently, Islamic banks were established in Abu Dhabi and Sharjah, and a new institution, Noor Bank, entered the Dubai market for Islamic financial services.

Dubai's ambition is to be a global hub for Islamic banking and finance.[3] The Dubai International Financial Centre (DIFC), which has the autonomy to legislate and regulate institutions that choose to register under its auspices, will play a central part in the Islamic Bank hub.[4] It has already actively explored how Islamic finance can be used for investment in infrastructure.[5] Noor Bank has already registered with the DIFC, as has the Bank of London and the Middle East, an Islamic investment bank based in London, as its name suggests. The dispute resolution procedures in DIFC are based on English common law, which many see as more compatible with *Shari'ah* than the civil laws that apply throughout the Arab world.[6]

However, the DIFC does not have sufficient resources to act as lender of last resort for institutions registered under its auspices. Only the UAE Central Bank in Abu Dhabi has the resources, but it is under no obligation to bailout institutions registered under the DIFC. The major local Islamic banks, including the Dubai Islamic Bank, are regulated by the UAE Central Bank, but fortunately they have yet to experience a loss of confidence or a run on deposits. If they did, the UAE Central Bank would certainly assist.

The legal framework for Islamic banking in Kuwait

The law providing for the establishment of the Central Bank of Kuwait and its regulation of the banking system was passed in 1968. When the Kuwait Finance House (KFH) was established in 1977 as the first Islamic bank in the country, it was exempted from the banking regulations as it was deemed not to be a bank. The Ministry of Finance had a minority stake in the equity of the KFH as a political symbol of the government's support, and it was therefore to exercise regulatory responsibilities rather than the Central Bank. This arrangement prevailed until 2003, by which time the KFH had become a major financial institution not only in Kuwait, but globally as it was the second largest stock market listed Islamic financial institution worldwide after Al Rajhi Bank of Saudi Arabia.

The Ministry of Finance never performed normal regulatory functions as it was not equipped to play such a role, hence the KFH enjoyed considerable freedom to develop its business as it saw fit. It became the leading institution in Kuwait for real estate finance, and its retail banking business included a major share in vehicle finance. There were, however, criticisms from the other banks that its activities constituted unfair competition, as well as some concern from customers concerning the monopoly it enjoyed in Islamic banking in Kuwait. In response to these criticisms and reservations by the Central Bank of Kuwait about possible systemic risks, the government of Kuwait decided that the KFH should come under the authority of the Central Bank and that the 1968 Law should be amended and extended to make provision for Islamic banking.[7]

Following this change in government policy, in 2003 an additional section, No. 10, was included in Chapter 3 of the Banking Law to specifically make provision for Islamic banking.[8] The legislation was not only designed to provide regulatory provision for the KFH, but also to allow other entrants to establish Islamic banks. Subsequently, the Boubyan Bank was established and the Kuwait Real Estate Bank converted all its operations into being *Shari'ah*-compliant and was renamed the Kuwait International Bank. As the legislative changes were introduced rather late, Kuwait had the advantage of being able to draw on the experiences of other jurisdictions, as well as the work conducted by the Accounting and Auditing Organization for Islamic Financial Services (AAOIFI) and the Kuala Lumpur-based Islamic Financial Services Board (IFSB), where the KFH has an Islamic banking subsidiary.

Section 10 of the Central Bank of Kuwait Law, although introduced as an amendment, is more comprehensive than most specifically Islamic banking laws. Article 86 of Section 10 outlines Islamic banking deposit and financing facilities, including *murabaha*, *musharaka* and *mudarabah*. The Article clarifies the remit of Islamic banks by stressing that they conduct direct investment operations both on their own account and on behalf of their clients, including through partnership arrangements. Islamic banks can establish subsidiary companies or hold equity in existing companies and become directly involved in economic activity. In other words, they should not be classified as mere financial intermediaries like conventional banks. Article 86 also provides for foreign Islamic banks operating in Kuwait, although none have yet opened branches in the country. Rather, the direct investment has been outward, notably the activities of the KFH in Turkey and Malaysia, which are regulated by the authorities in the host countries and not by the Central Bank of Kuwait.

While Article 86 recognised that Islamic banks often established subsidiary companies as part of their normal operations, Article 87 introduced restrictions on such activity. Each Islamic bank operating in Kuwait would henceforth be allowed to establish only one subsidiary company with a minimum capital of Kuwaiti dinar (KD) 15 million, of which the bank should have a majority shareholding of at least 51 per cent. This provision was to prevent Islamic banks establishing numerous small companies outside their control that, if they got into difficulties, could undermine the financial stability of the bank with potentially adverse consequences for bank depositors and the Central Bank of Kuwait if it was forced to intervene to inject new capital to keep the bank solvent.

Articles 88–92 concern the procedures for the establishment and registration of new Islamic banks, which are similar to those for conventional banks with a minimum capital requirement of KD 75 million, or KD 15 million in the case of a foreign Islamic bank establishing a branch in Kuwait. Founder shareholders should subscribe a minimum of 10 per cent of the capital, but not more than 20 per cent, to ensure diversity of ownership as concentration can result in conflicts of interest.

Under Article 93 each Islamic bank in Kuwait must have an independent *Shari'ah* Supervisory Board comprising at least three members appointed by the bank's general assembly in line with AAOIFI and IFSB recommendations. The memorandum of agreement and articles of association of each Islamic bank should specify how its *Shari'ah* Supervisory Board is established and its powers and procedures. Where conflicts arise among members of a *Shari'ah* Supervisory Board that cannot be resolved internally, these can be referred to the Fatwa Board of the Ministry of Awqaf and Islamic Affairs. This body has the final authority, but this has never arisen in practice, which is fortunate as the Fatwa Board members have no specialised knowledge of *fiqh muamalat* pertaining to Islamic finance. Article 93 stipulates that the *Shari'ah* Supervisory Board should prepare an annual report of its opinions of the bank's operations, which should be submitted to the general assembly of shareholders and published in the bank's annual report.

Article 94 gives the Central Bank authority to open accounts with Islamic banks and accept deposits from Islamic banks provided the terms of these facilities conform with Islamic financial principles. Article 95 authorises the Central Bank to provide emergency funding for Islamic banks for a six-month period, renewable for a further six-month maximum. It can also purchase and sell Islamic bank securities. All these operations and the instruments used should be in accordance with Islamic financial principles. The Central Bank can also issue instruments that conform to Islamic financial principles, notably *sukuk*, although these are not specifically cited in the law. There have been a number of corporate *sukuk* issuances in Kuwait, but no sovereign *sukuk*.

Article 96 of the Central Bank of Kuwait Law distinguishes between the rights of current or sight depositors and investment depositors with Islamic banks. The former have the right to withdraw their funds on demand and have their deposits guaranteed with no liability for losses. Investment depositors participate in the Islamic bank's profits and losses in proportion to their share of total deposits. Therefore, their deposits are not guaranteed and their capital is potentially at risk in a similar manner to equity investors. In practice, investment account depositors have never suffered from capital losses in Kuwait, but if losses do arise there would be no obligation on the Central Bank of Kuwait to offer compensation under Article 96.

Article 98 provides the Central Bank with considerable powers to regulate the business of Islamic banks, but these are consistent with its powers over conventional banks.[9] It can specify the maximum financing of a single project to avoid excessive concentration exposure, the maximum equity holdings and the maximum deposit the bank can accept from a single customer. Under Article 99, it is recognised that Islamic banks may own residential property to facilitate Islamic financial transactions such as *murabaha*, *ijara* and diminishing *musharaka*, but apart from these cases, as with conventional banks, the banks should not own private property unless it is used for business premises for a branch or staff accommodation, or acquired as a result of an unfulfilled obligation by a client.

Overall, the addition to the Central Bank of Kuwait Law to accommodate Islamic banks represents an impressive piece of legislation. It seems to have achieved its purposes and it provides a template that could benefit other jurisdictions not only in the GCC, but more widely where new laws governing Islamic finance are being considered. It is not, however, a piece of comprehensive legislation designed to transform the whole financial system to being *Shari'ah*-based, but rather an attempt to support a parallel Islamic banking system within existing bank legislation. The policy has essentially been pragmatic, although it is insufficient to win support from fervent advocates of a wholly Islamic system as in the case of Iran.

Malaysia's Islamic Financial Services Act

Another example of good practice is Malaysia, where government policies have encouraged the development of Islamic banking since the 1980s when Islamic banking and *takaful* legislation was enacted. Unlike Kuwait, the policy choice was to enact legislation with the sole aim of facilitating Islamic banking and insurance operations. The conventional financial system functioned under its own legislation rather than having hybrid legislation catering for both sectors. Inevitably, over time the existing legislation needed reform in the light of changes in banking practices, including those of Islamic banks. New legislation was therefore passed in 2013, the Islamic Financial Services Act, to supersede the Islamic Banking Act of 1983 and the Takaful Act of 1984. The updating drew on over thirty years of experience of Islamic banking regulation in Malaysia. The policy choice of combining legislation on Islamic banking with *takaful* was innovative, with the aim of the Malaysian act being to cover the entire Islamic financial sector with one piece of legislation; an approach that has not been adopted anywhere else.

A similar approach was also adopted for the conventional sector as parallel provision in the Financial Services Act combined provision for insurance with banking. The rationale for this approach is that banks often offer insurance products to their clients, with Islamic banks providing *takaful* either in-house or the products of third-party providers. The earlier legislation did not distinguish between different types of *takaful*, with little attention to organisational structures such as *mudarabah* and *wakala* models. Provision for these was spelled out in greater detail in the Islamic Financial Services Act, which provided for bank assurance models. However, the disadvantage of this approach is that banking skills and practices are distinct from insurance, and the scholars who serve on the *Shari'ah* boards of banks have less knowledge of *takaful* issues than other more specialised scholars. Furthermore, few Islamic banks offer *takaful* products themselves. One advantage of the Islamic Financial Services Act from a *takaful* perspective is that it also covers Islamic capital markets, including *sukuk*. As *takaful* operators represent a substantial proportion of *sukuk* investors, this provision provides the assurance that the regulatory authorities have responsibility to ensure the market functions in a transparent and efficient manner.

The aim of the Islamic Financial Services Act is to ensure, first, the safety and soundness of Islamic financial institutions; secondly, the integrity and orderly functioning of the Islamic money and foreign exchange markets; thirdly, a safe, efficient and reliable payments system and Islamic payment instruments; fourthly, the fair, responsible and professional business conduct of Islamic financial institutions; and, fifthly, the protection of the rights and interests of consumers of Islamic financial services and products.[10] Conditions for licences are set out in detail, including capital adequacy, defined as paid-up capital, not authorised capital. The amount is not specified, however, in the Act, the requirements being set by Bank Negara which enjoys considerable regulatory discretion. Foreign institutions operating in Malaysia are expected to maintain a surplus of assets over liabilities so that in the event of failure the government of Malaysia and Bank Negara will not be liable to make up any shortfall.

The Islamic Financial Services Act also sets out fit and proper criteria for appointments and business conduct, with authorised persons only to undertake business for which they were approved. For example, those authorised to provide general *takaful* cannot undertake family *takaful* and vice versa. Licences and authorisation may be revoked if operations are contrary to *Shari'ah*, or if misleading, inaccurate or incomplete information has been provided. Licences will also be revoked if there has been a failure to comply with Bank Negara directives, if the business has ceased to be viable or if activities are pursued that are detrimental to customers, participants and creditors.

The Islamic Financial Services Act has comprehensive provisions for *Shari'ah* compliance, with the duties of institutions spelled out in Part IV. Any non-compliance should be reported immediately to the *Shari'ah* Advisory Board and non-compliant business should be halted immediately. The institution has to submit its plan for rectifying non-compliance within thirty days. An assessment may subsequently be carried out to determine if rectification is satisfactory. Penalties for non-compliance are severe, with any person contravening *Shari'ah* being subject on conviction to a prison term of up to eight years or a fine of up to Malaysian ringgit (RM) 25 million.

The conditions for the autonomy of banks and their *Shari'ah* advisory councils are also spelled out, with each institution's *Shari'ah* Advisory Council having discretion in the interpretation of *Shari'ah* law. Institutions are bound by the rulings of their *Shari'ah* Advisory Councils, but the banks determine the functions and duties of board of directors, *Shari'ah* Advisory Councils and senior management in relation to *Shari'ah*. Banks also determine the fit and proper criteria for the disqualification of *Shari'ah* Advisory Council members. The *Shari'ah* governance provisions include the requirement that licensed Islamic financial institutions must appoint a *Shari'ah* Advisory Council, with additional councils established for specific tasks, such as the supervision of payments or fund management. In the case of banks, their powers include the determination of the requirements and standards necessary for *Shari'ah* Advisory Council appointments and its duties and functions. *Shari'ah* Advisory Council members can be dismissed for breaches of duty, but they are not liable to dismissal for reports made in good faith to the bank. Nor can council members be sued for statements made in the discharge of their duties. Qualified privilege and a duty of confidentiality apply.

The bank's obligations include providing all documents the *Shari'ah* Advisory Council requests. It is also responsible for conducting an audit on *Shari'ah* compliance through the appointment of an independent *Shari'ah* auditor. The bank determines who is appointed and their remuneration. The auditor appointed should provide opinions additional to those of the *Shari'ah* Advisory Council through an independent report to the bank, but will have no liability for breach of confidentiality.

How the new Malaysian legislation works over time remains to be seen, but it clearly provides a detailed template for other Muslim majority countries that want to make comprehensive regulatory provision for Islamic finance. Malaysia is, however, a common law jurisdiction, hence, some modifications would be required if a similar law was to be enacted in Arab countries, where civil law applies.

Islamic perspectives of monetary policy

While there have been some studies of the role of money in an Islamic economy, both historically[11] and idealistically,[12] there has been no detailed critique of monetary policy choices and instruments from an Islamic perspective. A major objective of monetary policy is the control of inflation, with many central banks having inflation targets, usually around 2 per cent per annum. This represents zero inflation in reality, as empirical evidence suggests there is a qualitative improvement in goods and services each year, which means the current year's output is 2 per cent better in terms of specification or functionality than the previous year's.

The challenges presented by inflation in Muslim majority economies have already been discussed in Chapter 3 when fiscal policy was considered, with the rates shown in Table 3.2. The very high rates in countries such as Sudan and Iran undoubtedly bring injustices as the affluent are more able to protect themselves than the poor, who are vulnerable to rises in the cost of basic foodstuffs. In countries such as Egypt and Pakistan rates are more moderate, but are on an upward trajectory due to failures in fiscal policy. Interestingly, there appears to be no relationship between inflation and the money supply, broadly defined to include bank savings deposits as well as demand deposits, as a proportion of GDP. Malaysia and Morocco have the highest ratios, but the lowest rates of inflation, suggesting that there is little need to be concerned with the monetisation of economies. Countries with relatively low levels of development of financial intermediation, such as Sudan and Pakistan, seem to be more vulnerable to inflation. In other words, policies of monetary targeting are of little relevance to the Islamic world.

Much of the discussion of money by Islamic economists has taken place in an empirical vacuum, with no examination of data on the money supply and its relationship with macro-economic variables. There has also been no critique of existing monetary policies pursued by Muslim majority countries. Instead, there are nostalgic references to the early years of Islam when gold dinars and silver dirham served as money;[13] and criticisms of the introduction of paper currencies by governments.[14] There have even been some suggestions that an Islamic gold dinar should serve as a reserve currency for Muslim countries.[15]

Practical obstacles to an Islamic currency union

In reality, far from being stable measures of value, the prices for gold and silver are very volatile, with markets often driven by speculative buying and selling. On 11 September 2011 the gold price peaked at US$1,895, but a week later it had declined to US$1,598 with a subsequent longer-term fall to US$1,204 by the end of 2011, followed by a modest recovery to US$1,378 by March 2014.[16] Of course, it can be argued that it is the US dollar that is volatile and not gold, but there has been similar volatility against the euro and even greater volatility against the Japanese yen, Chinese renmimbi and Indian rupee. The price is also volatile against silver, making a bi-metallic standard as impractical as it was in the nineteenth century.[17]

These issues were debated when the IDB was established in 1974 as member states wanted to avoid using the US dollar as the unit of account, but instead introduce an Islamic dinar in which financing would be denominated. However, the par value of the new Islamic dinar was set at the equivalent to 1 Special Drawing Right (SDR), the unit of account of the IMF. The value of the SDR is determined by a weighted basket of four currencies, the US dollar, the euro, the Japanese yen and the pound sterling.[18] In the future, the Chinese renmimbi and Indian rupee are likely to be included in the basket when these currencies become fully convertible. It is notable, however, that there is no Muslim majority country whose currency is likely to be included as none of the economies are large enough to be of global significance.

There have been proposals for an Islamic currency union, but the economies of the Muslim world are too divergent, with very different exchange rate regimes, to make this feasible. In particular, countries with stronger currencies are unlikely to be willing to team up with the weaker, even in the spirit of Islamic solidarity. One way forward may be to have sub-regional currency groupings, as in the economies of the GCC.[19] Even this monetary integration between, in many respects, similar Muslim economies has proved to be problematic despite the countries already being integrated with a customs union and common market.[20] Originally, the idea was to follow the example of the eurozone countries, but the eurozone crisis caused the potential participants to downgrade their ambitions. Subsequent political disagreements between Saudi Arabia and Qatar have been a further setback.

The currencies of the economies of the Gulf are pegged to the US dollar, which has brought a degree of stability, especially as oil revenues and royalties are also denominated in dollars. However, in recent decades the source of imports for these countries has changed, with most payments for imports denominated in euros and, increasingly, in Asian currencies. Although the dollar peg is likely to remain for the coming decade, its longer-term viability is open to question, especially as oil and gas exports also largely go to Asia. The major disadvantage of the peg with the dollar is the inability to pursue an independent monetary policy, as when the Federal Reserve raises or reduces interest rates the Saudi Arabian Monetary Agency and the other central banks in the Gulf have to follow. However, their inflation rates and unemployment trends often diverge from those in the United States. In other words, they may be tightening monetary policy in periods when local conditions would suggest loosening is more appropriate.

Interest rate developments

From a *Shari'ah* perspective interest transactions are forbidden as they are equated with *riba*, an addition to a principal sum charged for borrowing. Although there has been much debate about the relationship between interest and *riba*, the premise of all Islamic financial institutions is that financing must be based on other factors, notably obtaining profit by risk-sharing rather than by transferring all risk to the client, who still has to repay regardless of circumstances.[21] It is regarded as fundamentally unjust if banks obtain high predetermined returns on lending while clients struggle to meet their obligations, perhaps due to a deteriorating economic climate which is not their fault.

Despite the *Shari'ah* prohibition on *riba* all Muslim majority countries use interest rates for monetary policy purposes. Indeed, interest rates are often considerably higher than in western countries, reflecting persistent inflation and the need to keep local rates at levels that encourage local companies and wealthy individuals to keep their capital in the country. Table 6.1 shows lending rates for some of the larger Muslim majority countries over the period from 2000 to 2012, with rates especially high in Azerbaijan, Bangladesh, Egypt, Indonesia, Iraq, Nigeria and Pakistan. Rates are significantly lower in Kuwait, Malaysia and Qatar, reflecting the lower rates of inflation in these countries and the much greater supply of savings in these more affluent economies, which reduces the cost of funding for both the commercial and Islamic banks. Furthermore, in all three of these relatively open economies interest rates have fallen in line with international trends in the period since the global financial crisis of 2008, whereas in countries such as Azerbaijan, Bangladesh

Table 6.1 Lending rates (%)

Country	2000	2004	2008	2012
Algeria	10.0	8.0	8.0	8.0
Azerbaijan	19.7	15.7	19.8	18.3
Bangladesh	15.5	14.8	16.4	13.0
Egypt	13.2	13.4	12.3	12.0
Indonesia	18.5	14.1	13.6	11.8
Iran	N/A	16.7	12.0	N/A
Iraq	N/A	12.9	19.5	13.0
Kuwait	8.9	5.6	7.6	5.0
Libya	7.0	6.1	6.0	6.0
Malaysia	7.7	6.0	6.1	4.8
Morocco	13.3	11.5	N/A	N/A
Nigeria	21.3	19.2	15.5	16.8
Pakistan	N/A	7.3	12.9	13.5
Qatar	N/A	7.0	6.8	5.4

Source: World Bank Database, Washington DC, 2014.

Table 6.2 Non-performing loans (%)

Country	2000	2004	2008	2012
Algeria	6.2	3.5	3.8	N/A
Bangladesh	34.9	17.5	11.2	N/A
Egypt	13.6	23.6	14.8	10.7
Indonesia	34.4	4.5	3.2	2.1
Kuwait	19.2	5.3	6.8	N/A
Malaysia	15.4	11.7	4.8	2.2
Morocco	17.5	19.4	6.0	N/A
Nigeria	22.6	21.6	7.2	N/A
Pakistan	19.5	11.6	10.5	N/A
Saudi Arabia	10.4	2.8	1.4	N/A
Tunisia	21.6	23.6	15.5	N/A
Turkey	9.2	6.0	3.4	2.5
UAE	12.7	12.5	2.3	7.6

Source: World Bank Database, Washington DC, 2014.

and Pakistan the economies are less integrated into the international economy. Being more isolated and marginal arguably makes the attainment of fairer funding costs more difficult, demonstrating that a lack of international engagement makes the attainment of Islamic financial goals more, not less, difficult.

There is a positive correlation between high interest rates on loans and the default rates shown in Table 6.2, although the causality can be debated. The high interest rates may reflect the perceived risks in a climate where failure to meet debt commitments is commonplace.[22] Of course, lenders bear some responsibility for defaults, as arguably with better risk appraisal they would not have approved the loans in the first place. Being more selective with financing would only restrict the supply of credit, however, and force many clients to turn to unscrupulous unofficial money lenders who charge even higher rates.[23] Therefore, clients may prefer bank loans, even if they struggle to pay the high interest charges, as they are preferable to the alternatives. Furthermore, it is only in Bangladesh, Pakistan, Egypt and Tunisia that default rates can be considered as unacceptable, but in all these countries the situation has improved, and even the economic disruption associated with the Arab Spring does not appear to have had an adverse impact, although admittedly some of the data for 2012 is missing. Default rates in Malaysia, Indonesia and Turkey are encouragingly low even by the standards of mature economies.

Most countries with Muslim majority populations borrow externally, either for project funding from international development assistance agencies such as the World Bank, or to obtain assistance with deficits as in the case of the IMF.[24] Funding has also been provided by regional allies, usually with political strings, as in the case of Egypt, which has a long history of calling on the Gulf states for budgetary support.[25] Such support has been given on

Table 6.3 Interest on new external debt (%)

Country	2000	2004	2008	2012
Algeria	6.2	3.5	3.8	N/A
Azerbaijan	5.4	2.7	3.7	2.5
Bangladesh	2.5	1.0	1.2	0.9
Egypt	5.1	2.7	2.8	3.3
Indonesia	4.2	3.4	4.3	4.0
Iran	5.9	3.8	5.6	N/A
Kazakhstan	8.3	1.8	3.0	4.8
Malaysia	5.8	3.0	4.7	9.6
Morocco	3.6	3.4	4.3	2.9
Nigeria	1.0	0.8	0.8	1.8
Pakistan	6.3	2.1	2.2	2.0
Sudan	1.7	3.5	2.9	2.1
Tunisia	4.0	3.7	2.8	1.7
Turkey	8.2	5.6	5.5	4.2

Source: World Bank Database, Washington DC, 2014.

a concessional basis, with the interest rates charged well below the cost of funding on international capital markets. As Table 6.3 shows, the interest paid on these loans has fallen significantly in recent years, with countries such as Bangladesh facing very modest financing charges. There have been no requests for special concessions because of the *Shari'ah* prohibition of *riba*, but rather recipient countries have simply accepted existing financing methods. They have little reason to complain, however, as, although interest payments are required, the low charges, often below global inflation rates, means that servicing the debt is not burdensome. Ironically, it is Malaysia that has paid more, as an increasing amount of its debts have been covered by the issuance of *sukuk*, both by the government itself and by state-owned corporations.[26]

Broadening the available monetary tools

There has been no critique of quantitative easing from an Islamic perspective, even though it has been the major method of stimulating demand in the US economy,[27] and to a lesser extent in the UK economy,[28] following the global financial crisis of 2008. There have been pressures on the European Central Bank to adopt similar policies due to the slow recovery since the eurozone crisis. Quantitative easing involves creating new money to purchase bonds, driving prices up and hence the yields down. This lowers the cost of financing, helping to reduce the costs of servicing government debt and facilitating additional spending, including expenditure on investment. Extending the asset purchases to corporate bonds could widen the scope of the stimulus.

Although the objectives of quantitative easing, notably the potential stimulus to real economic activity, may be applauded by Islamic economists and finance specialists, the methods are likely to be viewed as unacceptable. The buying of interest-based financial instruments is not permissible under *Shari'ah*, and manipulating interest rates by monetary means makes the position even worse. There is concern that such policies interfere with the finance pricing in the original contracts governing the security issuance, with windfall gains or losses for the parties involved that cannot be justified. There is also apprehension about the potential inflationary impact of quantitative easing, even though there is no evidence that this has occurred in the United States or the United Kingdom given the spare capacity in both economies.

There is a history of printing money and excessive debt finance through the issuance of government bonds, notably in the Ottoman Empire,[29] and more recently in Muslim majority countries with chronic government deficits such as Iran and Pakistan. However deplorable such policies may be, they are different in nature to contemporary quantitative easing, which involves setting employment and inflation targets for phasing out the policy. In contrast, the printing of money is usually a measure of last resort motivated by short-term financing needs because of fiscal and expenditure policy failures. No Muslim majority country has yet attempted a policy of quantitative easing, not least because as capital markets are underdeveloped such policies are unlikely to be effective in any case.

Malaysia is the only country with an inter-bank money market, but central bank intervention in the market is to ensure that there is sufficient liquidity, not to pursue an active monetary policy.[30] The most popular monetary instruments are *mudarabah* inter-bank deposits, first introduced in 1994, which pay a profit rate rather than interest and run from overnight to twelve months.[31] The profit rate is supposed to represent the receiving bank's return on the investment funds, but the rate is subject to negotiation between the parties and its relationship with the bank's profits is far from clear. *Shari'ah* scholars insist that, as the deposit is governed by *mudarabah* rules, the actual profit rate must be determined at the end of the investment period and cannot be predetermined, although in practice the indicative rate at the time the deposit is made is the actual rate. To move away from this would create an uncertainty premium. In September 1999, the scheme was enhanced when a *mudarabah* inter-bank tender was introduced under which bids are submitted for funds through an automated system. Again, the relationship between the tender rates offered and the profitability of the bidding banks is opaque.

As an alternative deposits based on *wadiah* acceptances were introduced, whereby there is an agency agreement with the receiving bank which earns a fee in return for its safekeeping of the funds. Such contracts are based on *amanah*, or trust, with the depositor guaranteed the return of the deposit. There is no return on the funds deposited, which potentially makes such deposits unattractive. To incentivise depositors a discretionary *hiba* or gift may be paid for the use of the funds. This is rather arbitrary, however, and there is no formula for the determination of the *hiba*.

The government of Malaysia first issued profit-based investment instruments in 2005 in which Islamic banks could place excess liquidity. The profit rates are declared unilaterally by the government on the advice of Bank Negara. However. as neither the government nor the central bank is a profit-making institution, it is unclear what the rates offered represent. The rates seem to vary with the supply of funds, with higher deposits lowering the rates. They also appear to be related to the interest paid on conventional treasury bills, although there cannot be a formal link as this would be unacceptable from a *Shari'ah* perspective. There is nevertheless recognition that benchmarks serve a useful purpose, and that the use of interest for pricing purposes may be allowed provided the payments represent profit shares or rents and not interest. Overall the government and central bank of Malaysia have done much to enhance Islamic finance by developing these instruments, but it is evident that further work is needed on the detail if these instruments are to be internationally credible.

Notes

1. See at: http://www.centralbank.ae/en/index.php?option=com_content&view=article&id=148&Itemid=106.
2. Federal Law No. 6 of 1985, Article 5.
3. Babu Das Augustine, Deputy Business Editor, 'Dubai races to become global Islamic finance hub', *Gulf News*, Dubai, 24 November 2013.
4. See at: www.difc.ae.
5. Habib Ahmed, *Islamic Finance of Infrastructure Projects*, Dubai International Financial Centre, 2012, pp. 1–35.
6. Rodney Wilson, *Legal, Regulatory and Governance Issues in Islamic Finance* (Edinburgh: Edinburgh University Press, 2012), pp. 17–38.
7. Rodney Wilson, 'Approaches to Islamic banking in the Gulf', in Eckart Woertz (ed.), *Gulf Financial Markets* (Gulf Research Centre, Dubai, 2011), pp. 221–38.
8. See at: http://new.cbk.gov.kw/en/legislation-and-regulation/cbk-law/chapter-three.jsp.
9. See at: http://new.cbk.gov.kw/en/legislation-and-regulation/cbk-regulations-and-instructions/instructions-for-islamic-banks.jsp.
10. Act 759, Islamic Financial Services Act, 2013; Part II, Regulatory Objectives and Powers and Functions of Bank; Section 6, Regulatory Objectives.
11. Masudul A. Choudhury (ed.), *Money in Islam: A Study in Islamic Political Economy* (Hove: Psychology Press, 1997), vol. 3.
12. Ziauddin Ahmed, Munawar Iqbal and M. Fahim Khan (eds), *Money and Banking in Islam* (Jeddah and Islamabad: International Centre for Research in

Islamic Economics, King Abdul Aziz University and Institute of Policy Studies, 1983).

13. Ahamed Kameel Mydin Meera and Moussa Larbani, 'The gold dinar: the next component in Islamic economics, banking and finance', *Review of Islamic Economics*, 8(1) (2004): 5–34.

14. Umar Ibrahim Vadillo, *The Return of the Islamic Gold Dinar: A Study of Money in Islamic Law and the Architecture of the Gold Economy* (Kuala Lumpur: Madinah Press, 2004).

15. Khaled Hanafi, 'Islamic gold dinar will minimize dependency on US dollar', *Money File, The Case for Gold*, Cairo, 8 January 2003.

16. Data from World Gold Council, London, available at: http://www.gold.org/investment/interactive-gold-price-chart.

17. Chau-nan Chen, 'Bimetallism: theory and controversy in perspective', *History of Political Economy*, 4(1) (1972): 89–112.

18. See at: https://www.imf.org/external/np/exr/facts/pdf/sdr.pdf.

19. Oker Gurler, 'Role and function of regional blocs and arrangements in the formation of the Islamic common market', *Journal of Economic Cooperation*, 21(4) (2000): 1–28.

20. Emilie Rutledge, *Monetary Union in the Gulf: Prospects for a Single Currency in the Arabian Peninsula* (Abingdon: Routledge, 2008).

21. Mohammad Farooq, 'The *riba*-interest equation and Islam: re-examination of the traditional arguments', *Global Journal of Finance and Economics*, 6(2) (2009): 99–111.

22. John M. Culbertson, 'The term structure of interest rates', *Quarterly Journal of Economics*, 71(4) (1957): 485–517.

23. Amit Bhaduri, 'On the formation of usurious interest rates in backward agriculture', *Cambridge Journal of Economics*, 1(4) (1977): 341–52.

24. Jane Harrigan, Chengang Wang and Hamed El-Said, 'The economic and political determinants of IMF and World Bank lending in the Middle East and North Africa', *World Development*, 34(2) (2006): 247–70.

25. Lisa Blaydes, 'Electoral budget cycles under authoritarianism: economic opportunism in Mubarak's Egypt', *Proceedings of the Annual Meeting of the Midwest Political Science Association*, 2006.

26. Wahida Ahmad and Rafisah Mat Radzi, 'Sustainability of *sukuk* and conventional bonds during financial crisis: Malaysia's capital market', *Global Economy and Financial Journal*, 4(2) (2011): 33–45.

27. Arvind Krishnamurthy and Annette Vissing-Jorgensen, *The Effects of Quantitative Easing on Interest Rates: Channels and Implications for Policy*, Paper No. w17555 (Washington DC: National Bureau of Economic Research, 2011).

28. Michael Joyce, Ana Lasaosa, Ibrahim Stevens and Matthew Tong, 'The financial market impact of quantitative easing in the United Kingdom', *International Journal of Central Banking*, 7(3) (2011): 113–61.

29. Christopher G. A. Clay, *Gold for the Sultan: Western Bankers and Ottoman Finance 1856–1881: A Contribution to Ottoman and to International Financial History* (London: I. B. Tauris, 2000), vol. 20.
30. Obiyathulla Ismath Bacha, 'The Islamic inter-bank money market and a dual banking system: the Malaysian experience', *International Journal of Islamic and Middle Eastern Finance and Management*, 1(3) (2008); 210–26.
31. See at: www.iimm.bnm.gov.my.

PART TWO

♦ ♦ ♦

COUNTRY EXPERIENCES

The economic diversity of the Islamic world is a result of four major factors: resource endowments, demography, economic history and politics. Attributing differences to religion or culture is much more problematic, and there is no economy that can be identified as Islamic. Indeed, it is not clear what the term 'Islamic economy' means in practice, and the utopian literature on Islamic economics is of little use for policy-makers. Dismissing religious and cultural factors as irrelevant to economic decision-making, however, misses the deeper point. For the faithful life can have no meaning apart from through belief and simply striving for material possessions will never fulfil spiritual needs. Policy-makers are held to be responsible for their actions, which will be judged in a wider social context. High levels of GDP and rapid growth demonstrate material success, but policy-makers should also be concerned with social justice. Ultimately, it is human relations that matter and not merely economic achievement.

Although the OIC economies surveyed in this book cannot be categorised as Islamic, the quality of economic decision-making can be evaluated in terms of how far it is consistent with *Shari'ah* teaching. Assessing the degree of social and economic justice is far from being straightforward, however, not least because there is little reliable up-to-date data on income distribution. Similarly, economic inclusion, which is important from an Islamic perspective, cannot easily be measured. Unemployment rates, which were discussed in Part One, are only one measure of exclusion, and the extent of unemployment is under-estimated in any case in most OIC countries as there is little point in being registered as unemployed unless there are benefits or social security payments.

The country coverage starts with Turkey, a country that is overwhelming Muslim, but has a secular constitution dating from the founding of the republic. Due to its geographical position, Turkey has always been regarded as a bridge between Europe and the Islamic world. A greater emphasis on Islamic values potentially tips the country eastward and away from Europe. In reality, however, the policy choice is not between relations with Europe and the Islamic world, as one is not at the expense of the other. Rather closer economic relations with the Islamic world can actually deepen relations with Europe, as both can contribute to the country's economic strength. Turkey is of more value to Europe as an economy open to the east and playing a central role, rather than being an outpost of Europe cut off from its Muslim neighbours.

Recep Tayyip Erdoğan, the Turkish prime minister, likes to depict his country as a successful economic model which other Muslim countries should emulate. The size of the Turkish economy has quadrupled since the AK Party, which has a moderate Islamist ideology, came to power in 2003. However, a closer inspection of the Turkish economy reveals that, while living standards have improved substantially, much of the growth has been based on cheap credit, which has resulted in both public and private debt rising enormously. This includes dollar-denominated debt as investors have taken advantage of low interest rates in the United States to borrow cheaply, and then transfer the funds to Turkey where they can be lent out to construction companies, banks and credit card providers who can make attractive margins by providing funds locally at much higher rates. This type of 'carry trade', which involves making windfalls from interest rate differentials, is clearly in total conflict with *Shari'ah* teaching. It also makes the Turkish economy highly vulnerable to rising global interest rates, which proved to be the case in 2013, when the Federal Reserve started to wind down its monetary stimulus to the US economy through a tapering policy.

The Islamic Republic of Iran, as its country designation implies, prides itself as the only country in the Muslim world where the entire republican constitution reflects Islamist ideology. There is provision for a religious input to all policy, as legislation once approved by the Majlis, the Iranian parliament, is sent for vetting to the office of the supreme leader, Sayyed Ali Khamenei, which examines what is proposed on behalf of the clerical establishment. Policies can be, and often are, referred to the Guardian Council for consideration, which is chaired by the Supreme Leader, and consists of twelve members, six of whom are clerics.

The Islamic republic would like to see other Muslim countries introduce theocratic constitutions similar to its own, and its leaders are highly critical of the Arab monarchies where legislation is signed off by the king or sheikh without any input from *Shari'ah* scholars. However, Arab countries identify Iran as a Shi'a state, with its ideology based on the Ja'fari School of Islamic law, which Arab countries find unacceptable, apart from those with Shi'a majorities such as Iraq. Furthermore, while Iran's comprehensive Law on Usury Free Banking provided for the entire financial system to be managed in accordance with *Shari'ah* teaching, Arab critics note the continuance of the interest-based monetary policy and the absence of *Shari'ah* boards to approve and monitor the financing contracts offered by each bank.

Egypt's experience of Islamist rule under President Mohamed Morsi lasted barely over a year; too brief a period to witness any results. It soon became evident, however, that despite its long history of being in opposition since 1928, the Muslim Brotherhood, and its political vehicle, the Freedom and Justice Party, was ill-prepared for power. Most of its efforts went into writing an Islamist constitution, which proved unacceptable to many in Egypt, not least the military. There was much social meddling, with debates about women's rights or lack of rights, while the decaying state of the economy was ignored. Supporters of the revolution had economic aspirations, including better paid employment and reduced youth unemployment. However, under President Morsi many workers lost their employment as factories closed due to supply shortages and a chaotic security situation. Not surprisingly unemployment became worse than ever.

Although Egypt was seen as the leading country in the Arab world during the first decade of Nasser's rule in the 1950s, today it has little influence and its GDP lags far behind that of Saudi Arabia, and indeed Indonesia, Turkey and Iran in a broader OIC context, as Chapter 4 illustrated. Rather than being perceived as a successful economy, other OIC countries see Egyptian policy-making as incoherent and unstable. Egypt is classified as a lower middle income economy by the World Bank, whereas most OIC countries are in the high income or high middle income categories. Growth has declined since the Arab Spring resulted in the overthrow of the Mubarak regime, but then economic advance only helped a small business class and the senior military officers. There is little expectation that under President el-Sisi much will change.

Saudi Arabia is selected as the fourth country case, a resource-rich kingdom that manages the Islamic heartlands of Mecca and Medina where Muslims perform *hajj* and *umrah*. The governance of the kingdom has historically been in the hands of the house of Saud, whose support from the religious establishment has been conditional on the latter being given a free hand when it comes to maintaining Islamic social norms. Wahhabism, the dominant form of Islam in Saudi Arabia, stresses the literal interpretation of Quranic teaching. However, the Wahhabi clergy have little interest in economic issues, and are content to leave these decisions to government ministers. The current Grand Mufti of Saudi Arabia, Abdu'l-'Azīz ibn 'Abdu'llāh ibn Muḥammad ibn 'Abdu'l-Laṭīf Āl ash-Sheikh, serves as the head of the Permanent Committee for Islamic Research and Issuing Fatwa, but the committee does not get involved in economic policy issues or even in advising about Islamic banking and finance. Each Islamic bank in Saudi Arabia has its own *Shari'ah* board, which is completely autonomous, with no central authority.

Saudi Arabia is the largest Arab economy and a G20 member. Its economic status has been achieved not merely because of its position as, until recently, the world's largest oil exporter, but also because of good economic management and a long-term vision driving policy-making. It has been especially successful in establishing a major global petrochemical industry and in creating a consumer economy, which has resulted in many opportunities for local businesses. However, there has been no impact of Islam in the economic sphere, and while policy-makers in Riyadh may respect *Shari'ah* teaching in their private lives, it plays no role in public policy. Although Saudi Arabia hosts the world's largest Islamic financial institution, Al Rajhi Bank, there has always been much scepticism in the kingdom regarding Islamic finance, and indeed there was a reluctance to give Al Rajhi a banking licence back in the 1980s.

Islam was the key factor in the identity of Pakistan and Bangladesh, hitherto East Pakistan, as it was religious differences with the Hindu majority that resulted in the partition of the Indian subcontinent. However, neither state has been well governed since independence. There remains widespread corruption, with politicians enriching their own families or clans rather than making policies in the wider public interest. Islamic teaching condemns such dishonest practices, but the political culture of Pakistan and Bangladesh seems impervious to reform and change.

Although Islamic banking and finance can be found in both countries, it remains on the margins, and the ambitious initiative to transform the whole Pakistani system into being *Shari'ah*-compliant in the 1980s failed. The State Bank of Pakistan remains supportive of Islamic finance, but within the political classes opinions are mixed. The only attempts to consider how Islamic teaching might be applied to economic policy-making has been by academics, some of whom are among the most well-known Islamic economists, but their opinions have been ignored by governments. Meanwhile, both economies have performed relatively badly not only in relation to other OIC economies, but also in comparison with their larger neighbour, India.

Indonesia is the most populous Muslim country, but interest in Islamic economics and finance was slow to develop. This is in contrast to neighbouring Malaysia, where Islam is seen as an important aspect of Malay identity in relation to the Chinese and Indian segments of the population who are mostly non-Muslim. Encouragement of Islamic finance was one facet of the affirmative action programme designed to improve the economic conditions of the Malay majority. Trade and economic links with other OIC countries have also been favoured as a means of diversifying international relations, which might otherwise become ever more dependent on China. Malaysia's liberal visa policy has also encouraged large visitor numbers from the Gulf, giving a major boost to the tourist industry, the largest in the region.

In Indonesia, there has been no attempt to compete with Malaysia as an Islamic economic and finance hub. Islam is taken for granted, but *Shari'ah* teaching has no influence on economic policy-making. Islamist political parties such as the National Awakening Party (PKB) appear to have done better in recent elections, but this largely reflects a protest vote against the ruling parties because of perceived corruption, rather than enthusiasm for an Islamist policy agenda. The PKB in any case has little to say with regard to economic policy, its concern being good governance and Islamic social issues. Islamic banking and finance remains on the fringes in Indonesia, and although the central bank has become supportive, it has been an uphill struggle to attract even 5 per cent of total deposits.

Overall, the survey of OIC member state experiences reveals that Islam has little, if any, influence on economic policy-making and that the writings of Islamic economists have been largely ignored. Although this situation is often blamed on the politicians responsible for policy-making, the academic Islamic economists can arguably also share some of the responsibility. As illustrated in Part One, much of the writing is idealistic rather than being of practical use. There is no discussion of fiscal policy choices or how government should prioritise expenditure. An Islamic monetary policy has yet to be developed, and there appears to be no distinctive Islamic approach to development that has clear policy implications. The existing literature on Islamic economics and finance can serve as a starting point, but there remains much work to be done at the academic level if the range of policy options for OIC economies is to be extended and revaluated in the light of Islamic teaching.

ISLAM AND ECONOMIC MODERNISATION IN TURKEY

The Ottoman inheritance

Although Christianity and Judaism were practised widely in the lands that were to be included in the Ottoman Empire, Islam was from the start its official religion. Its role became more important following the conquest of Constantinople, hitherto the centre for Orthodox Christianity, and the conquest of Arab regions of the Middle East, which were predominately Muslim. After the defeat of the Mamluks in Egypt, the Ottoman sultan took on the title of caliph, the title of an undisputed Muslim leader. Although this enhanced the status of Islam in the Ottoman Empire, it brought the clergy under the control of the sultan and restricted their ability to express opinions that were critical of government policy.[1]

Strategic decisions were undertaken by the sultan, who had the power to issue decrees without consulting the religious authorities. Nevertheless, the Sunni clerics had considerable influence over day-to-day matters, and their authority was central to the regulation of the economy. Furthermore, as the sultan was not a religious scholar, his role being primarily political, matters pertaining to *Shari'ah* were dealt with by the sheik of Islam, the highest clerical position. For example, as only Muslims paid *zakat*, the religious authorities made Christians and Jews liable for *jizya*, a poll tax, so that they paid the state for the protection it provided for religious minorities.[2]

Ottoman law was inclusive as far as Muslims were concerned, as those of any ethnic background enjoyed precisely the same rights and privileges, whether Turk or Arab. This did not, however, stop the Arab provinces wanting as much autonomy as possible, and by the seventeenth century the Maghreb was only nominally under Ottoman control, and Egypt was virtually independent by the beginning of the nineteenth century. It seemed that nationalism remained a potent force, and was in many respects more significant than Islamic solidarity.

In any case, by the late eighteenth century, and especially during the nineteenth century, the Ottoman governments introduced European-inspired reforms, resulting in a degree of secularisation in practice, even if the public face of the empire remained Islamic. The government under the reforming sultans still sought to reinforce Hanafi Islam where it was seen as being under threat in the empire. Nevertheless, the clergy were eased out of influential positions and their leaders' influence on government was drastically reduced. The *jizya* was abolished and religious minorities played an increasing economic role, especially in trade and finance. Under the concept of Ottomanism all citizens, irrespective of religious affiliation, were to have the same tax and military responsibilities through conscription, a policy that many minorities resisted while at the same time supporting the concept of equal status under the law.

Secularist policies under Atatürk

To understand the contested public policies of contemporary Turkey it is important to appreciate the legacy of Mustafa Kamal Atatürk, the founder of the Turkish republic. Despite the attempts by Recep Tayyip Erdoğan to nudge Turkey to stress its Islamic credentials, secularist forces remain strong, drawing on a populist nationalist ideology. The opposition in Turkey want to ensure the continued separation of religion and the state, and despite over a decade in power, the Islamist governing Justice and Development Party (AKP) has made no attempt to restore religious institutions to their former power. Indeed, the falling out of Erdoğan with his erstwhile ally, Muhammed Fethullah Gülen, the influential preacher and Islamic opinion leader, makes it even less likely that religious institutions will see their role in public policy-making revived.

The policies of Atatürk changed Turkish society fundamentally and, perhaps to the regret of many Islamists, irreversibly, as it is unlikely that the AKP or any other party with an Islamic ideology would want a return to Ottoman values.[3] The alphabet was changed from Arabic script to a modified form of Latin, which had a positive effect on literacy as only a small minority of Turks could read Arabic.[4] When a Turkish translation of the Quran appeared this resulted in hostility from many clergy, as there was concern that if the devout could read the Quran for themselves this would undermine the authority of religious leaders to interpret the text as they saw fit without being challenged.[5]

Gender equality was central to Atatürk's thinking, with boys and girls studying together in mixed classes rather than being segregated as the clergy favoured.[6] In education the focus shifted from rote learning of the Quran in schools attached to mosques to a modern secular curriculum designed to equip school leavers and university graduates for work. Clothing which expressed

Islamic identity was prohibited, with men expected to adopt European fashion. Women could wear head scarfs if they wished, but there was no compulsion to cover the head, and increasingly urban women did not. Needless to say, these policies were opposed by many Muslim clerics, but they had no power to stop the social transformation.

Under Atatürk political power was concentrated in the Grand National Assembly (GNA), based in Ankara, which replaced the former Ottoman parliament in Istanbul. The GNA established its own army in 1920, which gained notable victories over the armed forces of the caliph and the Greek and Armenian armies. Subsequently, in 1924, the caliphate was abolished and the territorial integrity of the Turkish republic was firmly established. *Shari'ah* courts were abolished the same year, and the clergy were brought under the control of a newly established Ministry for Religious Affairs.[7]

As a nationalist, Atatürk wanted to ensure that Turkey, and specifically the GNA, was totally in control of economic and financial policy free from outside interference so that the full range of options could be debated as an expression of sovereignty and independence.[8] He was, however, pragmatic as far as economic policy was concerned, and believed that policies should be adapted as circumstances changed.[9] The initial policy was of state intervention, sometimes referred to as *etatism*, to take over foreign monopolies, notably the tobacco company which had hitherto been under French control as a result of a debt for equity swap by the Ottoman administration.[10] Tobacco was significant, as in the 1920s it was Turkey's major export. The cotton industry and the textile sector, the other major source of export earnings, were also taken into state ownership. The government established the first Turkish financial institution, Iş Bankasi, which, needless to say, was run on conventional lines with interest-based transactions in disregard of the Islamic prohibition of *riba*. A central bank was established in 1931 to manage the Turkish currency, supervise the banking system and pursue a monetary policy, again with no reference to Islamic injunctions.

The policy of state intervention was not ideologically driven, but partly reflected the unfavourable international economic developments that were to cumulate in the Great Depression of 1929–31.[11] In practice, the state-owned businesses enjoyed considerable autonomy from government, and in many respects the economic system could be characterised as a form of state capitalism. There were members of the GNA who favoured a more liberal approach to economic policy-making, notably supporters of the newly formed Liberal Republican Party, which proposed ending state industrial monopolies and attracting foreign direct investment. Although the First and Second Five Year Plans continued to emphasise the role of the state in the economy, Atatürk himself believed this was the only option given the depressed state of international markets. Relations between Turkey and the Soviet Union were cordial, but Atatürk had no ambitions to apply Stalinist economic policy. Rather, he looked to the West, in particular the United States, as an example of a resilient economy.[12]

Turkey in the twenty-first century

The purpose of this chapter is not to provide an economic history of Turkey, as there are many books and articles available on the subject.[13] Rather, detail is provided on the secularist economic policies under Atatürk, as his influence remains considerable and is likely to endure, not least as the one hundredth anniversaries of his ascent to power and the founding of the Turkish republic are celebrated. This section evaluates recent developments in the Turkish economy, which provides the context for future debates between the AKP, the Gülenists and the secularist opposition parties covered in later sections.

While the statistical data in the thematic chapters of Part One provided a snapshot in relation to other OIC countries, the time series data presented here enables the reader to evaluate how the Turkish economy has performed under the AKP.[14] As Table 7.1 shows, per capita GDP rose significantly over the period from 2005 to 2012, which indicates a substantial improvement in living standards. GDP growth was impressive in 2005–6 and again in 2010–11, when rates rivalled those of China and were very favourable in relation to other emerging markets. Growth was uneven, however, with dramatic falls in 2008 as a result of the global financial crisis, followed by contraction the following year. The subsequent recovery was too rapid to be sustainable, with growth running out of momentum by 2012. The table also provides data on the structure of GDP, with a modest decline in the share of agriculture, although it remains very significant given Turkey's substantial land area, abundance of fertile land and, in most years, a good supply of rainfall. Investment in agriculture has been substantial, and it should no longer be considered a backward sector. The share of industry in GDP remains high, reflecting the developed manufacturing economy which is a major source of employment. The share of industry is higher than in most European economies, illustrating the extent of the industrialisation of the Turkish economy in recent years. While it is now stagnant at between one-quarter and one-fifth of GDP, this contrasts with most other industrial economies where the share is falling.

The share of services and their value has risen over the last decade much of which is accounted for by tourist earnings. Turkey has become a major destination for beach holidays by European tourists, especially with the growth of direct flights by budget airlines from smaller airports in Europe to regional airports along the southern and western coasts of the country. Islamists do not approve of the scantily clad tourists staying in the beach resorts and their high alcohol consumption, but the visitors have become too economically important for their criticisms to carry much weight. Istanbul has, in contrast, developed as a major city destination for more conservative tourists from the Gulf,

Table 7.1 Statistical profile of Turkey

Indicator	2005	2006	2007	2008	2009	2010	2011	2012
GDP per capita (US$)	11,394	12,883	13,895	15,021	14,415	15,775	17,034	18,114
GDP growth (%)	8.4	6.9	4.7	0.7	-4.8	9.2	8.8	2.2
Agriculture/GDP (%)	10.6	9.4	8.5	8.5	9.1	9.5	9.0	8.9
Industry/GDP (%)	23.0	22.9	22.3	22.0	21.1	21.8	22.5	21.8
Services/GDP (%)	17.7	18.6	20.3	21.0	23.7	22.1	20.1	20.2
Services (US$ billion)	28.0	26.2	29.9	37.0	35.7	36.3	40.7	43.5
FDI flow (US$ billion)	10.0	20.1	22.0	19.5	8.4	9.0	16.5	12.5

Source: Organisation for Economic Cooperation and Development, Paris, 2013.

Islam and economic policy

many of whom have invested in the city's booming real estate sector by buying secondary residences. This type of tourism has been especially welcomed by the AKP.[15]

Foreign direct investment in the OIC economies was contrasted in Table 5.1 as a percentage of GDP. Table 7.1 shows the value of inflows of FDI in Turkey, which has been very high over the last decade.[16] European companies have made increased profits by investing in Turkey as a cheaper manufacturing base. Increasingly, there have been investment inflows from the Gulf, mainly in real estate, including hotels, shopping malls, and residential and commercial property.[17] Istanbul may no longer be a political centre serving the wider Muslim world, but it has certainly been revived as a commercial centre, all too rapidly for some residents who are concerned that overdevelopment may have negative environmental effects and at least partially destroy some of the city's historical inheritance.[18] Recep Tayyip Erdoğan has been accused of excessively favouring short-term commercial interests at the expense of long-term sustainability.

Turkey is the only Muslim country to be a member of the Paris-based Organisation for Economic Cooperation and Development (OECD), which as one of its responsibilities monitors the economic performance of member states. Table 7.2 compares leading social indicators for Turkey with the corresponding averages for the EU and the OECD overall. Given that Atatürk's ambition was to transform Turkey into a developed European state, these are appropriate comparators. Fertility rates have fallen substantially in Turkey, with just over two births per female, enough to sustain the population. This is in contrast to the EU and OECD where populations have started to shrink, especially those of Turkey's European neighbours in the Mediterranean.

Unemployment rates, although relatively high in Turkey, compare favourably with the EU and OECD averages, but admittedly the workforce is relatively smaller in Turkey because of lower female participation, especially by those from more conservative Muslim families.[19] Income inequality is much greater in Turkey than in the EU or OECD as measured by the Gini coefficient,

Table 7.2 Social indicators for Turkey

Indicator	Turkey	EU	OECD
Fertility rate (%)	2.02	1.59	1.70
Unemployment (%)	8.9	11.1	9.1
Gini coefficient	0.411	0.291	0.313
Inequality gap	15.1	7.4	9.5
Social spending/GDP (%)	12.8	25.1	21.9
Confidence in government (%)	56	41	43
Confidence in banks (%)	37	43	46

Source: Organisation for Economic Cooperation and Development, Paris, 2013.

where 0 represents equality and 1 maximum inequality. This is reinforced by the inequality data, which measures the gap between the richest and poorest 10 per cent. Despite the emphasis of the AKP on social justice, social spending as a percentage of GDP is much lower in Turkey than in the EU or OECD.

Although there is considerable, and indeed growing, inequality and low levels of social spending, which is contrary to the agenda of most Islamist political parties, the AKP retains much popular support in comparison with other EU and OECD governing parties. Nevertheless, its poll ratings have fallen as a result of corruption allegations. Confidence in banks has also fallen, only a small number of which are Islamic despite over a decade of AKP rule. Leading AKP politicians, including Recep Tayyip Erdoğan, have opened and addressed Islamic finance conferences in Istanbul and welcomed delegates from the Gulf, but the so-called participation banks, which by law still cannot be designated as Islamic, remain on the fringes.[20]

AKP economic policies

The election of the AKP in November 2002 reflected disillusionment with the previous government, which had presided over the 2001 economic and financial crisis, the latest in a series of recurrent crises experienced in 1994, 1999 and 2000. The impressive victory of the AKP was largely a protest vote against the government rather than because of enthusiasm for AKP policies, which were somewhat vague. There was no sudden desire to embrace an Islamist political or economic agenda; indeed, a major casualty of the 2001 crisis was Ihlas Finance, the largest Islamic bank in Turkey, which became insolvent due to poor risk management and inadequate liquidity. This severely damaged the image of Islamic banking among the general public.[21]

The IMF provided conditional funding to help the Turkish economy recover from the 2001 crisis, with assistance similar to that provided on many previous occasions, the major policy recommendations being that the government should get its finances in order and that the banking system should be strengthened by firmer regulation. Such policy recommendations, although implying a degree of temporary hardship, were well understood by the Turkish public, who were aware of the lack of sustainability of previous government policies, which lacked any strategy or direction. Therefore, when the AKP indicated that they would, if elected, accept and indeed fully implement the IMF recommendations, this gave the party added credibility in the eyes of Turkish voters. It was seen as a serious and economically responsible party, a safe pair of hands rather than as revolutionary.[22]

Once elected, the new AKP government kept to its word and implemented the IMF recommendations, which worked better than expected with rapid GDP recovery, increasing tax receipts and the economy underpinned by a stronger, if largely conventional, banking system. The AKP took the credit for this economic turnaround, and was duly rewarded by victory at the polls in the 2004 local elections and the 2007 national elections with substantially increased majorities. This provided the AKP with the opportunity to design its own economic policy framework, but it failed to introduce a radical programme and to a large extent this was an opportunity missed. Its policies involved raising the retirement age, the amalgamation of public insurance schemes and the partial rationalisation of health care expenditures. These amounted to tinkering rather than fundamental reform.[23]

The core of AKP support comes from the conservative owners of small- and medium-sized business of Anatolia where it won overwhelmingly in the 2011 elections; the main opposition Republican People's Party winning only in western Turkey and the European suburbs of Istanbul. For the AKP core supporters Muslim religious beliefs are taken for granted, but there is no support for Turkey becoming a theocracy or even abandoning secularism.[24] Rather, the key issues are seen as economic, and the AKP has positioned itself as a market friendly political party focused on improving the business climate and respecting property rights.

This has resulted in it winning the support of the influential association of Turkish businessmen, TÜSİAD,[25] as well of many in the independent Muslim business association, MÜSİAD,[26] which, since the 1990s, has been successful in attracting many members.[27] The AKP favours an outward looking Turkey, and has done much to encourage exports and FDI inflows. The tariff-free access to the EU market is appreciated, but less welcome have been EU pronouncements on human rights in Turkey, press freedom and other contentious issues.

In many respects, despite its Islamist underpinnings, the AKP can be described as a party without an ideology as its approach is pragmatic and even opportunistic. This partly reflects the Turkish context, as previous Islamist parties were banned, notably the Welfare Party of Necmettin Erbakan, which was shut down on the orders of the Constitutional Court in 1998 as it was allegedly acting in violation of Turkey's secular constitution.[28] The Welfare Party had its assets seized and its leaders were prohibited from political activity for a five-year period. To avoid this fate, the AKP was less explicit about Islamist policies, moving cautiously over matters of religion and religious symbols, notably women's head scarfs. Rather, it stressed its business credentials, success in implementing the IMF recovery programme and its economic aspirations for Turkey.[29]

The philosophy of Said Nursi

To understand the factors shaping contemporary Islamism in Turkey it is necessary to examine the philosophy of Said Nursi, who was born in eastern Anatolia in 1877 and died after a long and productive life in 1960. He was a religious scholar who wrote a commentary on the Quran exceeding 6,000 pages and became famous for his masterly contribution to debates on Islamic theology. Rather than looking back with nostalgia to a supposed golden age of Islam, Nursi confronted the realities of his time, including the stagnation and demise of the Ottoman Empire and the rise of a secularist Turkish republic under Mustafa Kamal Atatürk.[30]

The philosophy of Said Nursi is one of liberalisation and moderation in contrast to the fundamentalism associated with many of the Arab Islamist movements. Hence, Sufism, a form of Islamic mysticism which was widely practised in Turkey, is to be tolerated rather than being condemned as deviant. His response to the secularisation and westernisation, as advocated by Atatürk, was to declare that the Quran was an undying, inexhaustible sun that would inspire all those with faith. It was from this position, however, that he urged inter-faith dialogue.[31]

The power of Islamic teaching had to be re-invigorated and re-discovered, and its relevance for the modern world analysed and explained. Nursi urged a *jihad* of the word and positive action in contrast to military *jihad* and the negative condemnations of contemporary life by many Arab Islamists. True verified belief was seen as the most effective barrier to the spread of corrupt practices, but positive action through the maintenance of public order and security was also viewed as essential if the damage caused by the forces of unbelief was to be repaired by the healing truths of Islam.[32]

Said Nursi welcomed the age of science, reason and civilisation, but he saw materialism and atheism as enemies that had to be defeated. This defeat should come about by argument and debate, and never by force. He was a strong advocate of the power of ideas, which he saw as having a more profound and long-term impact than any military force. Although Nursi had many enemies on the political right in Turkey, and even more so in the military, he was totally opposed to communism which he saw as incompatible with Muslim beliefs. He favoured a market economy and saw the protection of property rights as essential for a well-functioning economy.

The Fethullah Gülen movement

The philosophy of Said Nursi had a profound influence on succeeding generations of Islamic thinkers in Turkey and beyond. In particular, Fethullah Gülen and his followers have taken many of the ideas on board while re-evaluating them in the light of the changed circumstances of the late twentieth and twenty-first centuries.[33] Said Nursi advocated the teaching of sciences in religious schools and the teaching of religion in secular schools alongside science and mathematics. Like Gülen and his followers, Nursi saw no conflict between religion and sciences.

Gülen believes it is unnecessary and undesirable for the state to get involved in applying *Shari'ah*. Islamic law applies to the private lives of Muslims, and the provisions of Islamic law should not be forced on anyone who does not want to observe *Shari'ah*. The payment of *zakat*, for example, is a religious duty for Muslims who want to ensure their wealth is purified, but if someone objects to paying, that is a matter for their conscience not for the state. Gülen is tolerant of other religions; indeed, he respects their beliefs and favours inter-faith dialogue. He has been personally involved in dialogue, having met the Chief Rabbi of Israel, the Pope in Rome and the Patriarch of the Greek Orthodox Church, in the latter case on several occasions. Gülen points out that the Ottoman Empire was multicultural and multiethnic, and tolerant and accommodating for minorities.

Critics of these meetings allege that Gülen attended only so that he would be seen as the spiritual leader of all Muslims. However, by not engaging in inter-faith dialogue the religious leaders of the Arab world are, in the view of Gülen, becoming more isolated and creating a vacuum. Gülen mounts a direct challenge to the Arab religious leadership, his aim being to Turkify Islam while at the same time to Islamise Turkish nationalist philosophy. The Arab religious leadership is contrasted to Anatolian tolerance, as it is seen as fanatic, imposing harsh restrictions that have no place in modern life. Gülen has progressive views on the role of women in society and the economy, believing that how they dress is a personal matter for them, and that no one should suppress the progress of women through the clothes they choose to wear.

Like Said Nursi, the Gülenists see education as the key to progress in the Muslim world, and much of their efforts have been devoted to the establishment of schools, with over 200 founded mainly in the Turkic republics of the former Soviet Union. Although the autocratic leadership of these republics has been intolerant towards Islamists, the Gülenists are careful not to get involved in politics, and instead keep focused on educational activities where they can use the resources of the movement to fill the gap in good quality education provision. The Gülenists stress their charitable work and cultural activities, which require no matching government funding. Their long-term ambition is to establish networks of progressive free-thinking Muslims, not to compete for short-term political advantage.

Gülen wants to see the Muslim world integrated into the existing global economic and political system, with the power of Islam steadily harnessed through engagement. He supports Turkish membership of the EU, the OECD and the G20, as well as its participation in western military alliances, notably the North Atlantic Treaty Organization (NATO). Gülen lives in self-imposed exile in the United States, where he is well aware of the power of western business and technological leadership. He, of course, would like to see the Muslim world playing more of a leadership role, but recognises that the first step towards this is a reformed, modernist Islam.

Factionalism and sectarianism are recognised as impediments to the strengthening of Islam. Gülen's responses is to stress inclusiveness, including in

Turkey where he urges respect for the views of the Alevi minority, although he belongs to the Sunni majority and designates himself as being within the Shafi'i School of Islamic jurisprudence, the most numerous in the Muslim world as it also is dominant in Indonesia and Malaysia. Sufism, which remains a potent religious belief in Turkey, should be accommodated and respected.[34] Gülen believes democracy is the best form of government, especially as it presents the voters with policy choices, and he supports republicanism.

However, although Gülen does not get involved in fractional disputes, some of his supporters undoubtedly have, and the falling out with Recep Tayyip Erdoğan is undoubtedly damaging the AKP, if not the Gülenists, who some believe represent a fifth column in Turkish society.[35] Nevertheless, the reformist Islamic message has a wide appeal, and some compare Gülen with evangelical Christian clergy because of the power of his preaching. A limiting factor impeding his influence in the wider Muslim world, however, is his association with Turkish nationalism, with the Ottoman inheritance greeted with suspicion, if not outright hostility, in many Arab countries.

Notes

1. Kemal H. Karpat, *The Politicization of Islam: Reconstructing Identity, State, Faith, and Community in the Late Ottoman State* (Oxford: Oxford University Press, 2001).
2. Ziauddin Ahmed and Ziauddin Ahmad, 'The concept of Jizya in early Islam', *Islamic Studies*, 14(4) (1975): 293–305.
3. Andrew Mango, *Ataturk* (London: Hachette, 2011).
4. Kaya Yılmaz, 'Critical examination of the alphabet and language reforms implemented in the early years of the Turkish republic', *Journal of Social Studies Education Research*, 2(1) (2011): 59–82.
5. Nilüfer Göle, 'Secularism and Islamism in Turkey: the making of elites and counter-elites', *Middle East Journal*, 51(1) (1997): 46–58.
6. Deniz A. Kandiyoti, 'Emancipated but unliberated? Reflections on the Turkish case', *Feminist Studies*, 13(2) (1987): 317–38.
7. Paul Stirling, 'Religious change in republican Turkey', *Middle East Journal*, 12(4) (1958): 395–408.
8. Malcolm Cooper, 'The legacy of Atatürk: Turkish political structures and policy-making', *International Affairs*, 78(1) (2002): 115–28.
9. Abdullah Takim and Ensar Yilmaz, 'Economic policy during Atatürk's era in Turkey', *African Journal of Business Management*, 4(4) (2010): 549–54.
10. Osman Okyar, 'The concept of *etatism*', *Economic Journal*, 75(297) (1965): 98–111.
11. Seyfettin Gürsel, 'Growth despite deflation: Turkish economy during the Great Depression', *Sixth Congress of the European Historical Economics Society*, Istanbul, 2005, pp. 1–33.

12. Malik Mufti, 'Daring and caution in Turkish foreign policy', *Middle East Journal*, 52(1) (1998): 32–50.

13. Sumru Altug, Alpay Filiztekin and Şevket Pamuk, 'Sources of long-term economic growth for Turkey, 1880–2005', *European Review of Economic History*, 12(3) (2008): 393–430.

14. Marcie J. Patton, 'The economic policies of Turkey's AKP government: rabbits from a hat?', *Middle East Journal*, 60(3) (2006): 513–36.

15. Medet Yolal, 'Blooming tulip: a decade of Turkish tourism', *Studia Universitatis Babes Bolyai-Negotia*, 4 (2010):15–24.

16. Ioannis N. Grigoriadis and Antonis Kamaras, 'Foreign direct investment in Turkey: historical constraints and the AKP success story', *Middle Eastern Studies*, 44(1) (2008): 53–68.

17. Ziya Öniş and Şuhnaz Yilmaz, 'Between Europeanization and Euro-Asianism: foreign policy activism in Turkey during the AKP era', *Turkish Studies*, 10(1) (2009): 7–24.

18. Arzu Kocabaş, 'Urban conservation in Istanbul: evaluation and re-conceptualisation', *Habitat International*, 30(1) (2006): 107–26.

19. Aysit Tansel and H. Mehmet Taşçi, *Determinants of Unemployment Duration for Men and Women in Turkey*, Discussion Paper Series, No. 1258 (Bonn: Forschungsinstitut zur Zukunft der Arbeit (IZA), 2004), pp. 1–42.

20. H. Saduman Okumus, 'Interest-free banking in Turkey: a study of customer satisfaction and bank selection criteria', *Journal of Economic Cooperation among Islamic Countries*, 26(4) (2005): 51–86.

21. Martha A. Starr and Rasim Yilmaz, 'Bank runs in emerging-market economies: evidence from Turkey's special finance houses', *Southern Economic Journal*, 73(4) (2007): 1112–32.

22. Ziya Öniş, 'The triumph of conservative globalism: the political economy of the AKP era', *Turkish Studies*, 13(2) (2012): 135–52.

23. Ihsan Dagi, 'Turkey's AKP in power', *Journal of Democracy*, 19(3) (2008): 25–30.

24. Fulya Atacan, 'Explaining religious politics at the crossroad: AKP-SP', *Turkish Studies*, 6(2) (2005): 187–99.

25. Mehmet Ugur and Dilek Yankaya, 'Policy entrepreneurship, policy opportunism, and EU conditionality: the AKP and TÜSİAD experience in Turkey', *Governance*, 21(4) (2008): 581–601.

26. Dilek Yankaya, 'The Europeanization of MÜSİAD: political opportunism, economic Europeanization, Islamic Euroscepticism', *European Journal of Turkish Studies and Social Sciences on Contemporary Turkey*, 9 (2009), available at: http://ejts.revues.org/3696#quotation.

27. A. Choudhury, 'The political economy of enterprise, polity and knowledge: a case study with respect to Musiad and Islamic banking and finance in Turkey', *Middle East Business and Economic Review*, 10(1) (1998): 87–95.

28. Chris Morris, 'Turkey bans Islamist party', *The Guardian*, 17 January 1998.

29. Ahmet Insel, 'The AKP and normalizing democracy in Turkey', *South Atlantic Quarterly*, 102(2) (2003): 293–308.

30. Şerif Mardin, *Religion and Social Change in Modern Turkey: The Case of Bediuzzaman Said Nursi* (New York: State University of New York Press, 1989).

31. Michel Thomas, SJ, 'Muslim–Christian dialogue and cooperation in the thought of Bediuzzaman Said Nursi', *Muslim World*, 89(3/4) (1999): 325–35.

32. Hamid Algar, 'The centennial renewer: Bediüzzaman Said Nursi and the tradition of Tajdid', *Journal of Islamic Studies*, 12(3) (2001): 291–311.

33. M. Hakan Yavuz, 'Towards an Islamic liberalism? The Nurcu movement and Fethullah Gülen', *Middle East Journal*, 53(4) (1999): 584–605.

34. Michel Thomas, SJ, 'Sufism and modernity in the thought of Fethullah Gülen', *Muslim World*, 95(3) (2005): 341–58.

35. Rachel Sharon Krespin, 'Fethullah Gülen's grand ambition: Turkey's Islamist danger', *Middle East Quarterly*, 16(1) (2009): 55–66.

CHAPTER

8

THE ISLAMIC REPUBLIC OF IRAN'S NATIONALIST ECONOMIC MODEL

Categorising Iran

Given the designation of Iran as an Islamic republic since the 1979 revolution, it would appear, at least superficially, to be the country best placed to have distinctive economic policies based on *Shari'ah* teaching. However, although the country is sometimes described as a theocracy, given the supposed power of the clergy, in the realm of economics at least this is far from being the case. The economic challenges from the Pahlavi era remained, notably how to diversify the economy away from oil and create a more sustainable development model.

The structures for governing the economy and determining policy continued as before the revolution, with the Ministry of Finance and Central Bank retaining control over fiscal and monetary policy, respectively. Furthermore, the short terms of ministers of finance following the disruption of the revolution only served to strengthen the hands of the bureaucrats who opposed change. There was much political in-fighting following the revolution as the forces opposed to the Pahlavi dynasty were a loose coalition, with some stressing their Islamic credentials more than others.[1] This also applied in the economic sphere, although most of the supporters of the revolution had no knowledge of Islamic economics or finance, and hence any debate was uninformed and led nowhere.

The most significant Islamist reform in the financial sphere was the Law on Usury Free Banking, which was enacted in 1983.[2] Unlike the laws and regulations in Arab states discussed in Chapter 6, which provide for Islamic banking within systems still dominated by conventional banks, the Iranian law aimed to transform the entire banking system to being *Shari'ah*-compliant with the elimination of *riba*.[3] Although this was achieved, Iran has made no effort to export its model; conferences, both academic and professional, on Islamic banking and finance being dominated by Arab and Malaysian speakers with few Iranians present. Even the literature on the Iranian experience with Islamic banking and finance is very limited with much Arab scepticism about how Islamic the system actually is.

Iranians often claim that their country is unique or, in other words, different from all others. This notion of Iranian 'exceptionalism' means its Islamic model cannot be applied elsewhere. It is, of course, overwhelmingly Shi'a, while all other Muslim countries are Sunni with the exception of Iraq and Bahrain. Although Sunni and Shi'a worship separately and have different theologies, there is no distinctive Islamic economic or financial philosophy. The interpretation of Quranic teaching on economic and financial issues is the same. Most Shi'a identify with the Jafari School of Islamic jurisprudence, which has much in common with the Hanafi, Hanboli and Maliki Sunni schools. It is the Shafi'i School that has pronounced differences, but its main followers are the Sunni of southeast Asia. In other words, Iran is less exceptional than its self-image suggests, any distinctiveness owing more to nationalism than to religious factors.

Ideological debates and economic influence in the early years of the Islamic republic

The two key figures in the debate about the direction of economic policy in post-revolutionary Iran were Abolhassan Banisadr, who was to become the first president of the Islamic Republic of Iran, and Mohsen Nourbakish, who was to serve as the governor of the Central Bank and later as minister of finance. They came from very different backgrounds, but both had overseas doctorate degrees and were from wealthy families.

Banisadr spent most of his life in France, and was very influenced by the student uprising of 1968. Despite his affluent family, he tended to identify with the radical left and was supportive of labour unions. He, however, always regarded himself as an Islamist, and in Paris he became one of the Iranian exiles closest to Ayatollah Ruhollah Khomeini. The ayatollah had no interest in economics, but he trusted Banisadr and relied on him for advice on economic issues. Banisadr was to accompany Khomeini on his victorious homecoming to Iran, and immediately became very involved in politics. He championed the causes of Mujahedeen radicals and served with them on the front line during the war between Iraq and Iran, although his critics saw this as a publicity stunt, as a final and unsuccessful attempt to sustain his position as president. Banisadr became interested in Islamic finance, and in the early 1970s studied for his doctorate on the topic at the Sorbonne in Paris. This research was in the subject area of political economy, with Banisadr's motive in undertaking the work largely idealistic, as were his views on government.[4]

Mohsen Nourbakish, in contrast, was a technocrat who was not directly involved in the Iranian revolution, but he was favoured by the bazaar merchants who were opposed to the shah and did not want continuous revolution, which was seen as being detrimental for business. Nourbakish was a well-known economist, with a doctorate from the University of California, but he displayed little interest in Islamic economics or finance. He was originally nominated to be minister of finance, but this was rejected by Abolhassan Banisadr who wanted to see a candidate with a background in Islamic economics like his own. However, once Banisadr was forced to stand down, Nourbakish was appointed as governor of the Central Bank, serving until 1986. Subsequently, in 1989, he was appointed as finance minister under the new pro-business government of President Akbar Hashemi Rafsanjani, before being re-appointed as Central Bank governor in 1994, serving until his death in 2003.

While Nourbakish was a pragmatist, Banisadr's views were less accommodating to changing circumstances, which was to be his undoing. Nourbakish did not question the premises of conventional economics and, in any case, he was more interested in how it could help policy-making rather than economic theory. In contrast, although Banisadr was involved with how Islamic banking could be introduced, he made no recommendations on economic policy despite being a self-styled Islamic economist. He was concerned with the status of workers and adopted a leftist stance on employment issues, but this was probably more influenced by the student riots of 1968 he witnessed in France than by Islamic teaching.

Given that the economic challenges in the Islamic republic were the same as those faced before the revolution, many welcomed the continuity that Nourbakish brought. This especially applied in the case of those who supported the overthrow of the shah, but did not want to see the country becoming a theocracy. Though a Muslim, for Nourbakish religion was a private matter and he did not see it as being of relevance to economic policy-making. Although not a secularist, Nourbakish's policy-making was based on mainstream economic principles and not *Shari'ah*.

In particular, a conventional monetary policy was to be pursued based on the use of interest rates by the Central Bank to ensure stability and the control of inflation. The Islamic prohibition of *riba* was not seen as relevant for transactions between the Central Bank and the commercial banks. With fiscal policy, oil revenues continued to account for most government receipts, *zakat* being collected by the foundations (bonyads), which will be discussed later, and not by government. Government spending priorities were determined politically, with defence taking an increasing share as the war with Iraq intensified. There was no attempt to justify government expenditure in the light of Islamic teaching.

The influence of Mohammad Baqir al-Sadr

Banisadr and his contemporaries who supported the adoption of a new type of economic system based on Islamic values were profoundly influenced by the writings of Mohammad Baqir al-Sadr. This Iraqi Shi'a cleric founded the Dawa Party which embraced an Islamist ideology.[5] It was seen as a threat by Saddam Hussein, who in the aftermath of the Islamic revolution ordered the arrest and subsequent execution of Baqir al-Sadr.[6] His martyrdom in 1980 served to enhance his reputation and influence at a time of flux in neighbouring Iran, and strengthened those who urged the conversion of the entire financial system so that it adhered to Islamic teaching. His longer-term influence on economic policy-making in Iran was minimal, especially as Nourbakish came to prominence. Baqir al-Sadr's intellectual legacy remains potent, however, not only in Iran where he continues to be held in very high esteem, but among Islamic economists internationally, not least in the West.

Baqir al-Sadr was a scholar of *fiqh* rather than being a trained economist, but he was widely read and was able to define how a political economy based on Islamic teaching was positioned relative to other economic systems, notably socialism and capitalism.[7] He was writing at the time of the Cold War when the Soviet Union was still in competition with the West, and the United States in particular, for global dominance. The Communist Party had been a major force in Iraqi politics, emerging during the period of British occupation as one approach to liberation until it was ruthlessly supressed by the Baathist Party of Saddam Hussein in 1963. The fate of the Iraqi Communist Party was shared by the Tudeh Party of Iran, which translates as the party of the masses.[8] The party supported Mohammad Mosaddeq's campaign to nationalise the Anglo-Iranian Oil Company in the early 1950s, but with the overthrow of Mosaddeq in 1953 its followers were supressed.[9] Mosaddeq was a nationalist, and never a member of the Tudeh Party, but there can be little doubt that without communist support the nationalisation would not have been possible.

Baqir al-Sadr was highly critical of socialism, which he viewed as a secular creed that was inconsistent with Islamic teaching.[10] In particular, he was against excessive state interference in markets, which he viewed as a natural way of conducting exchanges with many of the historical cities of the Muslim world, including Baghdad and Isfahan which owed their prosperity to trade and commerce. He viewed private ownership as normal, with those benefiting from the privilege of ownership ultimately accountable to the Almighty for their actions.[11] Leases imply responsibility of owners, who must ensure that any property they rent is fit for purpose. It is this responsibility that justifies the rent in an Islamic economic system. In contrast, in a pure socialist system rent is not viewed as a justified form of remuneration and there is no provision for private ownership. Of course, there would be inequality in wealth distribution in an Islamic economy, but some are better at managing resources than others, and with financial wealth there is an annual obligation to pay *zakat* which purifies the wealth-holding. The aim of holders of wealth should be social responsibility and not the personal gratification of material possessions, which can become a false God.

Baqir al-Sadr also saw profit as being legitimate and playing an important role in an Islamic economy. This was in contrast to the Marxist view, which identified profit as arising from the exploitation of labour. Marx saw a class struggle between the owners of capital, who obtained profits, and workers' wages, a zero-sum game where higher profits meant lower wages. For Baqir al-Sadr profit accrued from risk sharing, where those who are willing and able to take on risk being entitled to a proportion of business profits. This was the basis for the *mudaraba* and *musharaka* partnership contracts that Baqir al-Sadr favoured for Islamic banking and finance.[12]

Although Baqir al-Sadr favoured a market economy, he also favoured the state playing a direct role in a wide range of social and economic activities. He distinguished between public and state ownership, with educational establishments open to all under public ownership, but natural resources, which for security reasons were not accessible to the public, under state ownership. Of course, the state should manage natural resources such as oil and gas for the greater public good as this was how its monopoly over resources could be justified. In other words, Baqir al-Sadr helped to define the boundaries of state intervention, which were much more restricted than would have been the case under a socialist regime.[13]

Ironically, the position of Baqir al-Sadr was closer to that of Nourbakish, who favoured conventional economic management, than it was to Abolhassan Banisadr, who favoured an Islamist approach. Baqir al-Sadr provided a persuasive critique of capitalism in his seminal work, *Iqtisaduna*, meaning in translation, 'Our Economics'.[14] Baqir al-Sadr was highly critical of the materialist utilitarian foundations of capitalism, the greed of many business leaders and the injustices in remuneration. Nevertheless, Baqir al-Sadr could not be considered a leftist, and insofar as his ideology could be classified in secular terms it could be regarded as moderate, or middle of the road.

Economic data limitations

Oil revenues account for between 80 and 90 per cent of Iran's export earnings and almost half of the government budget revenues. These figures are approximate as there are few up-to-date statistics on Iran's economy, and the authorities are not collaborating with international agencies such as the IMF and World Bank. Even the annual financial reports of the leading banks in the country are several years out of date. This has resulted in the loss by Bank Melli of its status as the leading Islamic bank in the world to Al Rajhi of Saudi Arabia; indeed, it possibly ranks behind the Kuwait Finance House.[15] Even before 2010, however, comparing Iran with other economies was problematic at both the macro- and micro-levels, as if variables were converted at

Table 8.1 Inflation in Iran

	General index	Food	Clothing	Health	Transport
2004	36.1	31.3	40.8	31.5	43.3
2005	39.8	34.7	44.2	36.4	45.2
2006	44.6	39.3	47.9	41.5	48.3
2007	52.7	47.8	54.9	48.5	54.8
2008	66.1	62.2	66.5	59.9	64.4
2009	73.2	68.3	73.3	71.2	68.2
2010	82.3	79.4	81.9	85.3	78.4
2011	100.0	100.0	100.0	100.0	100.0
2012	130.5	144.6	147.8	124.7	129.5
2013	160.5	194.0	192.3	143.1	158.9

Source: Central Bank of Iran, 2014.

the official exchange rate this was misleading. For example, bank deposits and assets were exaggerated by the data, as taking the black market exchange rate would decrease the balance sheets by half in dollar terms.

The government of President Mahmoud Ahmadinejad blamed US sanctions for the country's economic difficulties, and withholding data or simply not collecting it made it more difficult for hostile foreign interests to assess the effectiveness of sanctions.[16] Of course, the lack of data also meant there was less solid evidence by which to judge the regime of Ahmadinejad. Given these factors, there was little incentive for the government to improve economic reporting. Gross mismanagement was, however, also to blame. When the more reformist minded president, Hassan Rouhani, took over in August 2013, it was difficult for the incoming government to know where to start. Restoring economic and financial data collection is proving to be a slow and burdensome task.

The only data that has been collected throughout has been that on inflation thanks to the efforts of the Central Bank to retain some degree of normality. As Table 8.1 shows, inflation has been a major challenge in Iran with an almost threefold rise in the general index over the period from 2004 to 2011, and a further 60 per cent rise between then and the end of 2013. Inflation has been highest for food and clothing, most of which is imported, with the foreign exchange rate falling rapidly. This has adversely impacted the poorest groups in Iran, who spend much of their income on food. Inflation for domestically supplied services such as health has been less marked, and that for transport has been moderated by domestic fuel subsidies, although in the long run these are not sustainable given the substantial deficit in government finances.

The informal economy

Much of Iran's economic activity is not officially enumerated and can be categorised as informal. Although such informal activity is found throughout the world, partly as a result of money laundering and tax avoidance, the size of the informal economy in Iran is thought to be particularly large, perhaps accounting for most of non-oil GDP. The informal network of unremunerated economic activities comprising foundations are referred to in Iran as 'bonyads'.[17] Their history dates back to the Pahlavi dynasty when the shah and his family controlled foundations which provided a source of income independently of the state. Most were officially charities, but in practice they were commercial enterprises that retained a tax-exempt status. There are parallels with Islamic foundations such as *waqf*, but these are dedicated to helping the poor and needy, which was often far from being the case with the bonyads.

Whoever controls the bonyads enjoys considerable powers of patronage, which was evident from the behaviour of the shah and his family who allocated funding as they saw fit, often ignoring the advice of government. The bonyads almost functioned as a parallel state with little or no accountability.[18] During and after the Islamic revolution the bonyads under the control of the Pahlavis were confiscated, but during the chaos of the revolution the state played only a limited role in the expropriations, with the semi-autonomous religious leadership seizing control of many, and others being taken over by the Revolutionary Guard. This included the largest bonyad, the renamed Foundation for the Oppressed and Disabled, whose major purpose was not to support the disabled, but rather to provide an independent source of income for the Revolutionary Guard, which was allegedly partly used for weapons purchases.

The bonyads enjoy tax exemption and customs privileges, preferential access to credit and foreign exchange, as well as regulatory protection from private sector competition. Using these privileges, the bonyads have been able to monopolise trade, in particular imports and the distribution of consumer and capital goods. As a consequence, the bonyads are estimated to control as much as 30–40 per cent of Iran's total GDP and to directly employ 5 million Iranians. This has resulted in the bonyads enjoying considerable popular support, with Supreme Leader Ayatollah Khamenei having a significant say over their policies. The Foundation for the Oppressed and Disabled is headed by Mohammad Forouzandeh, a former chief of staff of the Revolutionary Guards.[19] It manages over 400 companies valued at over US$12 billion, and it is considered the largest economic entity after the government with interests in shipping, petrochemicals, construction materials, dams, horticulture, tourism and transportation. The foundation uses the profits from these ventures to assist 120,000 families of veterans and victims of the 1980–8 Iran–Iraq War, but there is a lack of transparency over the division between spending on welfare and other purposes.

Despite their economic autonomy, the future position and power of the bonyads will depend on political developments in Iran. During the presidency of Ahmadinejad, who was a commander in the Revolutionary Guard during the 1980–8 Iran–Iraq War, the influence of the bonyads increased, especially those associated with the Guard. However, as the economy deteriorated, the reputation of the associates of Ahmadinejad, including those managing the bonyads, was undermined as many questioned their economic competency. In order not to suffer collateral damage, Supreme Leader Ayatollah Khamenei started to distance himself from Ahmadinejad, undermining the authority of the president. The election of President Hassan Rouhani in September 2013 has resulted in a change in the political climate. Rouhani would undoubtedly like to reign in the power of the bonyads and end their special privileges. However, he faces stiff resistance from the bonyads and, as the authority of the government bureaucracy was seriously undermined during the chaotic years of Ahmadinejad, it is proving difficult to restore government control of economic policy-making. Under Ahmadinejad economic decisions were politically driven. Hassan Rouhani and his ministers are more concerned with the wider public good and economic efficiency rather than with the narrow interests of pressure groups, but restoring normality is far from being straightforward.

The Islamic banking sector

While is clear that Iran's economy is far from being Islamic, and in practice there are widespread injustices, the one notable achievement of the Islamic republic from a *Shari'ah* perspective was to establish a usury-free banking system.[20] It was largely through the efforts of the Central Bank that resulted in the new law being drafted, as the commercial banks were sceptical and unenthusiastic, and although these institutions were state-owned they enjoyed considerable autonomy. It was only in 1985 that *Shari'ah*-compliant financing was introduced and most deposits were not Islamised until 1987.[21]

Iran's Islamic banking law provides for deposits on a *qard hassan* basis, the concept being that of an interest-free loan by depositors to the bank, the only type of lending permitted under *Shari'ah*. Those who drafted the law, however, recognised that depositors expect some return, especially in inflationary conditions. Hence, Article 6 of the law provides for non-fixed bonuses in cash or in kind. In practice, prizes are given to depositors, with the lucky account holders selected through a lottery. As gambling (*maisir*) is forbidden in Quranic teaching (*Sura* 2:219), it is unclear how awarding such prizes can be viewed as justified, especially as most depositors, as in any lottery, do not receive prizes.

Article 3 of Iran's Islamic Banking Law provides for term investment deposits, which the banks can use for *mudaraba* financing and direct investments, the so-called restricted *mudaraba* which the influential Iraqi Shi'a cleric Muhammad Baqir al-Sadr recommended. With restricted *mudaraba* contracts the bank acts as an agent and the depositor shares in the profits from the project being financed rather than receiving interest. The contract is regarded as just, as the depositor as financier (*rabb al mal*) is sharing in the risk with the businessmen or entrepreneur (*mudarib*) undertaking the project.[22] In practice, term investment deposits rates in Iran were determined by the Central Bank as part of its monetary policy without reference to particular projects.

In contrast to the customer-driven Islamic banking in the GCC, on the Iranian side of the Gulf the policies have been dictated by the government's economic priorities. Article 11 of the section of the Fourth Plan dealing with credit policy states that the banks are obliged to give priority in their lending to deprived and less developed regions and technologically advanced projects. While the former may be commendable from a social perspective, the article is contradictory, as high-technology projects are unlikely to be located in such areas. Under Article 12, housing finance is solely for construction and not for mortgages on existing properties. This is unhelpful for the development of a housing market in Iran, and limits the return that investors can expect from housing or commercial property.

Such quotas and restrictions mean that potentially profitable projects may not get undertaken, while resources are directed to sectors and areas where returns may be low. The quotas have resulted in an inefficient allocation of capital, with banks' autonomy to make financing decisions based on normal risk and return criteria severely curtailed. However, under Article 23 the Central Bank Guidelines encourage credit scoring, with banks urged to favour customers with good credit records and to limit credit to those who have not met their debt obligations by at least the amount of the outstanding debt.

Although the allocation of finance by the banks in Iran is state-directed at the sector level, the economy is gradually coming under private rather than state control. The public sector banks in Iran appear to be becoming more autonomous in their decision-making, a development welcomed by the Central Bank which appears to recognise that there are efficiency gains to be made from liberalisation. In particular, the use of commercial criteria rather than political patronage is implicitly supported, although the term political patronage is not, of course, used in Central Bank publications. Nevertheless, it is asserted that credit policies can affect sector growth rates. There was a reduction in direct controls over credit, which meant that the 'free' allocation increased from 35 per cent in 2004 to 75 per cent in 2008, although further liberalisation was frozen under Ahmadinejad. There has been no plan to privatise Iran's major commercial banks, which have been under state ownership since 1979, but there is no ideological objection to private banking by the authorities in Iran. The nationalisation was driven simply by expediency, as without state support in the aftermath of the revolution the banks would have become bankrupt. There was enormous capital flight in the late 1970s, with a substantial run down in bank deposits as upper- and middle-class Iranians, especially those influential under the shah, left the country for a life in exile. Arguably, the inefficiencies in the allocation of finance and the poor resultant returns was a result of government directives which would have applied regardless of whether the banks were under public or private ownership.

In 2001, in response to lobbying by industry, there was a significant policy change in Iran permitting the establishment of private banks. Bank Eghtesad Novin (EN) was the first institution established and is owned by a group of construction and industrial companies, including Behshahr, Behpak and Novin, with Bank Melli, the largest state-owned bank, together with the civil servants pension fund having a minority stake.[23] Given this ownership, it is clear that the dividing line between state and private ownership is blurred in Iran. More important than the actual ownership was the ethos of EN Bank, the aim being to provide more modern and innovative banking services for bank clients in line with international standards, rather than having the bureaucratic form-filling approach of the state-owned commercial banks.

Parsian Bank, which was also established in 2001, has experienced even more rapid growth with its total assets worth almost US$22 billion by 2010, making it the largest of the six private banks in Iran.[24] This compares with total assets of just under US$60 billion of Bank Melli, illustrating the increasing significance of the private banks, which now account for over 16 per cent of total financing. As on the Arab side of the Gulf, the private banks are focused on consumer finance, especially vehicle and housing funding. This is in contrast to with the state-owned commercial banks, which are mainly involved in corporate finance, particularly import finance. The private banks aim to gain personal customers by offering an attractive range of accounts, and to encourage those with salaries to arrange direct transfers to their current accounts. In marketing terms, the focus is on middle-class and more affluent customers as the majority of Iranians, and virtually all the poorer classes, do not use banks, with most household payments being in cash.

Although Iran pays little heed to criticism from neighbouring countries and is unrepresented or under-represented at international Islamic banking and finance conferences, there are some signs that practices are changing in line with what happens elsewhere. In particular, since 2013 the Central Bank has permitted banks to set their deposit and financing rates within a price range rather than setting a single price. This means the banks can respond to market developments by reducing the cost of finance if there is insufficient demand, or increase the price if there is excessive demand. Hence, the banks have more control over their margins and therefore profitability. As the essence of Islamic banking is risk- and profit-sharing, this makes the objectives of *Shari'ah* in the field of finance more attainable. Centralised determination of margins makes profits meaningless, whereas liberalisation restores risk and return decisions to banks and their clients, which was viewed as a normal state of affairs by the advocates of Islamic finance.

Economic prospects

Iran's economy has performed extremely poorly in recent years largely because of populist policies pursued by Mahmoud Ahmadinejad, notably the fuel subsidies that encouraged waste and were unsustainable. Such policies, which result in economic distortions, are far removed from those recommended by Islamic economists. After taking office in August 2013 after a landslide election win, President Rouhani has succeeded in repairing some of the economic damage suffered by Iran during years of direct confrontation with the West under his predecessor. The official inflation rate had fallen to 32.5 per cent by May 2013, still very high but an improvement from the 40 per cent rate of mid-2013. The economy emerged from recession with GDP increasing by 1.5 per cent in 2014 after contracting by 5.6 per cent in 2012 and 1.7 per cent in 2013 according to IMF estimates.[25] However, the exchange rate remains under pressure, falling by 9 per cent during April 2014, which makes control of inflation more difficult.

Most of the difficulties the economy faced under Ahmadinejad were self-inflicted, with gross domestic mismanagement rather than sanctions causing much damage before 2013. The United States had maintained sanctions since 1979 and had become peripheral to Iran's economic interests. Oil and gas exports to the EU and Asia continued, but it was only after 2012 when sanctions were tightened and applied to much of the banking sector that they started to have a major impact. China proved a less satisfactory destination for Iran's energy exports as it took advantage of Iran's problems by offering lower prices. The reduced revenues from oil and gas resulted in a growing government deficit as well as an increasing balance of payments deficit, which caused the exchange rate depreciation and inflation.

Although the easing of sanctions can help to reduce the fiscal and balance of payments deficits, the serious damage to the economy under Ahmadinejad cannot easily be undone. Many of the most talented and best qualified young people have left Iran in search of better employment opportunities elsewhere, from nearby Dubai to more distant countries including Europe, North America and Malaysia. Kuala Lumpur has attracted post-graduate students from Iran, many of who have stayed on after graduation or have moved elsewhere, but have seldom gone back to Iran. There has been a considerable brain drain, which has reduced the supply capacity of the Iranian economy with long-term negative implications for growth.

The ending of sanctions would enable Iran to approach the IMF for financial assistance, but their standard package of measures involves cuts in government spending, achieved mainly by a reduction of subsidies and a widening of the tax base to reduce dependency on oil and gas revenues.[26] Such policies are inevitably unpopular as they involve a further squeeze on living standards, especially if it is the middle classes who bear the brunt of the tax rises. In essence, what the IMF is recommending is the resumption of normal economics. Given the opening up to the outside world and the accompanying policy developments, will Iran's economy become more or even less Islamic? The answer is no different, as the policies may have changed, but the original policies and the changes made have no connection with Islamic values.

Notes

1. Charles Kurzman, 'Structural opportunity and perceived opportunity in social-movement theory: the Iranian revolution of 1979', *American Sociological Review*, 61(1) (1996): 153–70.
2. Downloadable from the Central Bank of Iran website at: http://www.cbi.ir/sim plelist/1457.aspx.
3. Rodney Wilson, *Legal, Regulatory and Governance Issues in Islamic Finance* (Edinburgh: Edinburgh University Press, 2012), pp. 89–102.
4. Abū al-Ḥasan Banī Ṣadr, *The Fundamental Principles and Precepts of Islamic Government*, trans. Mohannad R Ghanoonparvar (Tehran and Lexington, KY: Mazda Publishers, Kentucky, 1981).
5. Talib M. Aziz, 'The role of Muhammad Baqir al-Sadr in Shii political activism in Iraq from 1958 to 1980', *International Journal of Middle East Studies*, 25(2) (1993): 207–22.
6. Rodger Shanahan, 'Shi a political development in Iraq: the case of the Islamic Dawa Party', *Third World Quarterly*, 25(5) (2004): 943–54.
7. Rodney Wilson, 'The contribution of Muhammad Baqir al-Sadr to contemporary Islamic economic thought', *Journal of Islamic Studies*, 9(1) (1998): 46–59.
8. Ali Mirsepassi-Ashtiani and Valentine M. Moghadam, 'The left and political Islam in Iran: a retrospect and prospects', *Radical History Review*, 51(4) (1991): 26–62.
9. Farhang Jahanpour, 'Iran: the rise and fall of the Tudeh Party', *The World Today*, 40(4) (1984): 152–9.
10. Talib M. Aziz, 'An Islamic perspective of political economy: the views of (late) Muhammad Baqir al-Sadr', *Al-Tawhid Islamic Journal*, 10(1) (1993): 1–25.
11. Parviz S. Rad and M. Ahsan, 'Theories of ownership and Islam: a case study of the Islamic Republic of Iran', *Review of Islamic Economics*, 9(2000): 127–44.
12. Mohammad Nejatullah Siddiqi, 'Islamic banking and finance in theory and practice: a survey of the state of the art', *Islamic Economic Studies*, 13(2) (2006): 1–48.
13. Rodney Wilson, 'The Islamic economic doctrine: a comparative study', *International Journal of Islamic and Middle Eastern Finance and Management*, 4(1) (2011): 104–6.
14. Muhammad Baqir al-Sadr, *Our Economics: Iqtisaduna*, trans., commentary and ed. Kadom Jawad Shubber (London: Books Extra, 2000).
15. Annual league tables are compiled by *The Banker* and Maris Strategies of London.
16. Ali M. Ansari, *Iran under Ahmadinejad: The Politics of Confrontation* (London: Routledge, 2007).

17. Ali A. Saeidi, 'The accountability of para-governmental organizations (bonyads): the case of Iranian foundations', *Iranian Studies*, 37(3) (2004): 479–98.

18. David E. Thaler *et al.*, *Mullahs, Guards, and Bonyads: An Exploration of Iranian Leadership Dynamics* (Santa Monica, CA: Rand Corporation, 2010), vol. 878.

19. Ali Alfoneh, 'The Revolutionary Guards' role in Iranian politics', *Middle East Quarterly*, 15(4) (2008): 3–14.

20. Ehsan Zarrokh, 'Iranian Islamic banking', *European Journal of Law and Economics*, 29(2) (2010): 177–93.

21. Mohsin S. Khan and Abbas Mirakhor, 'Islamic banking: experiences in the Islamic Republic of Iran and in Pakistan', *Economic Development and Cultural Change*, 38(2) (1990): 353–75.

22. Obiyathulla Ismath Bacha, 'Conventional versus *mudarabah* financing: an agency cost perspective', *International Journal of Economics, Management and Accounting*, 4(1/2) (1996): 33–50.

23. See at: http://english.enbank.ir.

24. See at: http://www.parsian-bank.com/e_banking.html.

25. Andrew Torchia, 'Politics, markets complicate Rouhani's rescue of Iran economy', *Financial Times*, Dubai, 1 May 2014.

26. IMF, Islamic Republic of Iran Article IV Consultation, Country Report 14/93, April 2014, pp. 12–27.

THE INFLUENCE OF THE MUSLIM BROTHERHOOD ON EGYPT'S ECONOMY

Hassan al-Banna

The Muslim Brotherhood has a long history in Egypt, having being founded by Hassan al-Banna in March 1928 in Ismailia, which was the location of the Egyptian headquarters of the Suez Canal Company.[1] There were many foreigners living in the town who were working for the company, and al-Banna disapproved in particular of the spread of British culture, which he viewed as being incompatible with Islamic values. Al-Banna was a schoolteacher and served as preacher at a local mosque. The Brotherhood was founded when he was asked to lead a group of Muslim workers dissatisfied with their employment and hostile to their British bosses.

In many respects al-Banna was comparable to a trade union leader, but he used religious networks to attract support, his views being nationalist and anti-colonial.[2] He was critical of the luxurious accommodation enjoyed by the senior British managers of the Suez Canal Company in contrast to the squalid lodgings provided for the Egyptian Muslim workers. Although not an economist, he was very concerned with social issues and was critical of the leadership of the ruling Wafd Party, which represented landowners and businessmen. Ironically, al-Banna came from a landowning family, but they were of relatively modest means. Al-Banna regarded the Wafd Party leadership as being too secular and pro-British, believing it to be ill-suited to govern a largely Muslim country such as Egypt.

The struggles of the Muslim Brotherhood

Al-Banna was an excellent organiser, establishing branches of the Muslim Brotherhood initially in the Nile Delta, but soon afterwards throughout Egypt.

Ten years after its founding it boasted over 500,000 members and could be categorised as the leading mass movement in the country. Its widespread grassroots support meant that it reflected the views of a significant segment of Egyptian society and its religious values and attitudes. However, although 90 per cent of Egypt's population is Muslim, many feel that religion should play either no role in government or a minimal role.

Admittedly, the Muslim Brotherhood-controlled Freedom and Justice Party won almost half the seats and emerged as the largest single party in the 2011–12 parliamentary elections following the overthrow of President Mubarak. Mohammad Morsi could legitimately claim that he was the first democratically elected leader of Egypt following the 2012 presidential elections. However, much of this support was fickle, reflecting the vacuum created by the outlawing of Mubarak's National Democratic Party and the organising abilities of the Muslim Brotherhood to get the rural poor to the polls. Many disliked the authoritarian nature of the National Democratic Party, which was founded in 1978 by Anwar el-Sadat as a vehicle to propagate his rule. However, the broadly centrist views of the party and its pragmatism and lack of ideology appealed to many Egyptians, especially the urban middle classes.

The Muslim Brotherhood throughout its long history has been subject to a succession of government crackdowns in 1948, 1954, 1965, and most recently in 2013 when it was once again outlawed. Nasser saw it as a direct threat to government, and the leadership of the Arab Social Union, the socialist party supported by those around Nasser, believed the Muslim Brotherhood was a competitor for popular support. It is notable, however, that when Sadat replaced the Arab Social Union with the National Democratic Party, the Muslim Brotherhood was tolerated and was not subject to further crackdowns. This was because the Brotherhood was no longer seen as an ideological competitor, and its constituency was the rural poor who could easily be bribed and cajoled by tribal leaders to vote for the National Democratic Party even if they were Brotherhood members.[3]

The Muslim Brotherhood faced competition from other Islamist groups, notably the Noor Party, which has more fundamentalist origins as it is the political wing of Egypt's Salafi Dawa movement. Its leaders see the demise of the Muslim Brotherhood as an opportunity to strengthen their own position as the sole remaining representative of Islamist political forces in Egypt. It seems to have abandoned much of its Islamist ideology, and supported the military and Field Marshal Abdel Fattah el-Sisi's successful bid for the presidency. The Salafi Dawa movement draws on the experience of the Prophet and his followers in the early years of Islam, and is often compared with Wahhabism in Saudi Arabia in terms of its fundamentalism.[4] Some Salafis deny any connection, and it is unclear if the Noor Party receives any financial backing from Saudi Arabia, which was opposed to President Morsi and has favoured el-Sisi.

The Nour Party has responded pragmatically to the changing political situation in Egypt, although many in government are suspicious of its true intentions and its political manoeuvring carries the risk of it also being outlawed. Not all its leaders agree with its new pragmatism, with some resigning, resulting in further splits among Islamists, many of whom regard the Nour Party as simply opportunistic and having abandoned its Islamic values.[5] Much Islamist political competition revolves around personalities rather than policies, and ideological commitment is often less than it appears. Flexibility and pragmatism are by no means confined to the Noor Party, as the Muslim Brotherhood itself became more moderate in the final years of the Mubarak regime prior to its ascent to power.[6] Whether this was a genuine change or simply a ploy to make the Brotherhood more acceptable is debatable. Clearly, those who supported the outlawing of the Brotherhood following the overthrow of President Morsi believed the latter.

The conflicting economic policies of the Muslim Brotherhood

Although the economy had deteriorated rapidly with the disruption that accompanied the Arab Spring and the overthrow of the Mubarak regime, the leadership of the Muslim Brotherhood failed to give priority to reinvigorating growth and development. Rather, most of its efforts were directed at enacting a new constitution that would enhance the role of Islam in Egyptian society.[7] This inevitably proved to be divisive as it was viewed by many as a step backwards, especially for the status of women, and the efforts to justify the new constitution proved a wasteful distraction. It seemed the Muslim Brotherhood, and its political wing the Freedom and Justice Party, was more concerned to show results to its core supporters rather than the wider public, who were more preoccupied with making a living than clauses in the constitution. The continued breakdown in security did not help, as the authority of the police was undermined by the revolution, and relations between President Morsi and the military became ever more strained. The lack of security undermined business confidence, with investment decisions put on hold and the inevitable negative consequences for economic activity, especially employment.

Power arguably came too suddenly and unexpectedly for the Freedom and Justice Party to develop a coherent economic policy for government. Throughout much of its eighty- five-year existence, the Muslim Brotherhood was a banned opposition party which criticised government rather than preparing for power. Its economic policy was a confusing series of ideas, mostly aimed at its conservative constituency, what one economist, Mohamed el Dahshan, depicted as a series of clippings.[8]

There appeared to be two competing ideologies influencing economic policy-making in the Freedom and Justice Party. The first was an interventionist tendency reflecting the organisation's traditional hierarchical structure, with

Abdel Hafez el Sawy, the leader of the Economic Council of the Freedom and Justice Party critical of Egypt's unproductive rentier economy, his response being to raise productivity by selecting prime sectors in which investment, including by the state, should be focused. Private investment was to be directed by the state to these so-called prime sectors, defined as encompassing basic industries such as steel-making, although it was not clear how this was to be achieved. In many respects such policies were similar to those pursued in the 1960s by the secularist Arab Social Union under Nasser, and it was not evident how these related to Islamic teaching.

The second strand of Islamist economic thought was associated with Khairat al-Shater, a leading businessman who was imprisoned by the Mubarak regime and had his assets twice confiscated. After the overthrow of President Morsi he was again imprisoned, where he remains. Al-Shater was the leading strategist for the Freedom and Justice Party, who formulated the 'Renaissance Project' to repair Egypt's economy. By the time the project was ready to be implemented Morsi's brief rule, which lasted only a year, had come to an end. Al-Shater argued for a liberal, market economy with a business-friendly climate which would encourage private sector investment. Had Morsi's government survived he might have been challenged by al-Shater, who wanted to run for president, but was not allowed to do so in the 2012 election as those with prison records were barred from standing.

Although some Muslim Brotherhood members, including Abdel Hafez el Sawy, but not Khairat al-Shater, spoke of moving to an Islamic economy, no time frame was proposed, nor indeed what this might involve in practice in terms of economic policy. Al-Shater suggested public – private partnerships to reinvigorate industry and control budget deficits through rationalising public spending, but it was unclear if this was simply another name for cutbacks, which few would have supported. The Freedom and Justice Party argued for, but never implemented, a minimum wage, an original demand of the Tahrir Square protesters. It also advocated strengthening competition with anti-trust legislation and introducing a progressive income tax, none of which were enacted.[9] It seems doubtful if Khairat al-Shater, as a leading businessman, supported any of these measures.

The Muslim Brotherhood has been heavily involved in charitable activity since its inception in the late 1920s, and as one-quarter of Egyptians live below the poverty line the stress on charity derives much popular support. Charity is viewed as crucial for social justice, but there is more stress on continuous handouts to the needy rather than on economic development measures to help the poor escape from poverty. Some Muslim Brotherhood members urged making *zakat* compulsory rather than the donations being voluntary, but there is little transparency over *zakat* in Egypt, and the proceeds are unlikely to be sufficient to make much of an impact on poverty alleviation. Finding funds to meet the Muslim Brotherhood's commitment to charity would have been problematic if the Morsi government had survived. The Freedom and Justice Party estimated that reviewing all oil and gas export deals could provide US$18 billion for state coffers, but this seems wildly optimistic and would probably have resulted in even less investment in energy. Repossessing previously state-owned land from owners who obtained it through corruption was also proposed, but the pilot schemes conducted by the transitional government in 2011 failed to produce much revenue.

The two sectors that the Muslim Brotherhood were reluctant to touch were the military and tourism. The former were exempt from budget reductions as it was feared that might result in a coup d'état, which of course happened in any case. Tourism was exempt because one in nine Egyptians was dependent on the industry, even though members of the Muslim Brotherhood saw beach tourism as immoral and disliked the veneration of pre-Muslim archaeological sites.[10] The Freedom and Justice Party, however, promised to protect tourist sites which had been subject to some plundering in the aftermath of the revolution with the break down in law and order. Members of the Muslim Brotherhood favoured restrictions on sales of alcohol, but these were unlikely to apply to tourists. There was a desire to attract more tourists from Muslim countries, especially from the Gulf, but with the exception of Qatar, the other countries of the Gulf were hostile to the Muslim Brotherhood, and arrivals of Muslim tourists actually declined.

Overall, apart from the commitment to relieve poverty through charity and social programmes, there was little that was distinctively Islamic about the economic agenda. There was a pledge to eradicate the corruption that vilified the market economy in the eyes of many Egyptians, but apart from the arrest of the entourage of Mubarak, including his business-minded sons, no concrete action was taken, and it is far from certain that if the Morsi presidency had survived it would have made much impact on reducing corruption, which remains endemic in Egyptian society, largely reflecting the influence of money on law enforcement or lack of enforcement and the substantial income and wealth disparities.[11]

Fiscal policy choices

In Egypt fiscal policy choices are very constrained regardless of whether the government is democratically elected or authoritarian. Government finances have been in deficit for decades as it is politically very difficult to restrain state expenditure, let alone have cutbacks, while at the same time the tax base is very narrow and evasion is widespread. Although there was reasonable, if unimpressive, economic growth in the final years of the Mubarak presidency, the benefits mainly accrued to senior government officials, top military officers and an increasing number of wealthy business families, while the poor saw few benefits. There was a growing middle class, but many felt insecure as inflation eroded their purchasing power and few had substantial savings to draw on if conditions worsened. Economic hardship was only partly responsible for the Arab Spring, which was driven more by political factors, notably the frustration of being denied any voice in the country's future and perceptions of widespread corruption, including at the highest levels of government. Nevertheless, there was a feeling the economy was being mismanaged, but perhaps unrealistic expectations of what a post-revolutionary government could achieve.

President Morsi was ill-equipped to deal with fiscal issues as he had little understanding of economics and surrounded himself with advisers who were more concerned with their status in the Muslim Brotherhood hierarchy than the national interest. His advisers were often in conflict with each other, resulting in confusion and uncertainty, and it remained unclear to most of the advisers how Morsi reached decisions. On 9 December 2012, he issued a decree raising taxes, but the Freedom and Justice Party feared this would make the government unpopular.[12] Subsequently, Morsi rescinded the decree in deference to the party, but such volte faces did little for Morsi's public image and reputation.

As Egypt's foreign exchange reserves diminished, it became clear that the country needed assistance from the IMF which had a long experience of dealing with Egypt. The government of President Morsi asked the IMF for a loan of US$4.8 billion to replenish its reserves and to ensure that the country could continue to meet its international payment obligations.[13] As is usually the case, the IMF was only prepared to make the loan subject to Egypt pursuing reform policies to reduce both the fiscal deficit and the balance of payments deficit. Although assurances were given to the IMF by Essam al-Haddad, who had emerged as the senior adviser to President Morsi, the organisation was not convinced that the appropriate measures would be undertaken. Egypt had already reneged on payments to British Gas and British Petroleum under the gas and oil exploration and production agreements, and both companies demanded that arrears should be settled before there was any further investment. Oil and gas, along with tourism, are crucial for the balance of payments, but the outlook for these sectors under the Muslim Brotherhood looked grim.

It was in any case ironic that an Islamist government should be seeking interest-based loans. Islamic banking is underdeveloped in Egypt, with the first credit union, the Mitr Ghamr Savings Bank, founded in 1963, being nationalised under Nasser in 1971 as it was deemed to be too much associated with the Muslim Brotherhood.[14] In the Sadat era, the Faisal Islamic Bank was established in 1977, but the main aim of the government and central bank in granting its licence was to attract investment from the Gulf. The bank's Islamic credentials were viewed with suspicion, but tolerated because of the capital it brought.[15] During the Mubarak era, there were no new initiatives to establish or attract Islamic banks, although Banque Misr, a state-owned bank, offered some Islamic products. When an Islamic investment company, Al Rayan, collapsed

Table 9.1 Government expenditure in Egypt (LE billion)

Year	2010	2011	2012	2013
Expenditure	365	402	471	588
Interest	72	85	104	146
Subsidies	103	123	150	197
Defence	23	26	26	29

Note: LE 7.12 = US$ 1.

Source: Ministry of Finance, Cairo, 2014.

in 1988 no effort was made to save it or to compensate depositors.[16] Although some of Morsi's entourage paid lip service to Islamic finance, in reality nothing was done to encourage Islamic banking through legal or regulatory changes.

As Egypt's debt has increased the interest burden has become much greater, more than doubling over the period from 2010 to 2013, as Table 9.1 shows. The failure to get public finances on a sounder footing had a major adverse effect on the fiscal balance. By 2013 almost one-quarter of total government expenditure was accounted for by interest payments to both foreign and domestic creditors. There was some debate within the Freedom and Justice Party about issuing Islamic *sukuk* rather than bonds as a means of financing the deficit, and as a consequence legislation was passed by the Egyptian parliament in March 2013 providing for *sukuk* issuance, the one and only concrete measure undertaken in Islamic finance during the period of the Morsi government.[17] However, the timetable for sovereign *sukuk* issuance was to start in 2014, and as the Islamist government had already been swept from power, the plans for *sukuk* were abandoned.

Table 9.1 also shows government spending on subsidies, which accounted for more than one-third of state expenditure, more than the education or health budgets.[18] The subsidies are mainly on fuel and foodstuffs, but they are much less effective in helping the poor than social security payments, as it is the more affluent Egyptians that have vehicles and they benefit most from the fuel subsidies.[19] Furthermore, the food subsidies benefit urban dwellers more than the rural poor who supply more of their own food. Subsidies in Egypt date from the 1920s, however, and there has been much resistance to cutbacks as the 1977 food riots demonstrated, which nearly brought down the Sadat government. The argument that subsidies helped to ensure social stability was largely accepted by the Muslim Brotherhood, and, given this context, the Morsi government could not be expected to reduce the subsidies as the IMF urged.[20] On the contrary, during the year the Islamists were in power the subsidies rose by almost one-third, which was clearly not sustainable.

The figures for defence expenditure in Table 9.1 seem surprisingly low given the power of the military in Egyptian society and the size of the army in

Table 9.2 Government revenue in Egypt (LE billion)

Year	2010	2011	2012	2013
Revenue	268	265	304	350
Income tax	77	89	91	118
Property tax	9	9	13	16
Consumer taxes	67	76	84	92
Trade taxes	15	14	15	17

Source: Ministry of Finance, Cairo, 2014.

particular. However, as around one-fifth of the economy, including many businesses, are controlled by the military this provides a further revenue stream.
In addition, there is US$1.6 billion each year allocated by the United States,
largely to ensure that the army ensures continuing peace with Israel. Much of
this is for equipment imported from the United States rather than to cover the
wages bill, hence it also benefits American exports while ensuring that training and servicing links with the United States remain strong. The empirical
evidence suggests, however, that military expenditure has a negative effect on
economic growth in Egypt, while the impact of civilian spending is broadly
positive.[21] While in power, the Muslim Brotherhood were reluctant to interfere
in military matters, however, fearing a coup d'état, although that was what
happened anyway.

Egypt has a wide range of taxation, with income tax the largest single
source of government revenue followed by sales tax, as Table 9.2 shows. The
income tax regime is progressive, with those on low incomes, which applies in
the case of most Egyptians, paying either no tax or 10 per cent. Those with
incomes between LE 5,000 and LE 20,000 pay a 10 per cent rate, with 15 per
cent paid on incomes between LE 20,000 and LE 40,000, 20 per cent on
incomes between LE 40,000 and LE 10 million, with a maximum rate of
25 per cent for incomes in excess of that which was introduced by the Islamist
government in 2013.[22] Under the Mubarak regime the top rate was reduced
from 34 per cent to 20 per cent in 2006, a move criticised as unjust by both
those on the left of the political spectrum and many Islamists. The move to
reverse this under Morsi was therefore unsurprising, and in any case a 25 per
cent top rate is modest by global standards.

In practice income tax is mostly paid by government employees and those
working in state sector enterprises or large listed companies. Most of those in
small- and medium-sized businesses, especially in rural areas, pay no tax as
evasion is widespread. Corruption in tax administration is also prevalent, as
tax inspectors have low salaries and inevitably many accept illegal payments in
return for not investigating too far into business and personal accounts.

It is more difficult to evade sales taxes and although the rate in Egypt is
a modest 10 per cent, sales taxes are becoming more significant relative to

income tax and may well become the most important source of revenue by 2020. Islamists in Egypt have little to say about these issues, and as most of their supporters paid no tax in any case there was no agitation to reduce taxes, but there was support for the rich paying more and progressive income tax, although this is not discussed in traditional *fiqh*.

Unemployment policy

Egypt has a very youthful population and as a consequence of high rates of population increase in the 1980s and early 1990s there were many new entrants to the job market in the period from 2010 onwards. Many enter higher education which delays employment search, but it also increases expectations of the type of employment graduates would hope to obtain.[23] In the 1960s, under Nasser all university graduates were guaranteed employment, mainly in the armed forces, civil service and bloated state sector companies, but this was unsustainable because of the costs involved with ever rising numbers of graduates. Many sought to emigrate and seek employment in the economies of the Gulf, Europe and North America, but immigration restrictions severely limited these opportunities for all but the most highly qualified.

The unemployment data is collected through surveys, in which the numbers refer to those of working age who are not employed or seeking work. As there is no unemployment social security benefit system there is no register of the unemployed. There are many in part-time employment that would prefer to work for full-time salaries, but these are not included in the unemployment statistics. There are also many in the informal sector, who are not counted in the unemployment statistics as their work is casual, or in the case of the rural areas, seasonal.

Male unemployment increased significantly in 2011, as Table 9.3 shows, and there can be little doubt that the frustrations of young men at their poor employment prospects was a contributory factor to the Arab Spring. Egypt's economy had been growing during the final decade of the Mubarak regime, but most felt no benefit from the growth which largely brought gains for a small clique of businessmen with political connections. The rise in unemployment

Table 9.3 Unemployment trends in Egypt (%)

	Male	Female	Total
2010	4.8	22.8	8.9
2011	9.1	23.6	12.4
2012	9.6	24.7	13.0
2013	10.0	25.0	13.4
2014	9.9	24.8	13.4

Source: Central Agency for Public Mobilization and Statistics, Cairo, May 2014.

was partly caused by a delayed effect of the global economic crisis that was then exacerbated by the revolution, with GDP growth falling from over 7 per cent in 2008 to under 2 per cent by 2011. Labour-intensive sectors, such as tourism, construction and manufacturing, fared especially badly, but worse was to come for these activities following the coming to power of the Muslim Brotherhood.

The tourist sector, which employed 3.5 million workers, suffered both during the year of rule by President Morsi and after his overthrow. The subsequent violent clashes between the army and the Muslim Brotherhood resulted in most tourist operators winding down their Egyptian operations and expanding elsewhere, notably in Turkey and Morocco. There was in fact no violence in the Red Sea resorts, but perceptions matter, and the kidnapping of tourists in Sinai generated negative publicity. Morsi also failed to get the manufacturing sector working again with 3,500 factories remaining closed.

The labour market in Egypt is dominated by males, who numbered 19.1 million workers in 2014, almost four times larger than the female workforce with 4.8 million workers. As Table 9.3 shows, female unemployment is much higher than male unemployment, even though there remain many young women who are not seeking jobs because of family commitments. The Muslim Brotherhood in Egypt favours education for women, but many have mixed views on the role of women in the workforce and family responsibilities. The traditional view is that women should marry early and start having children, taking on a domestic role while their husbands work and provide the main financial support. This model has broken down in recent decades, however, not least because most men cannot find sufficiently lucrative employment to support their families. This resulted in falling population growth as couples struggled to support children, and under Mubarak family planning was encouraged.[24]

The family planning policies pursued under Mubarak were criticised by many in the Muslim Brotherhood, some believing that there was a foreign conspiracy to limit the number of Muslims. Although under Morsi family planning programmes continued to receive financial support, there was a reversion to the social attitudes of the past that favoured having more children, even if there were questions regarding the effects on family and state budgets. During Morsi's year in power there were 2.6 million children born, bringing the population to 84 million, with the birth rate rising to thirty-two per thousand people, the highest rate since 1991.[25]

Economic development

Former presidents Morsi and Mubarak had no vision for Egypt's longer-term development, and it seems that President el-Sisi also lacks a coherent economic strategy. Egypt's economy has underperformed not only the economies of east and southeast Asia over the last four decades, but also most of the economies of the Islamic world. The country has by far the largest population in the Mediterranean, but produces little that is distinctive with most of its exports comprising raw materials. The manufacturing sector remains weak, and compares very unfavourably with that of Turkey. El-Sisi is targeting 7 per cent GDP growth and 8 per cent unemployment by 2017/18, but it is unclear how this will be achieved.[26] He has stated that the budget deficit and public debt should return to 'safe levels' without specifying what these are and how each can be reduced. [27]

Many supporters of President el-Sisi like to draw comparisons between him and Nasser as they that believe he has the popular mandate to be a strong leader, re-establishing law and order and repressing dissidents, not least the Muslim Brotherhood. Better security is seen as essential for the restoration of business confidence and for the necessary investment in order to raise economic growth and promote development following three years of disruption. The popular perception, probably correct, is that the army and police are more enthusiastic about taking orders from one of their own with a military background. In contrast, President Morsi and his Islamist government were never trusted by the military, even though el-Sisi was appointed as defence minister.

El-Sisi's limitations lie in his lack of knowledge of economics and finance, which would not necessarily be a problem if leading economists, of which Egypt has plenty, could be attracted to head the Finance Ministry and other positions involving economic policy-making. So far, most have been unwilling to come forward to serve as, despite el-Sisi's overwhelming election victory, they fear his government could soon become unpopular if the economic challenges cannot be addressed. El-Sisi himself has spoken of establishing new cities in the desert to accommodate the country's growing population, a policy first advocated by Nasser, who also favoured grand projects. He envisages the state playing a leading role in the investment, rather than simply introducing incentives for the private sector and relying on the market. However, these plans are likely to be costly, and given Egypt's substantial budget deficit and high level of debt it seems unlikely that the investment is affordable.

Foreign direct investment amounted to US$2.8 billion in the first half of 2014 according to Hassan Fahmi, chairman of the General Authority for Investment and Free Zones (GAFI), compared with US$3 billion during the previous year.[28] However, non-petroleum exports declined, while demand for foreign exchange increased due to increasing food imports and rising prices for foreign-sourced building materials, including steel and cement as local supplies have fallen. There has also been an escalating demand for imports of petroleum products, notably natural gas and petrol, encouraged by fuel subsidies that cost the government US$15 billion a year, a fifth of the state budget. Help has come from the GCC countries, which have granted Egypt more than

US$12 billion in soft loans since the ousting of former president Mohamed Morsi. They all support el-Sisi, with the notable exception of Qatar, but are nevertheless cautious about providing further finance given the fragile state of Egypt's economy and the high probability that the loans will not be repaid. This would not matter if the loans yielded political dividends, but what these might be is unclear. Egypt is of less strategic value today than in Nasser's time, not least as the states of the Gulf largely trade with Asia rather than Europe, making the Suez Canal less important. Nasser was able to play off the Cold War protagonists against each other, but modern Russia has no interest in Egypt and the pivot to Asia by the United States has downgraded its relations with the Middle East. In short, if President el-Sisi is serious about economic development, Egypt will have to take on most of the task itself rather than relying on foreign assistance.

Notes

1. Aly Abd al-Monein Said and Manfred W. Wenner, 'Modern Islamic reform movements: the Muslim Brotherhood in contemporary Egypt', *Middle East Journal*, 36(3) (1982): 336–61.

2. Ninette S. Fahmy, 'The performance of the Muslim brotherhood in the Egyptian syndicates: an alternative formula for reform?', *Middle East Journal*, 52(4) (1998): 551–62.

3. Sana Abed-Kotob, 'The accommodationists speak: goals and strategies of the Muslim Brotherhood of Egypt', *International Journal of Middle East Studies*, 27(3) (1995): 321–39.

4. Quintan Wiktorowicz, 'Anatomy of the Salafi movement', *Studies in Conflict and Terrorism*, 29(3) (2006): 207–39.

5. Abdel-Rahman Youssef and Mostafa Hashem, 'The Nour Party's precarious future', *Sada: Middle East Analysis*, 9 May 2014.

6. Robert S. Leiken and Steven Brooke, 'The moderate Muslim brotherhood', *Foreign Affairs*, 86(2) (2007): 107–21.

7. Mahdi Darius Nazemroaya, 'Egypt's constitutional referendum: did President Morsi hijack democracy?', *Global Research*, Cairo, 2013.

8. Mohamed el Dahshan, 'Where will the Muslim Brotherhood take Egypt's economy? Egypt's Islamists scramble to develop economic policy staying within the dictates of religion', *YaleGlobal*, 6 February 2012.

9. Nader Habibi, *The Economic Agendas and Expected Economic Policies of Islamists in Egypt and Tunisia*, Middle Eastern Brief No. 67 (Waltham, MA: Crowne Centre for Middle Eastern Studies, Brandeis University, 2012).

10. Joan C. Henderson, 'Representations of Islam in official tourism promotion', *Tourism, Culture and Communication*, 8(3) (2008): 135–45.

11. Daniel Treisman, 'The causes of corruption: a cross-national study', *Journal of Public Economics*, 76(3) (2000): 399–457.

12. Alaa Bayoumi, 'The many faces of Mohamed Morsi', *Al Jazeera*, Doha, 13 December 2012.

13. Roula Khalaf, 'Morsi adviser blames IMF for delaying Egypt $4.8bn loan agreement', *Financial Times*, Dubai, 9 June 2013

14. Ann Elizabeth Mayer, 'Islamic banking and credit policies in the Sadat era: the social origins of Islamic banking in Egypt', *Arab Law Quarterly*, 1 (1985): 32.

15. Rodney Wilson, 'Arab government responses to Islamic finance: the cases of Egypt and Saudi Arabia', *Mediterranean Politics*, 7(3) (2002): 143–63.

16. Sherin Galal Abdullah Mouawad, 'The development of Islamic finance: Egypt as a case study', *Journal of Money Laundering Control*, 12(1) (2009): 74–87.

17. Abhinav Ramnarayan, 'Egypt plans to issue *sukuk* in early 2014', *Reuters*, Cairo, 23 May 2013.

18. Dalibor Rohac, 'Solving Egypt's subsidy problem', *Cato Institute Policy Analysis*, No. 741, Washington DC, 6 November 2013.

19. Hans Löfgren and Moataz el-Said, 'Food subsidies in Egypt: reform options, distribution and welfare', *Food Policy*, 26(1) (2001): 65–83.

20. John William Salevurakis and Sahar Mohamed Abdel-Haleim, 'Bread subsidies in Egypt: choosing social stability or fiscal responsibility', *Review of Radical Political Economics*, 40(1) (2008): 35–49.

21. Suleiman Abu-Bader and Aamer S. Abu-Qarn, 'Government expenditures, military spending and economic growth: causality evidence from Egypt, Israel, and Syria', *Journal of Policy Modelling*, 25(6) (2003): 567–83.

22. Ernst & Young and the Institute of Chartered Accountants in England and Wales (ICAEW) provide annual tax guides on Egypt. See at: http://www.icaew.com/en/library/subject-gateways/tax/tax-by-country/egypt.

23. Ragui Assaad, 'Unemployment and youth insertion in the labour market in Egypt', in Hanaa Kheir-El-Dinn (ed.), *The Egyptian Economy: Current Challenges and Future Prospects* (Cairo: American University in Cairo Press, 2008), pp. 133–78.

24. Abdel R. Omran and Farzaneh Roudi, 'The Middle East population puzzle', *Population Bulletin*, 48(1) (1993): 1–40.

25. Kareem Fahim, 'Egypt's birth rate rises as population control policies vanish', *New York Times*, 2 May 2013.

26. Sara Aggour, 'Al-Sisi targeting 7% GDP growth, 8% unemployment by 2017/2018', *Daily News Egypt*, 20 May 2014.

27. Ben W. Heineman, 'General Sisi's greatest enemy: the Egyptian economy', *The Atlantic*, New York, 27 March 2014.

28. Noha Moustafa, 'Managed devaluation? The Egyptian pound is continuing to lose ground against the dollar and other currencies', *Al-Ahram*, No. 1198, Cairo, 22 May 2014.

10

PIETY, INCLUSION AND
MATERIALISM IN SAUDI ARABIA

A model of economic success

Although Mecca and Medina were successful centres of trade at the time of the Prophet, much of what was to become the Kingdom of Saudi Arabia was until the 1950s a relative economic backwater. Prior to its unification as a state in 1933, the Arabian Peninsula comprised often warring tribal groups with an economy based on animal rearing, apart from the major area of settled agriculture in Azir in the southwest bordering Yemen. The tribesmen lived from day to day at a subsistence level with no investment that might have aided economic development. The discovery of oil in 1938 in the al-Hasa region was to transform the kingdom into a largely urban society, with the population acquiring middle-class values and enjoying increasing material prosperity.

The economy remains dependent on oil, which accounts for 90 per cent of total government revenues, 88 per cent of export earnings and 35 per cent of GDP.[1] Saudi Arabia, however, should not simply be regarded as a rentier economy, a term that is disparaging with negative connotations as it implies a state where revenue comes from the ownership of natural resources rather than from productive effort and that the government survives through patronage.[2] Corruption is often associated with systems of patronage, but, as shown in Chapter 4, Saudi Arabia is one of the least corrupt countries in the Islamic world and is widely viewed as a safe destination for foreign investment with sound protection of property rights. Furthermore, although the state plays a major role in resource allocation, the private sector continues to thrive and expand, accounting for half of the country's GDP. The free market economy is well entrenched and the state has been consistent in favouring and promoting business.

The public service is rather bloated in Saudi Arabia as there have been pressures for the state to increase employment of local nationals, many of whom aspire to have secure jobs in government. Nevertheless, key ministries are well run and function efficiently, notably the Ministry of Finance, the Defence Ministry and the Ministry of Petroleum. The Saudi Arabian Monetary Agency is arguably the best bank regulator in the Middle East. Although the commercial banks have got into difficulties at times of low oil prices, there has never been a bank failure in the kingdom and there is much confidence in the stability of the financial sector. State sector enterprises are in many cases centres of excellence, notably Aramco, the state oil company.[3] In terms of e-government portals, the systems in Saudi Arabia compare with the best in the world.

Islam and the economy

Saudi Arabia is the heartland of the Islamic world, with the two most important centres for Muslims being Mecca and Medina. It is the duty of Muslims to perform *hajj* as the fifth pillar of Islam, and *umrah* has become increasingly popular in recent years as travel becomes easier and the living standards of Muslims worldwide rise making it more affordable. The growing numbers performing *hajj* and *umrah*, which exceed 3 million each year for *hajj* alone, have proved to be a logistical challenge for the Saudi Arabian government, but major improvements are being made to the local transportation infrastructure with the Haramain high-speed rail project. This 450-km high-speed inter-city rail transport system, due to open in 2015, will link the Muslim holy cities of Medina and Mecca via King Abdullah Economic City, Rabigh, Jeddah and King Abdulaziz International Airport.

The spending of pilgrims is the most concrete example of Islam having an impact on the economy of Saudi Arabia, if only at regional level.[4] At national level, outside the banking sector, the impact is largely invisible despite religion being supposedly the key determinant of Saudi Arabian culture and values. The monarch is depicted as the guardian of the two holy mosques of Islam, a reference to Mecca and Medina, but it is not clear what this means in practice today, apart from the government funding of the Haramain rail project. Although Saudi Arabia has long been classified as both a Muslim state and an industrial country, at least in terms of extractive industry, the implications of these dual characteristics and how they interact are ill-defined and uncertain.[5] There is little to distinguish economic policy in the kingdom from anywhere else, and in no sense could it be depicted as drawing on Islamic teaching. The informal pact between the ruling House of Saud and the Wahhabi religious leadership may have served to legitimise the monarchy, but it had no influence on economic policy-making. The short-lived Umma Islamic Party, which was established as a Saudi Arabian response to the Arab Spring in 2011, had no economic agenda, its main aim being to destabilise the relationship between the religious umma and the royal family.

At the micro-economic level of individual businesses, there are also questions about what attributes constitute Islamic values.[6] There have been empirical surveys of business' operations in Saudi Arabia where respondents have stressed their commitment to Islamic values, but what this means in practice if difficult to decipher.[7] In areas such as marketing, however, Islamic culture determines what is acceptable and what is inappropriate, and arguably engagement with public opinion in Saudi Arabian does have an impact on business practice, especially on what to promote through advertising and what methods to use.[8] There is also increasing discussion of the *halal* economy, originally with reference to meat, but now encompassing a wide range of products from alcohol-free mouthwash to leather goods guaranteed not to contain any pig skin. *Shari'ah* compliance is enforced for all products made in Saudi Arabia and all imports, but this has not proved to be a problem for suppliers who are very willing to comply if this means obtaining profitable contracts.[9]

Fiscal policy

Fiscal policy largely involves the management of oil revenues, with government spending reflecting development and security priorities rather than being shaped by Islamist ideas on welfare spending. Saudi Arabia maintains a healthy budget surplus and has little debt but substantial financial reserves. This largely reflects caution and conservative forecasts of oil prices as the Ministry of Finance seeks to avoid the situation that has arisen in neighbouring Iran, where excessive spending commitments are increasingly funded by debt as oil production declines and prices are at best static. Iran would be in even greater difficulty if oil prices fell below US$70 per barrel, but Saudi Arabian government finances would still be sustainable if oil prices temporarily collapsed, resulting from, for example, an economic crisis in China.

From an Islamic perspective the main criticism of deficit finance is that it usually involves government borrowing and the payment of interest, which for many equates with the forbidden *riba*. This concern was unlikely to have figured in policy-making at the Ministry of Finance in Riyadh. Since the 1980s, Saudi Arabia has issued development bonds that pay a fixed interest return, as well as floating rate notes that pay a variable interest return. The kingdom also sells treasury bills that run for short periods, typically ninety days, most of which are held by local banks who receive interest on their holdings. These instruments cannot be held by Islamic banks, and the government has yet to offer a general purposes sovereign *sukuk*. However, state majority-owned companies, including the Saudi Basic Industries Corporation (SABIC), have issued *sukuk*, and in 2012 the Ministry of Finance provided a guarantee for a *sukuk* to finance the expansion of King Abdul Aziz International Airport in Jeddah.[10]

Table 10.1 Expenditure on GDP at current prices (SR billion)

	2008	2009	2010	2011	2012	2013
Government	345	357	400	488	551	621
Private	523	592	639	682	785	833
Stock	87	96	123	104	110	107
Capital	444	414	484	569	615	651
Exports	1,210	756	982	1,411	1,498	1,453
Imports	662	608	653	742	807	860
Total	1,949	1,609	1,975	2,511	2,752	2,807

Note: SR 1 = US$ 3.75.

Source: Central Department of Statistics and Information, Riyadh, June 2014.

There are excellent statistics on the economy of Saudi Arabia with long data runs facilitating econometric analysis. Recent data for major expenditure indicators is shown in Table 10.1, which demonstrates in particular how the economy is increasingly being driven by private spending. Of course, as much of this spending is by public employees and companies winning government contracts, the state and the private sector can be regarded as complementing each other rather than the relationship being a trade-off. There are multiplier effects for private sector employment from state spending, and the non-oil economy remains substantially dependent on the oil revenues accruing to the state. For meaningful diversification the government would have to bring in more diverse revenue streams, such as VAT as advocated by IMF teams visiting the kingdom. The UAE, and Dubai in particular, raise substantial revenue from sales taxes, so there are precedents in the adjacent countries of the Arabian Peninsula. The table highlights how government spending increased substantially following the Arab Spring of 2011, as the Saudi Arabian government response was to award local citizens working in the public sector with substantial salary increases as part of its counter-revolutionary strategy.[11] This bought off potential discontent, but how sustainable such policies are is debatable, as to diversify the kingdom must be internationally competitive and substantial salary increases only add to costs.

Gross capital formation is also shown in Table 10.1, which almost doubled over the period from 2008 to 2013 from an already high level. Much of the capital formation represents investment in infrastructure, partly with the expansion of existing cities as well as work preparing new industrial sites. Most of the infrastructure expenditure is financed directly by government, which has the resources to ensure a steady upward trend. The exception was 2009 in the aftermath of the global financial crisis when earnings from oil exports fell, resulting in the government being more cautious and taking the decision to delay some major public works.

Even in 2009, however, there remained a substantial trade surplus and this widened subsequently, as Table 10.1 shows. Imports comprise a wide variety of capital equipment and consumer goods, most of which are sourced from Asia with a declining share for Europe. Exports are also destined largely for Asia, especially China, Japan and South Korea, with oil being the dominant export.[12] However, in recent years petrochemicals have become increasingly important, accounting for around 10 per cent of exports and bringing much value-added into the kingdom. SABIC accounts for most of these exports, with its overseas subsidiaries in Europe and Asia providing the stable and captive market envisaged when the company embarked on its long-term strategy of investing in plants worldwide.

Exchange rate and monetary policy

The Saudi riyal has been pegged to the US dollar for over four decades at a rate of 3.75 SR per dollar. The rationale for the peg was that as the oil price was denominated in dollars this brought stability. With the dollar being the dominant currency for international payments, the ability to maintain the peg to the dollar increased the credibility of the riyal and prevented speculative attacks by currency traders. The Saudi Arabian Monetary Agency (SAMA) enforced the peg by buying and selling dollars to maintain the equilibrium rate, which, given the kingdom's substantial financial reserves, proved to be a relatively straightforward task. The dollar anchor also restrained inflation, as with currency stability Saudi Arabia did not experience the price rises experienced by its neighbours, notably Iran and Iraq, where currency depreciation simply added to import price rises that triggered more generalised inflation.

Although the US dollar remains dominate, its role in international payments is being slowly eroded by the increasing use of Asian currencies, notably the Chinese renminbi, the Japanese yen and the Hong Kong and Singapore dollars. The liberalisation of the Indian economy is expected to result in free convertibility of the rupee, a move that would have regional implications, including for the Gulf, India's historical trading partner. These developments are of significance for Saudi Arabia as most of its oil and petrochemical exports are destined for Asian markets, which are also the leading source for its imports. Although trade with the EU has declined relatively during the last two decades, it remains more significant than trade with the United States, and is increasingly denominated in euros. Hence, as pointed out in Chapter 6, the dollar is unlikely to retain its special status as far as the economy of Saudi Arabia and the other states of the Gulf are concerned.

Although the nominal exchange rate between the riyal and the US dollar is fixed, divergence between the inflation rate in Saudi Arabia and the United States can result in real exchange changes taking account of relative prices.[13] As Saudi Arabia usually has a higher rate of inflation, reflecting supply bottlenecks and market inefficiencies, this causes an appreciation of the real exchange rate and introduces the possibility of the so-called Dutch disease.[14] This occurs when oil- and gas-exporting countries experience increasing export earnings that exert upward pressure on the exchange rate, crowding out production not only of non-oil exports, but also local supplies for the domestic market as imports become relatively cheaper. Although the nominal exchange rate for the riyal remained pegged, the real exchange increased, causing these effects.

The main counterbalance has been overseas investment, which has resulted in increased demand for foreign currencies, including US dollars. There is minimal opportunity cost for investment in the domestic economy given that the kingdom is not financially constrained. Indeed, outward investment can be beneficial for inward investment, with Saudi Arabia attracting more inflows than the rest of the Arab world combined. The investments by SABIC into its wholly-owned subsidiaries in Asia and Europe provide a captive market for its petrochemical output, increasing profitability and benefiting local stock market investors in Riyadh. The investments also help to ensure that the kingdom has income for future generations when the oil resources either become depleted or they are no longer in demand due to the development of alternative energy sources, the latter being the most likely scenario. There is no attempt to adopt *Shari'ah* screening with these investments, although the investments by SABIC are inherently compliant given their nature. There is some investment into international banks, however, which do not qualify as being *Shari'ah*-compliant because of their involvement with *riba*.

Despite the unease of many Islamic scholars, interest is used as a monetary policy instrument in Saudi Arabia. The rates tend to move with those in the United States given the peg with the dollar; indeed, the main objective is to use interest rate variations to maintain the peg rather than having a target for domestic inflation. Ironically, the United States has an inflation target with some built-in provisos regarding unemployment, and by having a fixed peg with the dollar interest rate movements in Saudi Arabia are indirectly affected by these domestic US economic variables rather than by inflation and unemployment within the kingdom. Having monetary policy determined by another country's economic priorities is a peculiar situation, but this has been the experience of Saudi Arabia since the 1970s. Fortunately for Saudi Arabia, however, there is evidence to show that low US interest rates are associated with high commodity prices.[15]

SAMA uses repurchase agreements, usually abbreviated to repos, as its main means of aligning local interest rates with those in US dollars to maintain the exchange rate peg. These sale and repurchase agreements involve the sale of securities by SAMA to the commercial banks, together with an agreement to buy back the securities at a later date. The repurchase price should be greater than the original sale price, the difference effectively representing the repo rate, which is a form of interest. The commercial banks are acting as a lender to SAMA, who is the borrower. The banks' holdings of the securities supplied by SAMA reduces their capacity to finance the private sector, curtailing economic activity. With reverse repo, also used by SAMA, the economy is stimulated as securities are purchased from the banks, which then have more cash to lend. The average daily repo rates are published by SAMA,[16] and the process is transparent, but there has never been any consultation with *Shari'ah* scholars concerning the legitimacy of this tool of monetary policy in the light of the prohibition of *riba*.

Islamic banking and finance

SAMA's major role is bank regulation rather than the active pursuit of monetary policy. Its record on regulation is viewed favourably, as fluctuations in oil revenue have inevitably been destabilising for the banking sector, but there has never been a bank failure in the kingdom, and depositors regard their deposits as safe. In recent years, the time of greatest stress was in 1998 following the Asia crisis of the previous year when the price of oil fell below US$10 a barrel, causing cutbacks in government spending and a loss of confidence in Saudi businesses, some of which could no longer service their bank debt. However, the nationalisation and SAMA-instigated restructuring of the National Commercial Bank, the kingdom's largest financial institution, resulted in a speedy recovery. The prompt intervention by SAMA strengthened the banking system and enabled it to emerge from the later global financial crisis of 2008 relatively unaffected.

Despite its regulatory success, SAMA has done little to cater for Islamic banking. Unlike in Kuwait and the UAE, which have amended their banking laws to cover Islamic banking, as discussed in Chapter 6, there is no legislative provision for Islamic banking in Saudi Arabia. The Banking Control Law of 1966 has never been revised or amended to ensure that all Islamic financial contracts are subject to a review by a *Shari'ah* board appointed by the bank, as has been the case in other jurisdictions. For the kingdom the issue is sensitive, as by identifying some banks as Islamic the implication would be that other banks are not Islamic, a hugely controversial matter in Saudi Arabia as its founder, King Abdul Aziz, was opposed to all banks, and it was only with reluctance that the National Commercial Bank, usually referred to as AlAhli Bank, was licensed by Royal Decree on 26 December 1953.[17]

The bank was the result of the merger of the two largest exchange dealers in Jeddah, the Saleh and Abdulaziz Kaki and the Salem bin Mahfouz companies. AlAhli Bank functioned as a conventional bank in many respects, as its financing was largely through loans and overdrafts on which interest was charged, although these were designated as service fees. Deposits were, however, largely placed into current accounts on which no interest was payable, with clients who wanted to earn a return on their savings in excess of SR 100,000 advised to invest in Khayrat AlAhli, an investment product based on the principles of *murabaha* and approved as being *Shari'ah*-compliant. The customer purchases commodities, then sells them to AlAhli Bank at an agreed higher price, including profits, to be settled at a deferred date. As the bank sets up and administers all the contracts from the perspective of the client, Khayrat AlAhli has the convenience of a treasury deposit. For clients seeking higher returns but with no capital guarantees, AlAhli Bank refers clients to its sister institution, NCB Capital, which is regulated by the Capital Markets Authority. It provides a range of mutual funds based on equity investments and *sukuk*, the most recent offering being the AlAhli Global Growth and Income Fund, which provides dividend opportunities twice a year from a diversified worldwide *Shari'ah*-compliant investment portfolio.[18]

AlAhli Bank provides both personal financing, mainly involving credit cards for consumer purchases and residential mortgages, and business finance. All its financing became *Shari'ah*-compliant in 2010, with *murabahah* being the most important financing method. There is full disclosure of the purchase price and scope for negotiation of the mark-up between the client and the bank, both commendable practices from a *Shari'ah* perspective. *Musharakah* private equity finance is also offered, with the bank and the client signing a partnership agreement to invest in a new venture and jointly share the profits and any losses. As the risks to the bank with this type of financing are considerable, the approval process involves a careful appraisal of the project, which has resulted in many rejections. *Ijara* leasing contracts are deemed to be less risky by AlAhli Bank, the leased asset typically being equipment or premises, with a right to buy option at the end of the leasing period. The controversial *tawarruq* contract is also offered, which involves trading commodities to finance a cash advance. The contract was revised in 2012 to make it more acceptable to the bank's *Shari'ah* board, with the bank serving as the client's agent and a third party rather than the bank conducting the repurchase, but many external *Shari'ah* scholars remain sceptical.[19]

The experience of the conversion of AlAhli Bank's financing to being *Shari'ah*-compliant shows how banks in Saudi Arabia have adopted this policy in response to customer demands, rather than because of official directives. The policy has essentially been market-led, with each bank making its own decisions about the extent and timing of moves towards *Shari'ah* compliance. All banks in the kingdom have now appointed *Shari'ah* boards, but there has been no official oversight of these boards, and SAMA does not have its own *Shari'ah* board to adjudicate where there are differences of opinion between bank board members.

The case of Al Rajhi's banking licence illustrates the caution of SAMA towards Islamic banking. Al Rajhi was first established as a family currency exchange business in 1957, and subsequently different members of the family opened their own branches. These were merged in 1978, making Al Rajhi a substantial financial business as it diversified from currency exchange into trade finance and handling remittances.[20] It was, however, unregulated, but the Al Rajhi family approached SAMA for a licence, requesting that it be designated as an Islamic bank as none of its operations involved *riba* and Islamic banks were already well established in neighbouring countries. The request was put on hold, however, and it was only in 1988 that the licence was granted on condition that Al Rajhi did not use the word 'Islamic' in its name and was incorporated as a joint stock company like the other banks.[21] It seems then that the major concern of SAMA was the large size of Al Rajhi and the fact that it had become a deposit-taker. Any failure by Al Rajhi would have caused systemic risks for the entire financial system and in these circumstances, given 'too big to fail' arguments, SAMA had little choice but to grant the licence.

Al Rajhi has subsequently grown to become the largest Islamic bank in the world with assets exceeding US$75 billion, deposits worth US$60 billion, a paid-up capital of US$4 billion and almost 7,500 employees. It has become a multinational bank with subsidiaries in Jordan, Kuwait and Malaysia. In Saudi Arabia, it has become the most profitable bank with the largest branch network. Arguably, had there been more government control it might not have achieved such success.

Employment issues

Since the development of oil and the subsequent rise in government spending, Saudi Arabia has been a magnet for migrant workers from other countries, not least from Muslim majority countries of the Arab world, Pakistan, Bangladesh and Indonesia. Many of the migrants have limited skills and work in the construction industry where Saudis are not interested in taking jobs due to the harsh working conditions. Others are better educated and include middle-class professionals doing jobs that Saudis aspire to but lack the skills to undertake, although this is changing as a result of policies favouring the employment of local citizens. Government employees are mostly Saudis, and in the private sector, hitherto dominated by foreign workers, the proportion of local citizens employed is steadily increasing.

Religion is not a factor in the allocation of work permits, but nationality is taken into account. Because of language Arabs had an advantage during the early years of oil production and development, with many working in the state sector as civil servants, teachers and doctors. However, it is these public sector jobs that were the first to be reassigned to Saudi citizens, with progress being slower in the private sector, especially in less well paid employment that was of little interest to local nationals. There has been a relative decline in the Arab non-Saudi workforce in the kingdom, and in recent years a decline in Muslim workers relative to non-Muslims. In hospital nursing, shops and household employment Philippine workers are often preferred because of their English language fluency, as English is the second language of most Saudis. Employment of Muslim Indonesian housemaids has declined relative to Christian Philippines, with language being a more important consideration than religion.[22] For many devout Muslims the kingdom was an employment destination of choice, not least because of its convenience for undertaking *hajj* and *umrah*. However, any pan-Muslim solidarity at personal and family level was not translated into state policy.

Most foreign nationals working in Saudi Arabia and the other Gulf states can only get work permits for two or three years, and obtaining citizenship is rare even for those who have had their work permits renewed many times and spent much of their life in the kingdom. This results in much career uncertainty, which reduces employee motivation.[23] As pressures for the replacement of expatriates with local citizens has increased, this has created resentments and undermined further the morale of foreign workers.[24] There can be little loyalty among migrant workers to Saudi Arabia, whether Muslim or non-Muslim, while the present work permit system continues. Most workers are solely in the kingdom for the money as they know they can never make it their home.

The Saudi economy, the fourth largest in the Islamic world, has been growing at a robust pace and has been successful in generating jobs. However, most of the jobs go to foreign workers, resulting in high unemployment among the rapidly growing Saudi labour force. The overall unemployment rate in 2013 was 5.8 per cent and has remained broadly stable since the end of 2009. Among Saudis, unemployment rates have risen from 10.5 per cent in 2009 to 12.1 per cent by 2012, with the rates especially high for youth and women. Despite total employment growth averaging near 8.5 per cent, employment growth for Saudi citizens was only 4.6 per cent over the period from 2010 to 2012, and Saudi employment as a percentage of total employment has actually declined since 2009.[25]

The government has attempted to absorb as many local citizens into the public sector as possible, especially into the military, but because of the rapidly expanding numbers entering the workforce, most cannot be guaranteed employment. Even in an oil-rich kingdom it is recognised that a bloated public sector is inefficient and unstainable. Therefore, much government effort has been devoted to trying to increase employment opportunities for local citizens in the private sector. Measures include increasing the cost of work permits for private sector employers and using the resultant revenue to subsidise the employment of Saudis for their first two years of job experience and training. It, nevertheless, remains more expensive to employ local nationals as their minimum wage is well above the rate for expatriates.

Employment trends in the private sector over the period from 2005 to 2013 are shown in Table 10.2. Employment of Saudi nationals has more than doubled over the period, but admittedly from a low base, and there was a

Table 10.2 Private sector employment in Saudi Arabia

Year	Saudis	Non-Saudis
2005	623,465	4,738,823
2006	713,751	4,866,989
2007	765,621	5,061,235
2008	829,057	5,392,890
2009	681,481	6,214,067
2010	724,655	6,266,545
2011	844,476	6,937,020
2012	1,134,633	7,352,900
2013	1,466,583	8,212,782

Source: Saudi Arabian Monetary Agency, *Annual Statistics*, Riyadh, 2014.

contraction in 2009 following the global financial crisis of the previous year. This did not affect the rise in the numbers of expatriates employed, which continued to increase steadily and actually accelerated from 2010 onwards, with over 8 million non-Saudis working in the private sector by 2013. The high salary awards given to local nationals in an attempt to buy off potential discontent in the aftermath of the Arab Spring meant that the employment of Saudis relative to expatriates became even more costly.

There is a very low female workforce participation rate in Saudi Arabia largely reflecting conservative social values which deter many women from seeking employment, even though the majority of university graduates are now women. The number of Saudi Arabian women working in the private sector increased from 32,185 in 2005 to 161,388 in 2013, a substantial rise but from a very low base. Many women want to work as it would increase family income and raise living standards, but family traditions, especially the attitudes of their mothers and mothers-in-law, often discourage workforce participation, even where their husbands are supportive.[26] There is little doubt that if more Saudi women worked, this could be the major way of tackling the inexorable rise in the number of expatriate workers.[27] As will be seen in Chapter 12, the high participation of Muslim women in the Malaysian workforce has been a significant factor in Malay economic empowerment. There is much that Saudi Arabia could learn from the Malaysian experience in this regard.

Notes

1. Saad A. Alshahrani and Ali J. Alsadiq, 'Economic growth and government spending in Saudi Arabia: an empirical investigation', IMF Working Paper, WP/14/3, Washington DC, 2004, p. 5.
2. Hazem Beblawi, 'The rentier state in the Arab world', *Arab Studies Quarterly*, 9(4) (1987): 383–98.

3. Steffen Hertog, 'Defying the resource curse: explaining successful state-owned enterprises in rentier states', *World Politics*, 62(2) (2010): 261–301.

4. Michael B. Miller, 'Pilgrims' progress: the business of the hajj', *Past and Present*, 191(1) (2006): 189–228.

5. William Ochsenwald, 'Saudi Arabia and the Islamic revival', *International Journal of Middle East Studies*, 13(3) (1981): 271–86.

6. Rodney Wilson, 'Islam and business', *Thunderbird International Business Review*, 48(1) (2006); 109–23.

7. Shahid N. Bhuian, 'An empirical examination of market orientation in Saudi Arabian manufacturing companies', *Journal of Business Research*, 43(1) (1998): 13–25.

8. Bjorn Bjerke and Abdulrahim al-Meer, 'Culture's consequences: management in Saudi Arabia', *Leadership and Organization Development Journal*, 14(2) (1993): 30–5.

9. A. H. Ayan, 'Halal food with specific reference to Australian exports', *Food Australia*, 53(11) (2001): 498–500.

10. Sara Hamdan, 'Saudi Arabia issues its first sovereign Islamic bond', *New York Times*, 25 January 2012.

11. Mehran Kamrava, 'The Arab Spring and the Saudi-led counterrevolution', *Orbis*, 56(1) (2012); 96–104.

12. Amy Myers Jaffe and Steven W. Lewis, 'Beijing's oil diplomacy', *Survival*, 44(1) (2002): 115–34.

13. Lucio Sarno, 'Real exchange rate behaviour in the Middle East: a re-examination', *Economics Letters*, 66(2) (2000): 127–36.

14. Robert E. Looney, 'Oil revenues and Dutch disease in Saudi Arabia: differential impacts on sectoral growth', *Canadian Journal of Development Studies/Revue canadienne d'études du développement*, 11(1) (1990): 119–33.

15. Jeffrey A. Frankel, 'The effect of monetary policy on real commodity prices', Paper No. w12713, National Bureau of Economic Research, Washington DC, 2006, pp. 1–41.

16. See at: http://www.sama.gov.sa/sites/samaen/FinanceExRate/RepoRate/Pages/Averagedailyreporate.aspx.

17. See at: http://www.alahli.com/en-us/about-us/corporate-profile/Pages/AlAhli-History.aspx.

18. See at: http://www.ncbc.com/microsite/GGIF/GGIF_En.asp.

19. Mohammad Nejatullah Siddiqi, 'Economics of *tawarruq*: how its *mafasid* overwhelm the *masalih*', *Tawarruq* seminar organised by the Harvard Islamic Finance Programme at London School of Economics, London, 2007, vol. 1.

20. See at: http://www.alrajhibank.com.

21. Jammaz al-Suhaimi, 'Consolidation, competition, foreign presence and systemic stability in the Saudi banking industry', Background Paper 128, Bank for International Settlement, Basel, 2001.

22. Rachel Silvey, 'Transnational domestication: state power and Indonesian migrant women in Saudi Arabia', *Political Geography*, 23(3) (2004): 245–64.

23. Shadid N. Bhuian, Eid S. al-Shammari and Omar A. Jefri, 'Organizational commitment, job satisfaction and job characteristics: an empirical study of expatriates in Saudi Arabia', *International Journal of Commerce and Management*, 6(3/4) (1996): 57–80.

24. Salah T. Madhi and Armando Barrientos, 'Saudisation and employment in Saudi Arabia', *Career Development International*, 8(2) (2003); 70–7.

25. Cornelius Fleischhaker, Martin Hu, Padamja Khandelwal, Jimmy McHugh, Haonan Qu and Niklas Westeiius, 'Saudi Arabia: Selected Issues', IMF, Washington DC, June 2013, pp. 14–22.

26. Eleanor Abdella Doumato, 'Women and work in Saudi Arabia: how flexible are Islamic margins?', *Middle East Journal*, 53(4) (1999): 568–83.

27. Eleanor Abdella Doumato, 'Education in Saudi Arabia: gender, jobs, and the price of religion', in Eleanor Abdella Doumato and Marsha Pripstein Posusney (eds), *Women and Globalization in the Arab Middle East: Gender, Economy, and Society* (Boulder, CO: Lynne Rienner Publishers, 2003), pp. 239–58.

FAITH AND POLITICAL ECONOMY IN PAKISTAN AND BANGLADESH

Islam in the subcontinent

Pakistan and Bangladesh emerged as a single country after the partition of India following independence in 1947. Partition was an attempt to split the subcontinent along religious lines, with East and West Pakistan predominantly Muslim and India predominantly Hindu. Given that religion was the rationale for the creation of these states, Islam might have been expected to play a major role in politics and economic policy, but in reality the influences on policy-making were more complex. Religion may have shaped the identity of Pakistan and Bangladesh and determined the territorial boundaries, but neither country today could be classified as an Islamic state, despite Islam being specifically referred to in their constitutions.[1]

Indeed, in the newly independent Pakistan religion was insufficient to serve as a unifying factor given the ethnic and linguistic differences between West and East Pakistan. The political differences were so great that war broke out in 1971, quickly resulting in Bangladesh becoming an independent state.[2] The countries are treated together in this study as it is instructive to compare and contrast their experiences since the 1970s. Both have faced major environmental and political challenges, but from an economic perspective Bangladesh has performed much better than its hitherto relatively more prosperous neighbour. Whether one can learn lessons from the other is debatable, not least as there remains much antagonism between these two Muslim countries despite over five decades of separation.

Despite partition, the Muslim population of India is larger than that of either Pakistan or Bangladesh, being the second largest in the world after Indonesia. It represents around 14 per cent of India's total population, but the Muslim community in India is diverse and scattered. Muslims in India mostly vote for the secular Congress Party or for regional parties, with relatively few supporting the Bharatiya Janata Party (BJP, India People's Party), the governing Hindu nationalist party.[3] There is no distinctive Islamic economic agenda in India, perhaps because if there was it would make little headway. The State Bank of India has refused to grant licences for any Islamic banks to open branches, although under the Cooperative Act, dating back from 1912 under the British Raj, some Muslim credit unions have been established, but most remain small local organisations.

Challenges facing the economies of Pakistan and Bangladesh

Islam does not have any place in policy-making in India, and the country's Muslims are mostly on lower incomes than their Hindu neighbours. In this study it makes more sense to focus on Pakistan and Bangladesh with their overwhelmingly Muslim populations. It is tempting to hypothesise whether Islam might have influenced economic policy-making in a united India if partition had not occurred, but such an exercise would be highly speculative and probably not very productive. For Pakistan and Bangladesh partition meant that both states emerged from a chaotic period of forced migrations and 'religious' cleansing, resulting in huge movements of people, with millions of refugees and massive economic disruption. Such conditions were not conducive to the creation of successful economies.[4]

To compound the problems of Pakistan and Bangladesh both have been subject to disasters beyond their control, which have resulted in severe loss of life and substantial material damage. Much of Pakistan lies in an earthquake zone with major quakes in 1974, 2005, 2008, 2011 and 2013. The 2005 quake was especially severe with an estimated 80,000 killed and 3.5 million people made homeless. As in other low income countries, the poor quality of building construction contributed to the death toll, with many continuing to be displaced a decade after the disaster.[5] Pakistan has also been subject to severe floods, the worst in 2010 displacing 20 million people, although most were able to return to their towns and villages later that year.

Bangladesh is subject to annual monsoon flooding because of its geographical position where the Ganges flows into the Bay of Bengal, resulting in storm surges and high tides combining with seasonal high river run-offs as the snow on the Himalayas melts. As three-quarters of Bangladesh is less than 10 metres above sea level, flooding is inevitable and the country does not have the money to build large-scale defences such as those in the Netherlands. Every year around 5,000 people are drowned by flooding and 7 million homes are damaged. The damage was especially severe in 1966, 1987, 1988, 1998 and 2007. The problems have been compounded by deforestation upstream in the Himalayas, but Bangladesh cannot stop it as the areas concerned lie within India.[6]

The other significant challenges facing Pakistan and Bangladesh are security and corruption. Security problems are most acute in Pakistan, especially in the areas bordering Afghanistan where the Taliban have waged a war of terror and the military have still not been able to restore law and order. Violent crime, including kidnapping, are an everyday occurrence in the major cities of Pakistan, including Lahore and Islamabad, although Karachi has long been the least safe city in the country. This lawlessness dates from the time of independence when many displaced people from India moved into Pakistan's major cities, creating an underclass that could easily be exploited by criminal gangs. Rural areas also lack security, especially the North West Frontier Province where the British were never able to completely control the tribes, a limitation subsequently inherited by the Pakistani military. Unfortunately, there is a history of military support fuelling corruption in Pakistan, including assistance from the United States.[7]

Security and the protection of property rights are preconditions for economic activity as uncertainty undermines investor confidence since businesses find it difficult to plan for the future. There is little doubt that capacity-building has suffered in Pakistan because of a lack of both domestic and foreign investment. The unwillingness of the private sector to invest has meant that there is more reliance on government, but the state has very limited resources and what finance it can provide often gets misallocated due to political factors and is poor value for money due to corruption. Instead of bringing economic benefits in Pakistan through trust and social solidarity, Islam in Pakistan is highly politicised and divisive. This is less the case in Bangladesh, although the country has not been immune to political turmoil, most recently in 2014 when the opposition Bangladesh Nationalist Party boycotted the elections won for the third time by Sheikh Hasina.[8] Both countries are predominately Sunni, which reduces sectarian rivalry, although in the case of Pakistan the Shi'a minority have been subject to harassment and violent attacks.

A comparative economic profile of Pakistan and Bangladesh

The quality and breadth of statistical data for Pakistan is less satisfactory than the data for Bangladesh, but it nevertheless covers most basic economic indicators. The population continues to increase rapidly, as Table 11.1 shows, with Pakistan having the world's third largest Muslim population after Indonesia and India, and ahead of Bangladesh, the fourth largest. The fertility rate for Pakistan is one of the highest in the world averaging 3.34 births per woman compared with 2.20 in Bangladesh where fertility rates have fallen significantly, largely reflecting the higher participation of its women in the workforce. The gap is unlikely to close soon given the more limited employment opportunities available to women in Pakistan and social attitudes that encourage women to stay at home.[9] Islamic teaching is no bar to women working in Bangladesh,

Table 11.1 Selected economic indicators for Pakistan

Year	2009	2010	2011	2012	2013
Population (million)	170	173	177	181	184
Inflation (%)	17.0	10.1	13.7	11.0	7.4
Federal government receipts (R billion)	1,679	2,052	2,236	2,424	2,775
Federal government expenditure (R billion)	2,101	2,577	2,678	2,794	3,826
Exchange rate (R per US$)	78.4	83.8	85.5	89.2	96.7
Exports (US$ million)	17,688	19,290	24,810	23,624	24,460
Imports (US$ million)	34,822	34,710	40,414	44,912	44,950
FDI (US$ million)	3,720	2,151	1,635	821	1,456

Source: State Bank of Pakistan, Core Economic Indicators, *Annual Report*, 2013, pp. 1–2.

Table 11.2 Basic economic indicators for Bangladesh

Year	2008	2009	2010	2011	2012	2013
Population (million)	144.7	146.7	148.6	150.6	154.7	N/A
GDP growth (%)	6.2	5.7	6.1	6.7	6.2	6.0
Inflation (%)	9.9	6.7	7.3	8.8	10.6	7.7
Tax revenue (% GDP)	11.3	11.3	11.5	11.8	12.5	13.5
Government expenditure (% GDP)	10.6	10.9	11.1	9.8	9.9	9.8
Exchange rate (Taka/$)	68.6	68.8	69.2	71.2	79.1	79.9
Exports (US$ million)	14,151	15,581	16,233	22,592	23,989	26,586
Clothing exports (US$ million)	10,700	12,348	12,497	17,914	19,090	21,516
Imports (US$ million)	19,481	20,291	21,388	32,527	33,309	33,576
FDI (US$ million)	748	961	913	775	1,191	1,300

Source: Bangladesh Bank, *Annual Report*, Appendix III, tables I, II and XIV, 2014.

but in Pakistan maintaining secluded family structures seems more important than earning money, at least among the less educated lower classes, although such attitudes are not shared by the more modernist middle and upper classes.

Inflation, which can be interpreted as a sign of government mismanagement, has been significantly higher historically in Pakistan than in Bangladesh. In both countries the rate has fallen in recent years, with the rate lower in Pakistan for the first time in 2013. As there are minimal economic relations between Pakistan and Bangladesh, there are no forces pushing for convergence for the two countries. Figures for GDP growth in Bangladesh show that it has exceeded 6 per cent in recent years, as Table 11.2 shows. There are no comparable figures for Pakistan, but the growth rate is significantly lower, at around 4 per cent.

There is a marked contrast in the taxation and public expenditure position in Pakistan and Bangladesh, with the former running a substantial deficit while the Dhaka government enjoys a consistent budgetary surplus. In Pakistan, the situation is even worse than it appears as there are state government deficits as well as the federal government deficit. Only 72 per cent of the federal budget was covered by tax revenue in 2013, the rest being financed by debt, a marked deterioration from 2009 when 80 per cent was covered. In Bangladesh, the surplus more than doubled over the same period, with relatively little tax evasion and strict controls on government spending which has actually fallen as a percentage of GDP.[10]

Both Pakistan and Bangladesh have trade deficits, but the deficit is much more serious in the former with imports worth almost twice as much as exports, while in the latter around two-thirds of imports are covered by export revenues. Exports of ready-made clothing from Bangladesh more than doubled over the period from 2008 to 2013, and these now comprise over 80 per cent of the country's exports. Most of these exports represent subcontracting to major global clothing retailers, with Bangladesh having a competitive advantage over China in its low labour costs. Women do most of the factory work, but in sweat-shop conditions, with insufficient attention paid to health and safety issues. A major factory collapse in 2013 resulted in over 1,100 fatalities, while previous years witnessed deadly fires.[11] FDI, mainly in the textile sector, has increased by 80 per cent over the period from 2008 to 2013, but this does not seem to have improved workers' conditions. FDI in Pakistan fell by half over the same period, largely reflecting a lack of investor confidence as a result of endemic corruption and a deteriorating internal security situation.[12]

Islamic banking in Pakistan

Although many of the leading advocates of Islamic banking are of Pakistani origin, and most still live there, the spread of Islamic banking has lagged behind that of the Gulf states and Malaysia. There have been three major initiatives in Islamic finance, but they have been poorly implemented and have had a very limited impact. The first was the Modaraba Companies and Modaraba (Floatation and Control) Ordinance of 1980 (Law No. 31), enacted by the federal government. This provided for the establishment of *modaraba* (*mudarabah*) partnership companies, which could be listed and traded like other registered companies.[13] Forty-one companies were established under the ordinance, but they had mixed fortunes due to the risky business climate in Pakistan. Twenty partnership companies were still in existence in 2014, but the investors have, for the most part, been disappointed with their returns.

The second initiative was by the Council of Islamic Ideology, which has lobbied for the elimination of *riba* from the Pakistan financial system since

Table 11.3 Islamic banking data for Pakistan

Year	2011	2012	2013
Number of accounts	1,249,636	1,892,023	1,990,179
% of total deposits	7.9	9.3	10.5
% of total financing	5.6	5.6	6.9
% of total investment	7.7	9.4	9.3
% return on advances	14.6	13.9	11.7
% return on deposits	5.5	5.2	4.6
No. of branches	726	874	1,030

Source: State Bank of Pakistan, *Annual Report*, Statistical Supplement, 2013, p. 16.

the 1950s. The government of General Muhammad Zia-ul-Haq was willing to take matters forward and in 1988 established a 'Commission for the Islamization of the Economy'. However, progress was slow after the untimely death of President Zia and it was only in 1997 that the *Blueprint for an Islamic Financial System* was finally published.[14] By that time government changes had resulted in a lack of political momentum and although some legislators favoured its implementation, the members of the Pakistan People's Party were obstructive and the Blueprint was shelved.

The third initiative, which was more market-driven than government-led, was to be the most successful. In December 2001, the State Bank of Pakistan issued detailed criteria for the establishment of Islamic banks following lobbying by the banks on behalf of customers who were opposed to *riba*. The following year this was passed into law with the Banking Companies (Amendment) Ordinance. This ordinance resulted in many of the commercial banks opening Islamic windows or separate Islamic branches through which *Shari'ah*-compliant financial products could be offered. This brought a favourable response from bank clients, with over 10 per cent of bank deposits being designated as Islamic by 2013, as Table 11.3 shows.[15] The State Bank of Pakistan has drawn up a strategic plan for the 2014–18 period that aims to increase the *Shari'ah*-compliant share of deposits to 15 per cent, a realistic and attainable target.[16] Its success will, however, depend on customer acceptance of Islamic finance rather than government banking policy.

The Dubai Islamic Bank Pakistan has become the most successful exclusively *Shari'ah*-compliant bank in the country with over 225 branches in fifty cities. It is a wholly owned subsidiary of Dubai Islamic Bank, the world's oldest *Shari'ah*-compliant commercial institution founded in 1975. The subsidiary in Pakistan was opened in 2005 and already has over 130,000 retail customers. Many are Pakistanis who work or have worked in the UAE and have already dealt with the bank there, especially for investment deposits and remittances, the latter being handled through an agreement with Western Union. The financial objective of many Pakistani professionals working in the UAE and other

Gulf economies is to save so that they can build a family home in Pakistan or extend and improve an existing home. Dubai Islamic Bank in Pakistan provides Islamic mortgages based on diminishing *musharakah* partnership contracts combined with an *ijara* rental agreement, with the bank receiving its profit from the rental paid by the client for the bank's share of the property.[17] Dubai Islamic Bank Pakistan can also provide mortgage protection insurance through its own *takaful* scheme. Similar products are provided in the UAE, and hence replicating these in Pakistan was a natural progression, especially as it already enjoyed client awareness and it was an opportunity to expand beyond their rather crowded home market.

Remittances between Muslim countries

Both Pakistan and Bangladesh benefit from high levels of remittances as their citizens take better paid jobs abroad, often in other Muslim countries, notably the oil-rich economies of the Gulf. Most of the migrants work in low paying jobs in construction, logistics and retailing, but increasing numbers work in professional occupations, such as doctors, accountants and financial services. These professionals represent a brain drain, but as their education has usually been paid for by their families and not the state, there is no subsidy from the poor sending countries to the rich host countries. In practice, remittances are better targeted than development assistance to governments, which all too often misallocate or expropriate aid. Remittances go directly to needy families, who spend the money carefully to maximise the benefits to children through education or cover medical expenses for older family members.[18] Evidence from Pakistan and Bangladesh suggests that both economic growth and poverty alleviation are positively correlated with remittances.[19] Inflation was the only negative effect identified in the case of Pakistan, to a large extent reflecting the supply constraints that bedevil its economy.[20]

Bangladesh produces accurate statistics on remittances, which are shown in Table 11.4. The value of remittances more than doubled over the 2007–13 period, and appeared to be unaffected by the global financial crisis. Most remittances come from Muslim majority countries, notably Saudi Arabia and the UAE, which account for almost two-thirds of the total, with Kuwait being the third most important Gulf economy from a Bangladeshi perspective. Most remittances from non-Muslim countries originate from the United States, the United Kingdom and, increasingly Singapore. Many of the Bangladeshis in Singapore are employed as house maids, but those in the United States and the United Kingdom are well qualified professionals earning high salaries. Many of these professionals, however, are accompanied by their families and over time remit less to Bangladesh as their families become more disconnected from the country. Remittances may still be sent to parents and grandparents, but all the younger family members live in the West.[21]

Table 11.4 Workers' remittances to Bangladesh (US$ million)

Country	2007	2008	2009	2010	2011	2012	2013
Saudi Arabia	1,735	2,324	2,859	3,427	3,290	3,684	3,829
UAE	804	1,135	1,755	1,890	2,003	2,405	2,829
United States	930	1,380	1,575	1,451	1,848	1,498	1,860
Kuwait	681	864	970	1,019	1,075	1,190	1,187
United Kingdom	887	896	790	827	890	987	992
Oman	196	220	290	349	334	401	601
Singapore	80	130	165	193	202	311	499

Source: Bangladesh Bank, *Annual Report*, 2014, p. 250.

Pakistanis and Bangladeshis who migrate to the United States and the United Kingdom and live there for an extended period of five years or longer can apply for and obtain American or British nationality, as can spouses living in south Asia up to the time of their wedding. This favourable treatment granted by largely non-Muslim states is in contrast to the restrictive nationality requirements of the Muslim states of the Gulf, which prevents their fellow Muslims from becoming citizens. Too often they are treated as second-class workers with much lower salaries than local nationals and suffer from workplace discrimination. Most come on two- or three-year contracts, and are not allowed to leave unless their employers agree to them being given exit visas. Most are not allowed to change employment as they are tied to their sponsors in contractual arrangements that resemble slavery. Clearly, pan-Islamic solidarity does not extend to workers from poor Muslim states with few employment rights. Even those who have their contracts renewed many times and have spent most of their lives in the Gulf are denied citizenship.[22] Marriage between foreign Muslims and local citizens is discouraged, but when it does occur spouses have no citizenship rights. Many Muslim migrants in the Gulf suffer from severe mental health problems because of their treatment.[23]

There has been a marked lack of inter-governmental discourse between Pakistan and Bangladesh and the Muslim countries that host their migrants. The Pakistan and Bangladesh embassies in Riyadh and Abu Dhabi deal with lost passports and other mundane matters, but the rights of migrant workers are seldom addressed. Many construction workers are recruited by gangmasters, who take much, if not all, of their first year salaries in return for obtaining visas and arranging transport and accommodation, but their profits are enormous in comparison to the meagre earnings of the migrants. As the gangmasters are often influential businessmen in Pakistan and Bangladesh little is done about the exploitation and abuses of workers. Governments of other sending nations, notably the Philippines, are more active in supporting their migrant workers in the Gulf, even though most of those involved are Christians rather than Muslims. There is a registrar of gangmasters involved in employing Pakistanis and Bangladeshis in the United Kingdom, which facilitates regulation, but there is no comparable organisation in the Gulf.[24] Although there has been much publicity concerning the exploitation of immigrant workers and the governments of the Gulf have established institutions to deal with worker's rights, there is no independent monitoring and trade unions are prohibited.

Micro-finance

Islamic finance is underdeveloped in Bangladesh, but the country is well known for its extensive experiences of micro-finance, which is often held up as a model for other countries. The best known institution is the Grameen Bank, whose founder, Mohammed Yunus, was awarded a Nobel Prize for his work in aiding the poor.[25] Although not an Islamic bank, many viewed the Grameen Bank as a model for how *Shari'ah*-compliant finance should be directed to those in need, instead of to middle and higher income Islamic retail bank clients as is typically the case in the Gulf and Malaysia. The Grameen Bank lends to those with no collateral to offer at interest rates that are significantly lower than those of conventional money lenders. The finance is mostly targeted at women working in handicraft activities with, for example, the acquisition of sewing machines funded for those providing clothing repairs or alterations. Grameen Bank can advise on how to make money from such activities, allocating funding to those who seem highly motivated to work. Despite the lack of collateral offered, repayments are prompt, as the women fear being stigmatised as bad debtors by their peers if they did not honour this commitment.

Grameen Bank does not exploit this loyalty as it is organised as a mutual holding company, controlling local credit unions but without shareholders. In contrast, Islamic banks, including the Islamic Bank of Bangladesh, are run on commercial lines and listed on the Dhaka and Chittagong stock exchanges, with shareholders expecting and receiving attractive dividends. The Islamic Bank of Bangladesh has proved sustainable, however, like other listed Islamic banks. In contrast, the sustainability of the non-profit-making Grameen Bank is open to question as with no equity capital it is dependent on subsidies from international development assistance organisations.[26]

Although Islamic micro-finance exists in Bangladesh, most micro-finance involves lending for interest. When Grameen Bank was founded there was no Islamic banking in the country and little knowledge about how it operated, hence Islamic micro-finance was not an option. For the last two decades there has been more awareness of Islamic finance, yet it remains on the fringes of micro-finance.[27] The question arises of why this is the case. Does it reflect government or development assistance organisation policy, or is it due to potential client resistance? As Islamic finance involves risk-sharing, perhaps this makes it institutionally unattractive when the risks are high, as with unsecured financing.

Partnership financing through *musharakah* assumes clients can act as co-investors, but in the case of Bangladesh the clients do not have the resources to make an up-front investment contribution. *Mudarabah* is a possibility as the client contributes their skills and entrepreneurship rather than capital, but it is not clear that low income micro-finance clients have such competencies. Most Islamic micro-finance in practice involves *murabahah* and *ijara* contracts, but this is often not what clients actually want, especially because of the high arrangement costs in relation to the very small amounts of finance sought, which makes the contracts expensive.[28]

The role of Pakistan and Bangladesh in intra-Muslim economic discourse

It is evident that despite their Muslim majority populations and the constitutional reference to Islam, neither Islamic economics nor Islamic finance is seriously applied in Pakistan or Bangladesh. There is little likelihood of this changing in the foreseeable future given the politics of the two countries. The main economic links with other Muslim countries are through labour migration and remittances, but the labour and immigration policies pursued by the host economies in the Gulf sour the relationship at a personal level, which consequently has a negative impact on intra-governmental Muslim relations.

The main concrete benefit Pakistan and Bangladesh have received from their participation in pan-Islamic organisations has been the development assistance from the IDB. However, the amounts have been modest in comparison with that destined for more affluent countries such as Turkey, which have drawn up many successful project proposals. Of course, the frequent electricity blackouts in Pakistan do not help, nor does the poor state of its infrastructure. In the case of Bangladesh, the frequent reoccurrence of natural disasters discourages aid providers and results in disaster fatigue, even though these highlight the need for assistance.

Despite their historical and political differences Pakistan and Bangladesh have many similar developmental needs. There is little doubt that they would be more effective in inter-Islamic economic forums if they had agreed positions and acted together. Unfortunately, this is seldom the case; yet acting as rivals damages both states with the result that they receive less assistance or are ignored. Pakistan, because of its geographical proximity to the Gulf, could act as a bridge for Bangladesh, generating much goodwill in the process. There seems little likelihood of this becoming reality, however, given the lingering state of bitterness between the two countries.

Notes

1. Nasir Islam, 'Islam and national identity: the case of Pakistan and Bangladesh', *International Journal of Middle East Studies*, 13(1) (1981): 55–72.

2. Hamza Alavi, 'The state in post-colonial societies: Pakistan and Bangladesh', *New Left Review*, 74(1) (1972): 59–81.

3. Robert L. Hardgrave, 'India: the dilemmas of diversity', *Journal of Democracy*, 4(4) (1993): 54–68.

4. Gyanesh Kudaisya, 'The demographic upheaval of partition: refugees and agricultural resettlement in India, 1947–67', *Journal of South Asian Studies*, 18(1) (1995): 73–94.

5. Robert Butler, Lewis Owen and David J. Prior, 'Flash floods, earthquakes and uplift in the Pakistan Himalayas', *Geology Today*, 4(6) (1988): 197–201.

6. Roy Brouwer, Sonia Akter, Luke Brander and Enamul Haque, 'Socioeconomic vulnerability and adaptation to environmental risk: a case study of climate change and flooding in Bangladesh', *Risk Analysis*, 27(2) (2007): 313–26.

7. Azeem Ibrahim, *US Aid to Pakistan: US Taxpayers have Funded Pakistani Corruption* (Cambridge, MA: Belfer Center for Science and International Affairs, John F. Kennedy School of Government, Harvard University, 2009), pp. 1–44.

8. Ali Riaz, *God Willing: The Politics of Islamism in Bangladesh* (Lanham, MD: Rowman & Littlefield, 2004), pp. 1–36.

9. Zeba Sathar, Nigel Crook, Christine Callum and Shahnaz Kazi, 'Women's status and fertility change in Pakistan', *Population and Development Review*, 14(3) (1988): 415–32.

10. Hassan Mirza and Wilson Prichard, 'The political economy of tax reform in Bangladesh: political settlements, informal institutions and the negotiation of reform', International Centre for Tax and Development Working Paper No. 14, Brighton, 2013, pp. 1–42.

11. Jason Burke, 'Bangladesh factory collapse leaves trail of shattered lives', *The Guardian*, London, 6 June 2013.

12. Najid Ahmad, Muhammad Farhat Hayat, Muhammad Luqman and Shafqat Ullah, 'The causal links between foreign direct investment and economic growth in Pakistan', *European Journal of Business and Economics*, 6(1) (2012): 20–1.

13. See at: http://www.secp.gov.pk/corporatelaws/pdf/jan_26_1981.pdf.

14. Hussain G. Rammal and Lee D. Parker, 'Islamic banking in Pakistan: a history of emergent accountability and regulation', *Accounting History*, 18(1) (2013): 5–29.

15. Ali Raza, Urooj Saddique, Umar Farooq, Saqib Awan and Atif Amin, 'Customers' satisfaction towards Islamic banking: Pakistan's perspective', *Arabian Journal of Business and Management Review*, 1(6) (2012): 71–9.

16. See at: http://www.sbp.org.pk/departments/pdf/StrategicPlanPDF/Strategy%20 Paper-Final.pdf.

17. See at: http://www.dibpak.com/Consumer-Financing/Home-Finance.

18. Arusha Cooray, 'The impact of migrant remittances on economic growth: evidence from south Asia', *Review of International Economics*, 20(5) (2012): 985–98.

19. Katsushi S. Imai, Raghav Gaiha, Abdilahi Ali and Nidhi Kaicker, 'Remittances, growth and poverty: new evidence from Asian countries', *Journal of Policy Modelling*, 36(3) (2014): 524–38.

20. Javed Iqbal, Misbah Nosheen and Ammara Javed, 'The nexus between foreign remittances and inflation: evidence from Pakistan', *Pakistan Journal of Social Sciences*, 33(2) (2013): 331–42.

21. Angela Dale and Sameera Ahmed, 'Marriage and employment patterns amongst UK-raised Indian, Pakistani, and Bangladeshi women', *Ethnic and Racial Studies*, 34(6) (2011): 902–24.

22. Mohammad A. Auwal, 'Ending the exploitation of migrant workers in the Gulf', *Fletcher Forum for World Affairs*, 34(2) (2010): 87–101.

23. Maha al-Ghafry, Marwa Saleh and Ziad Kronfol, 'Mental health issues among migrant workers in the Gulf Cooperation Council countries: literature review and case illustrations', Qatar Foundation Annual Research Forum, Doha, 2012, available at: http://www.qscience.com/doi/pdfplus/10.5339/qfarf.2012.AHPS2.

24. Deborah Smeaton, Maria Hudson, Dragos Radu and Kim Vowden, 'The EHRC triennial review developing the employment evidence base', Policy Studies Institute, London, 2010, pp. 151–3.

25. Pankaj S. Jain, 'Managing credit for the rural poor: lessons from the Grameen Bank', *World Development*, 24(1) (1996): 79–89.

26. Jonathan Morduch, 'The role of subsidies in microfinance: evidence from the Grameen Bank', *Journal of Development Economics*, 60(1) (1999): 229–48.

27. Habib Ahmed, 'Financing microenterprises: an analytical study of Islamic microfinance institutions', *Islamic Economic Studies*, 9(2) (2002): 27–64.

28. Rodney Wilson, 'Making development assistance sustainable through Islamic microfinance', *International Journal of Economics, Management and Accounting*, 15(2) (2007): 197–217.

ASIAN VERSUS MUSLIM IDENTITIES IN MALAYSIA AND INDONESIA

The contested Malaysian and Indonesian political economy

Islam spread to southeast Asia in the twelve and thirteenth centuries, the first notable conversion being by the ruler of Kedah, the northwestern Malaysian state, who abandoned the traditional Hindu faith. Other rulers on either side of the Straits of Malacca soon converted largely as a result of the increasing presence of Muslim traders both from south Asia and further afield in the Gulf. Like most states of the time, the social order was hierarchical, hence when the rulers converted, their subjects followed. By the time the Portuguese explorer Marco Polo arrived in 1292 Islam was well established. Arab traders were living in the region and actively involved in commerce, whereas contacts with the Hindu rulers of the Indian states were much reduced and never revived, the Indonesian island of Bali being the one remaining centre for Hinduism in the region.[1]

Chinese traders were also active in the coastal settlements, and the fifteenth-century ruler of Malacca, Iskandar Shah, established good relations with the Ming Dynasty through its envoy, Yin Qing.[2] Malacca became an important centre for the maritime spice route, and with Chinese support rival powers, notably Vietnam and Siam, were kept out of the lucrative trade. Although the Chinese were not Muslims, relations with the Malay rulers were cordial, with the Chinese confining their activity to business and making no attempt to threaten or change the social order. As the Malay states prospered with trade, the expatriate Chinese benefited substantially and arrived in ever increasing numbers, becoming dominant in urban commerce, while the Malays largely earned their livelihoods through agriculture and fishing, although the Malay elite worked in the royal courts of the state rulers, functioning as a kind of civil service.

The arrival of the Europeans was to have a profound effect both economically and politically on the Malay states. The Portuguese who settled in Malacca had no territorial ambitions, but the state benefited from being part of a worldwide empire, with Malacca serving as a transit centre between Portuguese-governed Goa in India and Macao in China. The Portuguese were Christians, but they made no attempt to convert the local Muslim population, although some Chinese Buddhists became Roman Catholics. This was also the case with the Dutch who built a Protestant Reform Church in Malacca, but this was largely to serve the Dutch traders not the indigenous population. The focus of the Dutch and later the British was on exploiting the natural resources of the region, not in interfering with the social or cultural values of the native population.[3] However, the rivalry between the Dutch and the British East India companies resulted in the governments of the Netherlands and the United Kingdom getting more directly involved, and this was ultimately to result in colonisation and the division of the Malay states into the separate countries of Peninsular Malaya, later Malaysia, and Indonesia. The colonial boundaries and the states created were to survive the Japanese occupation during the Second World War and the subsequent independent states created of Malaysia and Indonesia.

The post-independence New Economic Policy in Malaysia

Following the end of the Japanese occupation, the Indonesia National Union declared independence in August 1945, but it was not recognised by the Netherlands, the former colonial power, until 1949.[4] Independence for peninsula Malaya did not come until 1957, largely because following the ending of the Japanese occupation and the restoration of British rule a communist insurgency erupted, mainly involving ethnic Chinese who were influenced by events in China with the coming to power of Mao Zedong.[5] The British did not want to leave a destabilised Malaya because of their economic interests in the country's rubber and oil palm production, and hence independence had to wait until the resurrection was ended by British military force. Unrest continued in the jungles of North Borneo, and it was only in 1963 that these states and Singapore joined the Malaysian federation. The Sultanate of Brunei, although almost entirely Muslim, refused to join the Malaysian Federation, which would have resulted in Brunei having to share its considerable oil earnings; instead, it continued to be a British protectorate until 1984. Independence from the United Kingdom was amicable, not least as the British put down a revolt against the Brunei monarchy in 1962, and the sultan maintains strong links with London.[6]

Singapore only remained part of the Malaysian Federation for two years, as its largely Chinese population wanted to run their own affairs independently of the Bumiputera (Muslim Malays).[7] Racial tensions increased as the Chinese in Singapore felt they were being discriminated against by the federal policies of affirmative action, which granted special privileges to the Malays guaranteed under Article 153 of the Malaysia constitution.[8] The aim of this provision was to economically empower the Malay Muslim population, who despite being the political majority, were, apart from the royal elites, generally on much lower incomes than the ethnic Chinese who dominated the business community. As a result of Singapore becoming an independent state, the demographics of the Malaysian Federation tilted even more in favour of the Bumiputera, with the remaining Chinese comprising around one-quarter of the population, the Malays over 60 per cent and the Indians brought in by the British to work on the rubber plantations most of the remainder.

The affirmative action programme to raise the status of the Malay majority was formalised as the New Economic Policy following the race riots of 1969, which erupted in low income neighbourhoods largely as a result of the mistrust between the Chinese and Malay communities. The government response was to formulate a policy designed to raise the living standards of all ethnic and religious groups, while targeting resources to the Bumiputera majority to improve their educational performance and enhance their recruitment to positions as government employees and in wholly or partially owned state enterprises. Particularly controversial was the policy of having lower admissions grade requirements to university for Bumiputera. Chinese students resented this favouritism, as although they on average obtained better examination grades, this was insufficient to give them admission to the best universities.[9] Bumiputera also enjoyed preferential access to government scholarship programmes, resulting in Chinese parents having to pay expensive overseas fees themselves rather than having state assistance.[10]

Discriminatory policies favouring Bumiputera encompassed many areas of personal and business finance. Those looking for plots to build property resented the 7 per cent discount given to Malays; with the plots only offered to others if there was insufficient Malay demand. Companies listed on the Kuala Lumpur stock exchange were required to reserve 30 per cent of their shares for Muslim Malays, who prior to the new economic policy owned less than 2 per cent of shares in listed companies. Special mutual funds were also offered to Muslim Malay investors with guaranteed returns well above those available on bank accounts.

The New Economic Policy undoubtedly helped with poverty alleviation among the Muslim Malays, with the overall poverty rate falling from over half of the population in 1970 to less than 5 per cent by 2014, and even in the lower income rural areas the rate has fallen to below 10 per cent. Whereas in 1970 the equity stake in business of the Bumiputera was a mere 2.4 per cent, this has risen to 24 per cent. The rise in Bumiputera income has helped the whole society as it has increased demand in the economy, which has increased the turnover of Chinese businesses; hence, in many respects there has been a win-win situation.

The policy is not without its critics, however, including the Bumiputera beneficiaries as well as the Chinese and Indian communities. First, income inequalities within the Malay Muslim society have increased markedly as those who were associated with the state rulers and were already affluent have gained the most, increasingly flaunting their symbols of considerable wealth, especially expensive imported cars and luxurious villas. In contrast, the lifestyles of rural and urban low income Bumiputera have changed much less, as although there is no shortage of food, their living accommodation remains cramped and substandard.[11] Externally the excess of Bumiputera government employees and the top-heavy wholly or partially state-owned industries make Malaysia less competitive in a region of the world where competition is cut-throat. The rapid expansion of education has brought benefits to many, but there is criticism of standards and how far schools and universities equip their graduates for the workforce is debatable, as productivity remains uneven in Malaysia, especially in the state sector, and it is difficult to dismiss Bumiputera.[12]

One major success of the New Economic Policy has been the rise in the participation of women in the labour force, with over 56 per cent of women of working age in paid employment by 2014, a much higher participation rate than in most other Muslim majority countries, although not as high as in Thailand and the Philippines, or indeed Indonesia. There seem to be few barriers to women's economic empowerment, with women often better educated than their male peers and many occupying very senior positions, including that of Central Bank governor. In Malaysia there are increasing numbers of female *Shari'ah* scholars, with some serving on the *Shari'ah* boards of Islamic banks, a situation unheard of in Saudi Arabia and the Gulf. However, although there are more female than male university graduates and the vast majority of women in their twenties are employed, many subsequently quit work once they start having families. Many never return to work despite state childcare subsidies, a factor that may be explained by the relatively large number of children in Bumiputera families.[13]

Asian values and the role of *Shari'ah* in Malaysian and Indonesian law

As in the case of other Muslim majority states there are references to Islam in the constitutions of Malaysia and Indonesia. Under Article 160 of the Malaysian constitution Malays are defined as Muslims, the implication being that if they convert to another religion they cease to be Malay, and are therefore no longer entitled to the privileges accorded under the New Economic Policy. Despite being the world's most populous Muslim majority state, Islam does not have special constitutional provisions in Indonesia, although the constitution provides for everyone to have the right to worship according to their own religion or beliefs and states that the nation is based upon belief in one supreme God.[14] The Ministry of Religious Affairs officially recognises Islam,

Catholicism, Protestantism, Buddhism, Hinduism and Confucianism, but over 88 per cent of the population are Muslim, a much higher proportion than in Malaysia.

In east and southeast Asia there was a long tradition of religious tolerance with often people practising two religions simultaneously, Japan being a prime example where many people are both Buddhist and Shinto, the latter being a type of ancestor worship with, for example, adherents saying prayers and having special ceremonies on the birthdays of their deceased parents or grandparents. This does not preclude them being practising Buddhists at other times. Such dualism in worship is, of course, condemned in Islam, and indeed by other monotheistic religions, including Christianity and Judaism. However, as Hinduism and Buddhism were widely practised in Java, Indonesia's most populous island, prior to the coming of Islam, some believe that this legacy lives on. In particular, although Muslims in Indonesia cannot practise other religions, many are attracted by the diversity and mysticism of Sufi orders.[15] Although Islamic fundamentalism has gained ground in recent years, partly as a result of contacts with Muslims in the Middle East, tolerance remains deep-rooted in Indonesia. In particular, even the devout that pray on a daily basis, if not five times a day, are less likely to feel the need to apply their beliefs to all aspects of their lives, including their economic transactions and financial activity.

In the cultural context of Malaysia and Indonesia there is widespread acceptance of *Shari'ah* serving as a parallel, but not an exclusive, law. Family issues, including inheritance, are governed by *Shari'ah* law, but all commercial and financial dealings are governed by national law, including even Islamic banking and finance. There was legal continuity between the English common law in the case of Malaysia and the Dutch civil law in the case of Indonesia adopted during the period of colonial rule and the subsequent post-independence legal systems. This also applied to some extent in the Gulf, but there as the populations were much smaller, there was much less legislation and the amount of case law was only a small fraction of what it was in the more diverse and heterogeneous states of southeast Asia. There is no popular support for turning the countries into Islamic states even among the most Islamist, in contrast to the position in many states in the Middle East.

The questions inevitably arise as to what is meant by Asian values and how far they are compatible with Islamic teaching. Many view western values as incompatible with Islam, given that they derive from a Judeo-Christian tradition. These monotheistic religions, however, have arguably more in common with Islam than Hinduism or Buddhism, and the record of religious strife is as great in Asia as in Europe and the Middle East, as the experiences of northern Myanmar, southern Thailand, western China and the Indian subcontinent show. Classifying Islam as a religion of developing countries comparable to Hinduism or Buddhism is misleading and unhelpful.

In Malaysia the controversial opposition leader Anwar Ibrahim has written extensively on Asian values, which he sees as being associated with social complexity, but it is unclear what this means for economic policy.[16] The economic agenda of the opposition in Malaysia seems to be more motivated by vote winning than by Islamic or Asian values, the major differences revolving around personalities rather than policies.[17] Personality factors seem deeply embedded in the political culture of Malaysia, which grossly over-exaggerates minor differences. Writers have subsequently questioned whatever happened to Asian values and whether the concept simply applied to non-Western values with Asia artificially lumped together as somehow different.[18] Certainly, in a Malaysian context, although tourist advertising depicts the country as 'truly Asia, this seems to refer to its ethnic diversity not its value system, if this even exists.[19]

Malaysia has a strategic plan, the 2020 Vision, to become an advanced industrial country. The plan contains a spiritual dimension, hence the vision should not be viewed in entirely material terms, but it remains unclear what the spiritual vision actually is and whether the knowledge-based society envisaged will be predominately Islamic or multi-religious.[20]

In Malaysia, the United Malays National Organisation (UMNO) has been in power since independence, and although there are elections every four or five years, it has always been elected, though with varying majorities. Since 1973, it has governed through the Barisan Nasional coalition, which includes Chinese and Indian parties, though these have limited power bases. Most of the discussion of economic policy issues is within UMNO, and voters are not given competing agendas. The main issue has been the continuance of the New Economic Policy promoting Bumiputera empowerment, rather than arguments over tax and government spending priorities. Islam is seldom the subject of political discourse, and the government's promotion of Islamic finance is not disputed by other parties.

The political economy context of Indonesia

The political history of Indonesia since independence has been more dramatic, with Soekarno serving as the country's first president, an exponent of Indonesian nationalism who struggled, largely successfully, to create a unified and coherent state. Initially, Indonesia was a liberal democracy, but unbridgeable differences between the nationalists, communists and Islamists made the country ungovernable. Soekarno therefore moved to advocacy of 'guided democracy' in 1959, strengthening his own powers as president, winning the support of the army and suspending parliament.[21]

Liberals criticised this change of policy, prompting Soekarno's rhetoric to take on an increasingly authoritarian tone. Islamists and communists were both marginalised, which made the United States more sympathetic to the regime despite Soekarno's dictatorial tendencies. He was successful in getting control of the western part of New Guinea after the Dutch left with United Nations approval. From 1962 to 1966. Soekarno turned his attention to Malaysia, and was opposed to the inclusion of the territory of British Borneo, Sarawak and Sabah in the Malaysian Federation.[22] This time, however, Soekarno over-reached himself, as there was no international support for the inclusion of North Borneo in Indonesia, and the temporary withdrawal of Indonesia from the World Bank and the IMF in protest hurt the economy, which was badly in need of development assistance.

In September 1965, six army generals and one lieutenant were kidnapped and killed by a group of leftist officers, the allegation being that they were planning a coup to topple Soekarno. With his superiors murdered, General Suharto took control of the army, blaming the communists for the killings. Subsequently, the communists and their supporters were rounded up in what was to become the darkest period in Indonesia's history, with at least 400,000 people killed, many of whom were ethnic Chinese. Army units and civilian gangs were involved in the purges, but whether they were acting under orders is uncertain. General Suharto took power and deposed Soekarno, declaring a 'New Order', which was essentially nationalistic with the leftists largely eliminated and the Islamists continuing to be marginalised.[23]

The first task for Suharto was to repair the economic damage arising from the chaos and confusion of the final years of Soekarno. Investment, both foreign and domestic, had virtually ceased because of a lack of confidence, exacerbated by the purges of ethnic Chinese, who had played a much larger economic role than their numbers might suggest. The economy recovered, however, once Suharto successfully restored law and order. Recovery was helped by increasing oil revenue in the 1970s as oil prices quadrupled and production increased, further strengthening the position of Suharto. Oil revenue was used to finance the development of the country's infrastructure and poverty alleviation programmes, which had much popular support and made investment a more attractive proposition.[24]

Suharto was always careful in handling Islamic organisations, as he realised that repression could be counter-productive. Muslim leaders of organisations such as the Muhammadiyah and Nahdlatul Ulama were allowed more room than others to criticise Suharto. When Islam became a political alternative to express resentment, Suharto started to emphasise his own Islamic credentials, with a much publicised pilgrimage to Mecca in 1991. Practising, but moderate, Muslims were appointed to the top ranks of the army, and the Indonesian Association of Muslim Intellectuals (ICMI) was established in 1990 to provide a Muslim input into public policy. These moves neutralised Muslim opinion, and helped to stem the growth of mass public support for Islamist causes. Economic development also helped, with Indonesia classified as an 'Asian Tiger' economy by the World Bank. The autocratic nature of the Suharto regime was criticised by international human rights activists, but economic decision-making was aided by the lack of domestic dissent. Poverty alleviation was marked; in the 1960s more than 50 per cent of the population was classified as poor, while in 1993 this number had been reduced to 13.5 per cent of the population with social indicators such as school enrolment, infant mortality and life expectancy showing marked improvements.[25]

Suharto's governance system involved creating a political patronage system, with the opposition and potential critics bought off by providing them with senior government positions or investment opportunities through the award of state contracts. The system was corrupted, however, during the last decade of Suharto's rule when his children and close associates were able to establish and build large business empires purely because of their closeness to Suharto. Many Indonesians became critical at the high level of corruption, nepotism and collusion in government circles, but the government pointed to its impressive record of economic management. With the Asian Financial Crisis of 1997–8, the legitimacy of the regime started to collapse as Indonesia was the country that was most damaged. Riots against the regime erupted, with Jakarta turned into a battlefield in which violent rioters destroyed thousands of buildings, while more than a thousand people were killed. Suharto became more politically isolated and was forced to resign from the presidency, with his deputy Jusuf Habibie taking over in 1998 and declaring that there would be a new reformation.[26]

Habibie had to bow to popular pressures by increasing the power of the parliament and making the president accountable to the elected body. The parliamentary elections held in 1999 were to result in Habibie being replaced by Abdurrahman Wahid, but he was only to last two years until Megawati Soekarnoputri, the daughter of Indonesia's first president, was to become president herself. Megawati was far from being a reformer, but she allowed the reforms instigated by Habibie and continued by Abdurrahman Wahid to proceed, notably reducing the role of the military in politics.

The 2004 elections saw the emergence of two new parties, the Prosperous Justice Party, which advocated a greater role for Islam in public policy, and the Democratic Party, which was to be the election vehicle for Susilo Bambang Yudhoyono, a member of Megawati's cabinet, but with a more reformist position than the president. The Prosperous Justice Party received only 7 per cent of the vote, indicative of the limited public support for Islamist parties in Indonesia. The Democratic Party received a similar share, disappointing, but sufficient for Yudhoyono to stand for the presidency, winning over 60 per cent of the vote, compared with less than 40 per cent for Megawati. Yudhoyono's success was to be even greater in the 2009 election, with his share increasing slightly while that of Megawati slumped to under 27 per cent.[27]

With much of the political reform accomplished and democracy entrenched before Yudhoyono came to power, he focused more on economic reforms.[28]

Technocrats were appointed to key economic ministries, notably the Ministry of Finance, and the proportion of public debt to GDP was reduced to 25 per cent, indicative of strong public finances, with the growth rate exceeding 6 per cent. Yudhoyono was less successful with his pledges to reform the government bureaucracy and reduce corruption, which seems to be endemic in Indonesia. Indonesian presidents since Suharto have been limited to serving two five-year terms, but it was evident that as the end of Yudhoyono's presidency approached there remained widespread disillusionment concerning the extent of corruption. It remains to be seen if the new president, Joko Widodo, elected in 2014, will do any better.

The comparative macro-economic performance of Malaysia and Indonesia

Malaysia is an upper-middle income, highly open, economy which achieved an average growth of more than 7 per cent per year for over twenty-five years up to 2008. This included the period of the Asia crisis of 1997, which had a negative but less pronounced impact than in Indonesia. Growth has been lower in recent years, as Table 12.1 shows, but the goal of being a high-income developed country by 2020, first espoused by its longest serving prime minister, Mahathir Mohamad, is still attainable. The highly developed financial sector is helpful for economic growth, as is sustained FDI despite the capital controls that remain since the time of the Asia crisis.[29] Growth in 2014 may turn out to be 1 per cent higher than in the World Bank projection in Table 12.1. The country exports some oil and gas, but is much more diversified than Saudi Arabia and the Gulf, the most comparable Muslim majority country in terms of economic success being Turkey.

Indonesia is predicted to have a slightly higher GDP growth rate than Malaysia, but the difference in the projections is too small to describe its position as superior. In any case, Indonesia will remain a low-income developing country with its per capita GDP only one-third of that of Malaysia, reflecting its much larger population of almost 250 million. Indonesia is much more dependent on exports of raw materials and oil, mainly destined for China,

Table 12.1 GDP growth in Malaysia and Indonesia (%)

Year	Malaysia	Indonesia
2012	5.6	6.3
2013	4.7	5.8
2014	4.9	5.3
2015	5.0	5.6
2016	5.0	5.6

Source: World Bank Database, Washington DC, 2014.

Table 12.2 Current account balances of Malaysia and Indonesia (% of GDP)

Year	Malaysia	Indonesia
2012	6.1	−2.8
2013	3.8	−3.3
2014	3.5	−2.7
2015	5.1	−2.1
2016	5.1	−2.0

Source: World Bank Database, Washington DC, 2014.

and, despite its size, the economy is much less diversified than that of Malaysia. Much of the FDI investment in Indonesia involved extractive industries, which are not sustainable in the long run, whereas in the case of Malaysia the FDI has been in manufacturing industry and services.[30] This includes investment by multinational companies based in Japan that have built manufacturing facilities for electrical goods, including high-technology equipment. Skilled jobs have been created as a result, with Malaysia benefiting from technological transfers to widen its export base.[31]

Malaysia with its diversified range of exports maintains a trade surplus, as Table 12.2 shows, whereas Indonesia is vulnerable to commodity price developments and usually runs a deficit. Even prior to independence, it was apparent to the colonial government of Malaysia that overdependence on exports of rubber and oil palm increased vulnerability. Innovation in synthetics undermined the market in rubber and there were many substitutes for palm oil, resulting in a buyer's market. Malaysia is not a low-cost labour economy, and therefore the aim has been to manufacture differentiated goods aimed at the mid-market segment.

Apart from the Islamic finance sector there has been relatively little investment from the Islamic world as the need in Malaysia is for investment with embedded technology. The investment opportunities are in infrastructure, manufacturing and tourism, where companies from Japan, the United States, the EU and, to a lesser extent, China, have expertise to contribute.[32] Saudi Arabia and other Muslim countries can provide finance, but this is not in short supply internally given the size of Malaysia's banking system and its developed capital markets. In Indonesia, China has been the largest investor, and even though its resource needs are now growing less rapidly the existing commercial connections are likely to remain. The economic relations between Indonesia and other Muslim countries are very limited apart from the remittances sent by Indonesian migrant labourers working in the Gulf. Even this reveals little sign of religious preference as there are more Christian Philippines working in Saudi Arabia and the Gulf than Muslim Indonesians. In the case of Malaysia, the wages in the Gulf are insufficiently attractive to entice any Muslims to work in Saudi Arabia or the UAE.

ASEAN membership and relations with the Gulf

Both Malaysia and Indonesia are members of the Association of South East Asian Nations (ASEAN), a regional free trade grouping, the original objective being to strengthen economically, and perhaps politically, its member states in their relations with China.[33] Unlike the EU, which encompasses states with a largely Christian tradition, even if some profess to being secularist, the states of ASEAN share no common religious values, with Malaysia and Indonesia the only Muslim members, while the Philippines is largely Catholic Christian, Thailand and Myanmar are mostly Buddhist and Vietnam remains nominally communist, but with a substantial impact from Buddhist values.

From an economic perspective membership of ASEAN is much more beneficial for Malaysia and Indonesia than membership of the Organisation of Islamic Cooperation, which mainly concerns politics. Although there are excellent travel links between Malaysia and Indonesia and the Gulf, from a southeast Asian perspective the Arab world is distant, and has different economic and political challenges. The increased economic and political chaos of the core Arab countries makes Muslims in southeast Asia despair as Asian values stress orderliness and harmony, not rabble-rousing religious rhetoric and never-ending conflict.

ASEAN has had three rounds of ministerial discussions with the GCC, but no discussions with the Arab League or the Organisation of Islamic Cooperation. The GCC discussions in 2013 seemed to be more of a review of common interests, with potentially contentious issues such as conditions for migrant labour off the agenda.[34] Malaysia and Indonesia seem to have played a limited role in the meetings, and have made no effort to prioritise ASEAN relations with Muslim majority countries. Rather, they have been content to see the main extra-regional focus of ASEAN being on the Asia Pacific Rim, an area with no Muslim majority countries.[35] Most of the politics have involved discussing how ASEAN can collaborate with Canada, the United States, Chile, Australia and Japan, and circumvent China. Yet China has a Muslim population of over 60 million, far more than these states combined.

There is increasing movement of people within ASEAN, with nationals of member states issued with one-month free tourist visas on arrival in other member states. In the case of Malaysia, the largest group of visitors are from Singapore, also a major source for Indonesian visitors, with most tourists to Indonesia staying in the Hindu island of Bali rather than the Muslim states of the country. This does not reflect religious preferences, but rather the scenic attractions of Bali and its beach resorts. There is also labour migration of construction workers from Indonesia to Malaysia, some legal, but often illegal. There are regular round-ups of the illegal migrants, who are deported back to Indonesia, but they keep appearing again. Much of the urban development in

Malaysia could not have occurred without Indonesian construction workers, as few Malaysians are prepared to undertake this type of work.

Malaysia has been extensively marketed with some success as a tourist destination in Saudi Arabia and the Gulf. A liberal policy on obtaining visas has helped as it is simpler and cheaper to enter Malaysia than the EU or the United States. Four and five star accommodation, which many Gulf nationals want, is also cheaper. Religious factors also help, as Gulf visitors are well aware that Malaysia is a Muslim majority state with halal food widely available.[36] It has a good image in the Gulf as a modern, moderate Muslim state, indeed, a model many would like to see replicated in western Asia. Gulf institutions have invested heavily in the country, one of the largest developments being the Kuwait Finance House investment in the Pavilion shopping mall and adjacent apartments in downtown Kuala Lumpur, many of which have been sold to Kuwaitis as second homes.

Islamic banking and finance as a business proposition

The most significant Islamic influence on Malaysian economic policy-making has been in the field of Islamic finance where the country has played a pioneering role. Although Islamic banking developed first in the Gulf and Malaysia was a relatively late comer, it was the first country to have a coherent strategy to promote Islamic finance. This was implemented through the Islamic banking legislation enacted in 1983 and the Takaful Act the following year. Bank Islam Malaysia was the first institution to be awarded a licence, but in order to promote competition in the sector conventional banks were encouraged to open Islamic windows in the 1990s.

Competition intensified after the Asian financial crisis of 1997, which had a greater impact on conventional banks than on Islamic banks. A leading struggling conventional bank that served the Malay community, Bank Bumiputera, was recapitalised and reorganised, becoming Bank Muamalat.[37] Further competition ensued when the Islamic banking market was opened up to foreign banks, with Kuwait Finance House opening in 2005 and Al Rajhi Bank of Saudi Arabia establishing a Malaysian branch network in 2006.[38] The same year saw the establishment of the Malaysian Islamic Financial Centre (MIFC), an umbrella organisation that can advise on new ventures and also serves as a media centre for Islamic banking and finance, including *sukuk* and Islamic capital markets, worldwide.[39]

The development of Islamic banking in Indonesia has lagged far behind Malaysia, with the first institution, Bank Muamalat, not established until 1991.[40] Since then there has been a steady expansion with five Islamic banks established by 2014, as well as two foreign exchange dealing houses that claim to be Islamic.[41] Nevertheless, less than 5 per cent of deposits are with Islamic banks, a mere quarter of the proportion in Malaysia. The Malaysian market remains more dynamic, with Maybank Islamic becoming the third largest Islamic financial institution in the world after Al Rajhi Bank and Kuwait Finance House.

The strength of Islamic banking and finance in Malaysia is that it is viewed as a business proposition rather than as a political project. It, of course, fitted in well with the affirmative action programme to raise the economic status of the Bumiputera, but there was never a policy of converting the entire financial system to become Islamic. Islamic banking and finance was about widening choice and encouraging innovation, rather than looking to the past and a supposed golden age of Islam. The authorities were willing to work with the *Shari'ah* scholars interested in Islamic finance, appointing leading scholars to the *Shari'ah* advisory boards of the Central Bank and the Securities Commission. For their part, the scholars had no need to be critical of government, as is often the case in the Middle East, rather they were knocking on an open door with the government willing to take their advice seriously. Perhaps this is a case of Asian consensual values aiding *Shari'ah* standard setting and not conflicting with it.

Notes

1. Vincent J. H. Houben, 'Southeast Asia and Islam', *Annals of the American Academy of Political and Social Science*, 588(1) (2003): 149–70.
2. Victor Purcell, 'Chinese settlement in Malacca', *Journal of the Malayan Branch of the Royal Asiatic Society*, 20(1) (1947): 115–25.
3. Sinappah Arasaratnam, 'Some notes on the Dutch in Malacca and the Indo-Malayan trade 1641–1670', *Journal of Southeast Asian History*, 10(3) (1969): 480–90.
4. Heather Goodall, 'Port politics: Indian seamen, Australian unions and Indonesian independence, 1945–47', *Labour History*, 94 (2008): 43–68.
5. Wang Gungwu, 'Chinese politics in Malaya', *China Quarterly*, 43 (1970): 1–30.
6. D. E. Brown, 'Brunei on the morrow of independence', *Asian Survey*, 24(2) (1984): 201–8.
7. Len Ang and Jon Stratton, 'The Singapore way of multiculturalism: western concepts/Asian cultures', *Sojourn: Journal of Social Issues in Southeast Asia*, 10(1) (1995): 65–89.
8. Sharon Siddique and Leo Suryadinata, 'Bumiputra and Pribumi: economic nationalism (Indiginism) in Malaysia and Indonesia', *Pacific Affairs*, 54(4) (1981): 662–87.
9. H. E. N. G. Koon, 'The new economic policy and the Chinese community in Peninsular Malaysia', *Developing Economies*, 35(3) (1997): 262–92.
10. M. Shamsul Haque, 'The role of the state in managing ethnic tensions in Malaysia: a critical discourse', *American Behavioral Scientist*, 47(3) (2003): 240–66.
11. Wing Thye Woo, 'Understanding the middle-income trap in economic development:

the case of Malaysia', World Economy Lecture delivered at the University of Nottingham, Globalization and Economic Policy, 2011, pp. 1–12.

12. Firdaus Hj. Abdullah, 'Affirmative action policy in Malaysia: to restructure society, to eradicate poverty', *Ethnic Studies Report*, 15(2) (1997): 189–221.

13. Aihwa Ong, 'State versus Islam: Malay families, women's bodies, and the body politic in Malaysia', *American Ethnologist*, 17(2) (1990): 258–76.

14. Nadirsyah Hosen, 'Religion and the Indonesian constitution: a recent debate', *Journal of Southeast Asian Studies*, 36(3) (2005): 419–40.

15. Anthony Reid, 'Nineteenth century pan-Islam in Indonesia and Malaysia', *Journal of Asian Studies*, 26(2) (1967): 267–83.

16. Anwar Ibrahim, 'Universal values and Muslim democracy', *Journal of Democracy*, 17(3) (2006): 5–12.

17. Rodney Wilson, 'Islam and Malaysia's economic development', *Journal of Islamic Studies*, 9(2) (1998): 259–76.

18. Mark R. Thompson, 'Whatever happened to Asian values?', *Journal of Democracy*, 12(4) (2001): 154–65.

19. Wan A. Manan, 'A nation in distress: human rights, authoritarianism, and Asian values in Malaysia', *Journal of Social Issues in Southeast Asia*, 14(2) (1999): 359–81.

20. Hans-Dieter Evers, 'Transition towards a knowledge society: Malaysia and Indonesia in comparative perspective', *Comparative Sociology*, 2 (2003): 355–74.

21. Herbert Feith, 'President Soekarno, the army and the communists: the triangle changes shape', *Asian Survey*, 4(8) (1964): 969–80.

22. Frances L. Starner, 'Malaysia and the North Borneo territories', *Asian Survey*, 3(11) (1963): 519–34.

23. Jun Honna, 'Military ideology in response to democratic pressure during the late Suharto era: political and institutional contexts', *Indonesia*, 67 (1999): 77–126.

24. Richard Robison and Vedi R. Hadiz, 'Reorganising power in Indonesia: the politics of oligarchy in an age of markets', *Bulletin of Indonesian Economic Studies*, 41(1) (2005): 395–6.

25. Michael R. J. Vatikiotis, *Indonesian Politics under Suharto: Order, Development and Pressure for Change* (London: Routledge, 1993), pp. 1–49.

26. Douglas Webber, 'A consolidated patrimonial democracy? Democratization in post-Suharto Indonesia', *Democratization*, 13(3) (2006): 396–420.

27. R. William Liddle and Saiful Mujani, 'Indonesia in 2004: the rise of Susilo Bambang Yudhoyono', *Asian Survey*, 45(1) (2005): 119–26.

28. Wu Chong Bo, 'Policy moves for rejuvenating the economy by new Indonesian government and prospects for the future;, *Southeast Asian Affairs*, 1 (2005): 1–3.

29. Sajid Anwar and Sizhong Sun, 'Financial development, foreign investment and economic growth in Malaysia', *Journal of Asian Economics*, 22(4) (2011): 335–42.

30. Premachandra Athukorala and Jayant Menon, 'Developing with foreign investment: Malaysia', *Australian Economic Review*, 28(1) (1995): 9–22.

31. James B. Ang, 'Determinants of foreign direct investment in Malaysia', *Journal of Policy Modelling*, 30(1) (2008): 185–9.

32. Chee-Keong Choong and Kian-Ping Lim, 'Foreign direct investment, financial development, and economic growth: the case of Malaysia', *Macroeconomics and Finance in Emerging Market Economies*, 2(1) (2009): 13–30.

33. Subhash C. Sharma and Soo Y. Chua, 'ASEAN: economic integration and intra-regional trade', *Applied Economics Letters*, 7(3) (2000): 165–9.

34. Joint Press Statement of the 3rd ASEAN – Gulf Cooperation Council Ministerial Meeting, Wednesday, 27 November 2013, see at: http://www.asean.org/news/asean-statement-communiques/item/joint-press-statement-of-the-3rdasean-gulf-cooperation-council-ministerial-meeting.

35. Amitav Acharya, 'Ideas, identity, and institution-building: from the "ASEAN way" to the "Asia-Pacific way"?', *Pacific Review*, 10(3) (1997): 319–46.

36. Ala al-Hamarneh and Christian Steiner, 'Islamic tourism: rethinking the strategies of tourism development in the Arab world after September 11, 2001', *Comparative Studies of South Asia, Africa and the Middle East*, 24(1) (2004): 173–82.

37. Mohamed Ariff and Saiful Azhar Rosly, 'Islamic banking in Malaysia: unchartered waters', *Asian Economic Policy Review*, 6(2) (2011): 301–19.

38. Uzaimah Ibrahim, Aishath Muneeza and Rusni Hassan, 'Conflicts facing Islamic banking in Malaysia: dual banking system versus dual legal system', *Australian Journal of Basic and Applied Sciences*, 6(11) (2012): 246–51.

39. See at: http://www.mifc.com.

40. Mulya E. Siregar and Nasirwan Ilyas, 'Recent developments in Islamic banking in Indonesia', *Proceedings of the Fifth Harvard University Forum on Islamic Finance: Islamic Finance: Dynamics and Development* (Cambridge, MA: Center for Middle Eastern Studies, Harvard University, 2000), pp. 189–96.

41. Muhamad Abduh and Mohd Azmi Omar, 'Islamic banking and economic growth: the Indonesian experience', *International Journal of Islamic and Middle Eastern Finance and Management*, 5(1) (2012): 35–47.

POSTSCRIPT

There are fifty-six member states in the Organisation of Islamic Cooperation, and this study could cover only a small proportion otherwise it would have become unwieldy. Nevertheless, most of the major states are included, the notable omission being the Maghreb economies where Islam plays a minimal role in public policy-making, even allowing for the influence of Islamists in post-Arab Spring Tunisia. States such as Syria and Iraq were not included as the situation was too chaotic in both countries to draw any conclusions about the impact of Islam on economic policy. These countries, together with Yemen, Somalia and perhaps Libya can be regarded as failed states, which makes the formulation of economic policy virtually impossible unless security can be restored. This seems unlikely, given the weakness of central governments and the de facto partition of the countries.

In 2014, much of the comment and debate on the Middle East concerned the new so-called Islamic State, declared as a caliphate by Emir Abu Bakr al-Baghdadi, its titular head.[1] The organisation used to be called the Islamic State of Iraq and Syria (ISIS), but with Baghdadi regarding both states as creations of the infidel colonialists, he believes neither can any longer be recognised by pious Muslims. The Islamic State, although unrecognised internationally, can no longer be considered as a terrorist organisation as it has a territorial area larger than any European state, apart from Russia and Ukraine, plentiful oil resources, money and captured American and Russian military equipment with substantial firepower. It also has highly motivated jihadist fighters with extensive battlefield experience and a large number of European educated Muslims, often with considerable technical skills. Its members (perhaps citizens!) also have considerable communication skills, including how to exploit social media and use the internet more generally.

As the Islamic state has no formal government, it lacks a finance or economy ministry, and as it has no currency of its own, it has yet to establish a central bank, or indeed a banking or financial system. The law of the Islamic State is the *Shari'ah*, and the use of civil law is rejected, with the law solely interpreted by *Shari'ah* courts and enforced by the jihadist fighters. As the Islamic State, despite its battlefield successes, is under threat from its Arab and Kurdish neighbours, as well as from air strikes by the infidels, the main preoccupation of its commanders has been military matters, not the economy.

Nevertheless, some economic policy implications can be discerned. First, most of the economic priority has been to capture and take control of assets, especially the oilfields of Iraq and Syria. Oil export channels presented few problems as although the pipelines had been destroyed the Islamic State fighters were able to requisition and, if necessary, steal oil tanker trucks. Informal middlemen were willing to buy the oil, including those representing the Assad regime and illegal oil traders in eastern Turkey, some of whom were Kurds. Even oil exports from Kurdish areas that pass through Syria have been subject to levies by the Islamic State.

One of the Islamic State's senior officials, Hamad Hamid al-Ali has a background in finance and is believed to be responsible for money-making operations.[2] These extend to protection rackets in the form of levies on businesses in eastern Syria and Mosul, Iraq's second largest city which is under Islamic State control. Extortion also contributes to Islamic State revenues, notably holding hostages to ransom which has proved to be a lucrative activity. Funding also comes from Islamic State sympathisers in Saudi Arabia and the Gulf, as although the governments in Riyadh and Abu Dhabi attempt to curtail such transfers, in practice both the Saudi riyal and UAE dirham are fully convertible currencies and transfers through the banking system to middlemen are difficult to trace to the ultimate beneficiary.

Although the Islamic State does not issue its own currency, it has a largely cash-based economy, with, ironically, the US dollar widely circulated as well as the Iraqi dinar. Large cash withdrawals are monitored in Saudi Arabia and the Gulf, but there is little monitoring in Syria and Iraq. Most military equipment has been seized with no payments made, but purchases of ammunition are likely to be more important in the future. The jihadist fighters are motivated by comradeship and ideology rather than money, but they still have to be fed and accommodated, placing burdens on the new state, although this is certainly sustainable.

Less certain is how the Islamic State can move forward if it survives the threat of faction fighting and external military threats. Institution-building will be difficult as it is impossible to transform an informal into a formal state if there is no external recognition by its Arab neighbours or major powers. It is difficult to see how the Islamic State could enter the United Nations, for example, though it might not want to join such a secularist organisation in any case.

Although there is no Islamic banking in the Islamic State, which was very underdeveloped and in its infancy in Syria and Iraq in any case, it seems reasonable to assume that this would be a policy preference for Baghdadi and the higher religious council of the new state. In practice, establishing Islamic banking would be difficult as there would be no support from the IDB, the Islamic Financial Services Board or the Accounting and Auditing Organization for Islamic Financial Institutions. Other Islamic banks would be reluctant to provide correspondence facilities for institutions based in the Islamic State, let alone invest in subsidiaries or branches. In short, unless the Islamic State received political recognition, building formal economic or financial relations would be impossible.

A more fundamental question to ask is how Islamic is the Islamic State? Islamic finance involves risk-sharing and committed capital, but the Islamic State through its arbitrary demands for protection money increases business risks. Far from providing committed capital, it expropriates finance from those it exploits. It is a destroyer rather than a Creator of wealth. Furthermore, by increasing sectarian tensions it acts as a divisive force limiting the market for goods and services. There is no sectarian divide between Sunni and Shi'a in Islamic finance, but the leaders and followers of the Islamic State are probably unaware of this, and are largely ignorant of the details of how Islamic finance operates. Criminal behaviour in financial matters is inconsistent and totally at odds with the principles of Islamic finance. Yet such behaviour is a hallmark of the Islamic State.

It is apparent from this survey that although no Muslim majority state can be described as an Islamic economy, Islamic finance has made most progress in countries where the rule of law prevails and property rights are respected, notably the GCC states and Malaysia. These contracts are based on, and enforceable through, civil and common law which is rejected by some Islamists. However, far from being a hindrance to Islamic finance contracts, secular law facilitates these agreements and provides a framework for the protection of the parties involved, boosting confidence. Much of the conflict in the Islamic world over the role of *Shari'ah* is based on misunderstandings and ignorance, which a detailed study of what works and does not work can help to clarify. The aim of this study has been to make a modest contribution to such understanding

Notes

1. Jason Burke, 'The Isis leader's vision of the state is a profoundly contemporary one', *The Observer*, London, 24 August 2014.
2. Sam Jones, 'Opaque structure adds to the challenge of defeating ISIS', *Financial Times*, London, 25 August 2014.

BIBLIOGRAPHY

Chapter 1

Chapra, M. Umer (1992), *Islam and the Economic Challenge*, Leicester: Islamic Foundation, pp. 25–7.

Cizakca, Murat (1996), *A Comparative Evolution of Business Partnerships: The Islamic World and Europe, with Special Reference to the Ottoman Archives*, Leiden: Brill Academic Publishing, vol. 8.

Cizakca, Murat (2007), 'Democracy, development and *maqasid al-Shari'ah*', *Review of Islamic Economics*, 2(1): 101–18.

de Roover, Raymond (1958), 'The concept of the just price: theory and economic policy', *Journal of Economic History*, 18(4) (December): 418–34.

Ensminger, Jean (1997), 'Transaction costs and Islam: explaining conversion in Africa', *Journal of Institutional and Theoretical Economics*, 153(1) (March): 4–29.

Essid, M. Yassine (1987), 'Islamic economic thought', in S. Todd Lowry (ed.), *Pre-Classical Economic Thought: From the Greeks to the Scottish Enlightenment*, Recent Economic Thought Series, Rotterdam: Springer Netherlands, vol. 10, pp. 77–102.

Hemingway, Christine A. and Patrick W. Maclagan (2004), 'Managers' personal values as drivers of corporate social responsibility', *Journal of Business Ethics*, 50: 33–44.

Huse, Morten (2005), 'Accountability and creating accountability: a framework for exploring behavioural perspectives of corporate governance', *British Journal of Management*, 15(suppl.) (March): S65–S79.

Ibn Khaldun (1978 (1397)), *al-Muqaddima*, reprinted Dar al-Baz, Mecca, p. 467.

Ibn Taymiyyah (1982), *Public Duties in Islam: The Institution of Hisba*, trans. from original fourteenth-century text by Muhtar Holland, Leicester: Islamic Foundation, pp. 1–45.

Islahi (1984), Abdul Azim, *Economic Thought of Ibn Al-Qayyim*, Jeddah: International Centre for Research in Islamic Economics, pp. 13–14.

Janssens, Jules (2011), 'Al-Gazali between philosophy *(falsafa)* and Sufism *(tasawwuf)*: his complex attitude in the *Marvels of the Heart (Ajaib al-Qalb) of the Ihya Ulum al-Din*', *Muslim World*, 101(4): 614–32.

Lazonick, William (2011), *Business Organisation and the Myth of Market Behaviour*, Cambridge: Cambridge University Press, pp. 1–55.

Malthus, Thomas (1798), *An Essay on the Principle of Population*, London: J. Johnson, pp. 6–11.

Mardin, Serif (1969), 'Power, civil society and culture in the Ottoman Empire', *Comparative Studies in Society and History*, 11(3): 258–81.

Naqvi, Syed Nawab Haider (1997), 'The dimensions of an Islamic economic model', *Islamic Economic Studies*, 4(2): 1–23.

Ozay, Mehmet (1991), *Islamic Identity and Development: Studies of the Islamic Periphery*, London: Routledge, p. 57.

Robbins, Lionel (1932), *An Essay on the Nature and Significance of Economics Science*, London: Macmillan, pp. 12–15.

Shoshan, Boaz (1980), 'Grain riots and the "moral economy": Cairo, 1350–1517', *Journal of Interdisciplinary History*, 10(3): 459–78.

Chapter 2

Abbas, Ali J. and Manton Gibbs (1998), 'Foundations of business ethics in contemporary religious thought: the ten commandment perspective', *International Journal of Social Economics*, 25(9/10): 1552–64.

Adam, Nathif J. and Abdulkader Thomas (2004), *Islamic Bonds: Your Guide to Issuing, Structuring and Investing in Sukuk*, London: Euromoney Books, pp. 81–146.

Ahmed, Habib (2002), 'Incentive-compatible profit sharing contracts: a theoretical treatment', in Munawar Iqbal and David T. Llewlan (eds), *Islamic Banking and Finance: New Perspectives on Profit Sharing and Risk*, Cheltenham: Edward Elgar, pp. 40–54.

Ahmed, Mohammad Saeed, Zafar U. Ahmed and Syeda-Masooda Mukhtar (2001), 'International marketing ethics from an Islamic perspective: a value maximisation approach', *Journal of Business Ethics*, 32(2): 127–42.

Ajami, Riad A. (1982), 'The multinationals and Arab economic development: a new paradigm', in Robert A. Kilmarx and Yonah Alexander (eds), *Business and the Middle East: Threats and Prospects*, Oxford: Pergamon Press, pp. 178–99.

Alawneh, Shafiq Falah (1998), 'Human motivation: an Islamic perspective', *American Journal of Islamic Social Sciences*, 15(4) (Winter): 19–39.

Ali, Abbas J., Manton Gibbs and Robert C. Camp (2003), 'Jihad in monotheistic religions: implications for business and management', *International Journal of Sociology and Social Policy*, 23(12): 19–46.

al-Qardawi, Yusuf (1999), *Fiqh az-Zakat: A Comparative Study*, London: Dar Al Taqwa Publishing, pp. 65–100.

Al-Sadr, Muhammad Baqir (2000), *Our Economics: Iqtisaduna*, trans., commentary and ed. Kadom Jawad Shubber, London: Books Extra, pp. 182–3.

Bassiouni, M. Cherif (1993), 'Business ethics in Islam', in Paul M. Minus (ed.), *The Ethics of Business in a Global Economy*, Dordrecht: Kluwer Academic Publishers, pp. 117–22.

Beekun, Rafik Issa (1996), *Islam and Business Ethics*, Herndon, VA: International Institute of Islamic Thought, p. 1.

Borland, Brad (2001), 'Outward flows, inward investment needs in the GCC', *Arab Banker*, 16(2): 49–51.

Chapra, M. Umer (1992), *Islam and the Economic Challenge*, Leicester: Islamic Foundation, pp. 6–9.

Chapra, M. Umer (1993), *Islam and Economic Development*, Islamabad: International Institute of Islamic Thought, p. 122.

Chapra, M. Umer (2000), *The Future of Economics: An Islamic Perspective*, Leicester: The Islamic Foundation, pp. 74–6.

Elgari, Mohamed A. (2002), 'Islamic equity investment', in Simon Archer and Rifaat Ahmed Abdel Karim (eds), *Islamic Finance: Innovation and Growth*, London: Euromoney Books, pp. 151–9.

Haneef, Mohamed Aslam (1995), *Contemporary Islamic Economic Thought: A Selected Comparative Analysis*, Kuala Lumpur: Ikraq Books, p. 124.

Henry, Clement M. and Robert Springborg (2001), *Globalisation and the Politics of Development in the Middle East*, Cambridge: Cambridge University Press, pp. 99–133 and 168–93.

Henry, Clement M. and Rodney Wilson (eds) (2004), *The Politics of Islamic Finance*, Edinburgh: Edinburgh University Press, pp. 286–95.

Ibn Maja, K., 'al-Tijarat, Chapter Al-Haththt ala al-Makasib' (2003), cited in S. M. Hasanuzzaman, *Islam and Business Ethics*, London: Institute of Islamic Banking and Insurance, p. 12.

Ibn Taymiyyah (1982), *Public Duties in Islam: the Institution of the Hisba*, trans. from original fourteenth-century text by Muhtar Holland, Leicester: The Islamic Foundation, pp. 29–33.

Kavoossi, Masoud (2000), *The Globalisation of Business and the Middle East*, London: Quorum Books, pp. ix–x.

Khan, Kishwar and Sarwat Aftab (2000), 'Consumer protection in Islam: the case of Pakistan', *Australian Economic Papers*, 39(4): 483–503.

Koys, Daniel J. (2001), 'Integrating religious principles and human resource management activities', *Teaching Business Ethics*, 5(2): 121–39.

Laws of Malaysia (2013), Islamic Financial Services Act, No. 759, Kuala Lumpur.

Mohsin, Mohammad (1995), *Economics of Small Business in Islam*, Visiting Scholar Research Series, No. 2, Jeddah: Islamic Research and Training Institute, Islamic Development Bank, p. 41.

Naqvi, Syed Nawab Haider (1994), *Islam Economics and Society*, London: Kegan Paul International, pp. 29–34.

Naqvi, Syed Nawab Haider (2003), *Perspectives on Morality and Human Well-Being: A Contribution to Islamic Economics*, Leicester: The Islamic Foundation, p. 212.

Nuti, Dmenico Mario (1995), *The Economics of Participation*, Eminent Scholar Lecture Series, No. 11, Jeddah: Islamic Research and Training Institute, Islamic Development Bank, pp. 59–64.

Pomeranz, Felix (2004), 'Ethics: towards globalisation', *Managerial Auditing Journal*, 19(1): 8–14.

Pramanik, Ataul Huq (1993), *Development and Distribution in Islam*, Petaling Jaya, Selangor, Malaysia: Pelanduk Publications, pp. 11–27.

Rice, Gillian (1999), 'Islamic ethics and the implications for business', *Journal of Business Ethics*, 18: 345–58.

Rodinson, Maxime (1977), *Islam and Capitalism*, Harmondsworth: Penguin Books, pp. 137–57 and 185–94 (originally published by Éditions du Seuil, Paris, 1966).

Sabri, Sharaf (2001), *The House of Saud in Commerce: A Study of Royal Entrepreneurship in Saudi Arabia*, New Delhi: I. S. Publications, pp. 120–3.

Sakr, Naomi (2001), *Satellite Realms: Transnational Television, Globalisation and the Middle East*, London: I. B. Tauris, pp. 27–65.

Saleh, Nabil A. (1986), *Unlawful Gain and Legitimate Profit in Islamic Law*, Cambridge: Cambridge University Press, pp. 92–3.

Shehu, Salisu (1998), 'Towards an Islamic perspective of developmental psychology', *American Journal of Islamic Social Sciences*, 15(4) (Winter): 41–70.

Siddiqi, Muhammad Nejatullah (1985), *Partnership and Profit Sharing in Islamic Law*, Leicester: Islamic Foundation, pp. 11–18.

Siddiqi, Muhammad Nejatullah (1988), 'The guarantee of a minimum level of living in an Islamic state', in Munawar Iqbal (ed.), *Distributive Justice and Need Fulfilment in an Islamic Economy*, Leicester: The Islamic Foundation, p. 255.

Sirageldin, Ismail (2002), 'The elimination of poverty: challenges and Islamic strategies', in Munawar Iqbal (ed.), *Islamic Economic Institutions and the Elimination of Poverty*, Leicester: The Islamic Foundation, pp. 43–4.

Tayeb, Monir (1997), 'Islamic revival in Asia and human resource management', *Employee Relations*, 19(4): 352.

Usmani, Muhammad Taqi (2002), *An Introduction to Islamic Finance*, The Hague: Kluwer Law International, p. 11.

Vogel, Frank E. and Samuel L. Hayes (1998), *Islamic Law and Finance: Religion, Risk and Return*, The Hague: Kluwer Law International, pp. 168–9.

Wilson, Rodney (1997), *Economics, Ethics and Religion: Jewish, Christian and Muslim Economic Thought*, London: Macmillan, pp. 74–6 and pp. 208–9.

Wilson, Rodney (1998), 'The contribution of Muhammad Bäqir al-Sadr to contemporary Islamic economic thought', *Journal of Islamic Studies*, 9(1): 48.

Wilson, Rodney (1998), 'Islam and Malaysia's economic development', *Journal of Islamic Studies*, 9(2): 259–76.

Wilson, Rodney (2004), 'Screening criteria for Islamic equity funds', in Sohail Jaffer (ed.), *Islamic Asset Management: Forming the Future for Shariah-Compliant Investment Strategies*, London: Euromoney Books, pp. 35–45.

Yusoff, Nik Mohamed Affandi Bin Nik (2002), *Islam and Business*, Selangor, Malaysia: Pelanduk, pp. 1–12.

Chapter 3

Akhtar, Zia (2013), 'Charitable trusts and *waqf*: their parallels, registration process and tax reliefs in the United Kingdom', *Statute Law Review*, 34(3): 281–95.

Baer, Gabriel (1997), 'The *waqf* as a prop for the social system (sixteenth – twentieth centuries)', *Islamic Law and Society*, 4(3): 264–97.

Bosbait, Mohamed and Rodney Wilson (2005), 'Education, school to work transitions and unemployment in Saudi Arabia', *Middle Eastern Studies*, 41(4): 533–45.

Campante, Filipe R. and Davin Chor (2012), 'Why was the Arab world poised for revolution: schooling, economic opportunities and the Arab Spring', *Journal of Economic Perspectives*, 26(2): 167–88.

Davis, Nancy J. and Robert V. Robinson (2006), 'The egalitarian face of Islamic orthodoxy: support for Islamic law and economic justice in seven Muslim majority nations', *American Sociological Review*, 71(2): 167–90.

Hoxter, Miriam (1998), *Endowments, Rulers and Community: Waqf al-Haramayn in Ottoman Algiers*, Studies in Islamic Law and Society, Leiden: E. J. Brill.

Khan, M. A. Muqtedar, 'Islam and peace' (1998), *American Journal of Islamic Social Sciences*, 15(1): 158–62.

Kuran, Timur (1995), 'Further reflections on the behavioural norms of Islamic economics', *Journal of Economic Behaviour and Organization*, 27: 159–63.

Kuran, Timur (2001), 'The provision of public goods under Islamic law: origins, impact and limitations of the waqf system', *Law and Society Review*, 35(4): 841–98.

Kuran, Timur (2004), *Islam and Mammon: The Economic Predicaments of Islamism*, Princeton: Princeton University Press, p. 105.

Naqvi, Syed Nawab Haider (2003), *Perspectives on Morality and Human Well-Being: A Contribution to Islamic Economics*, Leicester: Islamic Foundation, pp. 143–83.

Parker-Jenkins, Marie (2002), 'Equal access to state funding: the case of Muslim schools in Britain', *Race, Ethnicity and Education*, 5(3): 273–89.

Razak, Mohamad Idham Md, Roaimah Omar Maymunah Ismail, Afzan Sahilla Amir Hamzah and Abul Hasan M. Sadeq (2002), '*Waqf*, perpetual charity and poverty alleviation', *International Journal of Social Economics*, 29(1): 135–51.

Razak, Mohamad Idham Md, Roaimah Omar Maymunah Ismail, Afzan Sahilla Amir Hamzah and Hashim, Mohd Adnan (2013), 'Overview of zakat collection in Malaysia: regional analysis', *American International Journal of Contemporary Research*, 3(8): 140–8.

Salim, Arskal (2008), *The Shift in Zakat Practice in Indonesia: From Piety to a Socio-Politico-Economic System*, Bangkok: Silkworm Books, pp. 17–60.

Sayari, Sabri (1996), 'Turkey's Islamist challenge', *Middle Eastern Quarterly*, 3(3): 35–43.

Tripp, Charles (2006), *Islam and the Moral Economy: The Challenge of Capitalism*, Cambridge: Cambridge University Press, pp. 77–102.

Wellisz, Stanislaw (1968), 'Dual economies, disguised unemployment and the unlimited supply of labour', *Economica*, 35(137): 22–51.

Wilson, Rodney (2010), 'Economy', in Amyn B. Sajoo (ed.) *A Companion to Muslim Ethics*, London: I. B. Tauris, pp. 141–3.

Chapter 4

Atherton, John (1992), *Christianity and the Market: Christian Social Thought for Our Times*, London: SPCK.

Baskan, Filiz (2004), 'The political economy of Islamic finance in Turkey: the role of Fethullah Gülen and Asya Finans', in Clement Henry and Rodney Wilson (eds), *The Politics of Islamic Finance*, Edinburgh: Edinburgh University Press, pp. 216–39.

Chapra, M. Umer (1992), *Islam and the Economic Challenge*, Leicester: Islamic Foundation, pp. 199–212.

Chapra, M. Umer (2000), *The Future of Economics: An Islamic Perspective*, Leicester: Islamic Foundation.

Crone, Patricia (2004), *Meccan Trade and the Rise of Islam*, Piscataway, NJ: Gorgias Press.

Feld, Lars P. and Stefan Voigt (2003), 'Economic growth and judicial independence: cross-country evidence using a new set of indicators', *European Journal of Political Economy*, 19(3): 497–527.

Hay, Donald (1989), *Economics Today: A Christian Critique*, Leicester: Inter-Varsity Press.

Huan-Chang, Chen ([1911] 2002), *The Economic Principles of Confucius and his School*, Ganesha Publishing (reprinted by University of Chicago Press).

Iannaccone, Laurence R. (1998), 'Introduction to the economics of religion', *Journal of Economic Literature*, 36 (September): 1465–96.

Ibn Khaldun (1989), *The Muqaddimah: An Introduction to History*, trans. Franz Rosenthal, ed. and abridged N. J. Dawood, Bollingen Series, 9th edn, Princeton: Princeton University Press, pp. 297–332.

Khan, Masood Waqar (1985), *Towards an Islamic Interest Free Economic System*, Leicester: Islamic Foundation.

Klein, Yaron (2006), 'Between public and private: an examination of *hisba* literature', *Harvard Middle Eastern and Islamic Review*, 7: 41–62.

Kuran, Timur (1997), 'Islam and underdevelopment: an old puzzle revisited', *Journal of Institutional and Theoretical Economics*, 153(1): 41–71.

Naqvi, Syed Nawab Haider (2003), *Perspectives on Morality and Human Well-Being: A Contribution to Islamic Economics*, Leicester: Islamic Foundation, pp. 143–83.

Novak, Michael (1982), *The Spirit of Democratic Capitalism*, Lanham, MD and London: Madison Books and Institute of Economic Affairs.

Palmier, Leslie (1978), 'Corruption and development', *Institute for Development Studies Bulletin*, 9(3): 30–2.

Payutto, Ven P. A. (1992), *Buddhist Economics: A Middle Way for the Market Place*, Dhammavijaya, available at: www.buddhistinformation.com/buddhist_economics htm.

Rodinson, Maxime (1977), *Islam and Capitalism*, Harmondsworth: Penguin Books (originally published by Éditions du Seuil, Paris, 1966).

Rosser, J. Barkley and Marina V. Rosser (2004), *The Transition between the Old and New Traditional Economics of India*, unpublished paper, March, available at: http//cob.jmu.edu/rosserjb/oldnewtransindia.doc.

Sleeman, John (1976), *Economic Crisis: A Christian Perspective*, London: SCM Press.

Stackhouse, Max, Dennis McCann and Shirley Roels (eds) (1995), *On Moral Business: Classical and Contemporary Resources for Ethics in Economic Life*, Grand Rapids, MI: Eerdmans, pp. 370–411.

Tawney, R. H. (1926), *Religion and the Rise of Capitalism*, New York: John Murray and Harcourt Brace (republished by Penguin Books, London, 1938).

Tripp, Charles (2006), *Islam and the Moral Economy: The Challenge of Capitalism*, Cambridge: Cambridge University Press, pp. 77–102.

Weber, Max ([1905] 1930), *The Protestant Ethic and the Spirit of Capitalism*, English translation, London: Allen, Unwin & Scribners.

Wogman, Philip (1986), *Economics and Ethics: A Christian Enquiry*, London: SCM Press.

Chapter 5

Ahlquist, John S. (2006), 'Economic policy, institutions, and capital flows: portfolio and direct investment flows in developing countries', *International Studies Quarterly*, 50(3): 681–704.

Ahmed, Habib, Mehmet Asutay and Rodney Wilson (2014), *Islamic Banking and Financial Crisis: Reputation, Stability and Risks*, Edinburgh: Edinburgh University Press, pp. 1–14.

Amin, Ruzita Mohd and Zarinah Hamid (2009), 'Towards an Islamic common market: are OIC countries heading the right direction?', *IIUM Journal of Economics and Management*, 17(1): 133–76.

Anwar, Syed Aziz and M. Sadiq Sohail (2004), 'Festival tourism in the United Arab Emirates: first-time versus repeat visitor perceptions', *Journal of Vacation Marketing*, 10(2): 161–70.

Chaudhuri, Kirti N. (1985), *Trade and Civilisation in the Indian Ocean: An Economic History from the Rise of Islam to 1750*, Cambridge: Cambridge University Press.

Crone, Patricia (2004), *Meccan Trade and the Rise of Islam*, Piscataway, NJ: Gorgias Press.

Khalifa, A. S. (2003), 'The multidimensional nature and purpose of business in Islam, accounting, commerce and finance', *Islamic Perspective Journal*, 7(1/2): 1–25.

Lewer, Joshua J. and Hendrik Van den Berg (2007), 'Religion and international trade: does the sharing of a religious culture facilitate the formation of trade networks?', *American Journal of Economics and Sociology*, 66(4): 765–94.

Meenai, Saeed Ahmed (1989), *The Islamic Development Bank: A Case Study of Islamic Co-operation*, London: Kegan Paul.

Neyaptı, Bilin, Fatma Taşkına and Murat Üngörb (2007), 'Has European Customs Union Agreement really affected Turkey's trade?', *Applied Economics*, 39(16): 2121–32.

Rauh, Nicholas K. (1993), *The Sacred Bonds of Commerce: Religion, Economy, and Trade Society at Hellenistic Roman Delos, 166–87 BC*, ed. Thomas Hocker, Amsterdam: J. C. Gieben.

Scott, Linda M. (2009), 'Religion and commerce', *Advertising and Society Review*, 10(4): 1–3.

Seznec, Jean-François (2008), 'The Gulf sovereign wealth funds: myths and reality', *Middle East Policy*, 15(2): 97–111.

Smith, George Leslie (1973), *Religion and Trade in New Netherland: Dutch Origins and American Development*, Ithaca, NY: Cornell University Press.

Valeri, Mark (2010), *Heavenly Merchandize: How Religion Shaped Commerce in Puritan America*, Princeton, NJ: Princeton University Press.

Watt, William Montgomery (1972), *The Influence of Islam on Medieval Europe*, Edinburgh: Edinburgh University Press.

Wilson, Rodney (1998), 'The contribution of Muhammad Bāqir al-Sadr to contemporary Islamic economic thought', *Journal of Islamic Studies*, 9(1): 46–59.

Winrow, Gareth (1997), 'Turkey and the newly independent states of Central Asia and the Transcaucasus', *Middle East Review of International Affairs*, 2: 30–45.

Wright, Louis Booker (1943), *Religion and Empire: The Alliance between Piety and Commerce in English Expansion, 1558–1625*, Chapel Hill, NC: University of North Carolina Press.

Yasir, Tariq Mohammad and Aihu Wang (2014), 'Is the Organisation of Islamic Cooperation promoting trade among members?', *Pakistan Journal of Statistics*, 30(1): 113–28.

Zamani-Farahani, Hamira and Joan C. Henderson (2010), 'Islamic tourism and managing tourism development in Islamic societies: the cases of Iran and Saudi Arabia', *International Journal of Tourism Research*, 12(1): 79–89.

Chapter 6

Ahmad, Wahida and Rafisah Mat Radzi (2011), 'Sustainability of *sukuk* and conventional bonds during financial crisis: Malaysia's capital market', *Global Economy and Financial Journal*, 4(2): 33–45.

Ahmed, Habib (2012), *Islamic Finance of Infrastructure Projects*, Dubai International Financial Centre, pp. 1–35.

Ahmed, Ziauddin, Munawar Iqbal and M. Fahim Khan (eds) (1983), *Money and Banking in Islam* (Jeddah and Islamabad: International Centre for Research in Islamic Economics, King Abdul Aziz University and Institute of Policy Studies.

Augustine, Babu Das (2013), 'Dubai races to become global Islamic finance hub', *Gulf News*, Dubai, 24 November.

Bacha, Obiyathulla Ismath (2008), 'The Islamic inter-bank money market and a dual banking system: the Malaysian experience', *International Journal of Islamic and Middle Eastern Finance and Management*, 1(3): 210–26.

Bhaduri, Amit (1977), 'On the formation of usurious interest rates in backward agriculture', *Cambridge Journal of Economics*, 1(4): 341–52.

Blaydes, Lisa (2006), 'Electoral budget cycles under authoritarianism: economic opportunism in Mubarak's Egypt', *Proceedings of the Annual Meeting of the Midwest Political Science Association*.

Chen, Chau-nan (1972), 'Bimetallism: theory and controversy in perspective', *History of Political Economy*, 4(1): 89–112.

Choudhury, Masudul A. (ed.) (1997), *Money in Islam: A Study in Islamic Political Economy*, Hove: Psychology Press, vol. 3.

Clay, Christopher G. A. (2000), *Gold for the Sultan: Western Bankers and Ottoman Finance 1856–1881: A Contribution to Ottoman and to International Financial History*, London: I. B. Tauris, vol. 20.

Culbertson, John M. (1957), 'The term structure of interest rates', *Quarterly Journal of Economics*, 71(4): 485–517.

Farooq, Mohammad (2009), 'The *riba*-interest equation and Islam: re-examination of the traditional arguments', *Global Journal of Finance and Economics*, 6(2): 99–111.

Gurler, Oker (2000), 'Role and function of regional blocs and arrangements in the formation of the Islamic common market', *Journal of Economic Cooperation*, 21(4): 1–28.

Hanafi, Khaled (2003), 'Islamic gold dinar will minimize dependency on US dollar', *Money File, The Case for Gold*, Cairo, 8 January.

Harrigan, Jane, Chengang Wang and Hamed El-Said (2006), 'The economic and political determinants of IMF and World Bank lending in the Middle East and North Africa', *World Development*, 34(2): 247–70.

Joyce, Michael, Ana Lasaosa, Ibrahim Stevens and Matthew Tong (2011), 'The financial market impact of quantitative easing in the United Kingdom', *International Journal of Central Banking*, 7(3): 113–61.

Krishnamurthy, Arvind and Annette Vissing-Jorgensen (2011), *The Effects of Quantitative Easing on Interest Rates: Channels and Implications for Policy*, Paper No. w17555, Washington DC: National Bureau of Economic Research.

Meera, Ahamed Kameel Mydin and Moussa Larbani (2004), 'The gold dinar: the next component in Islamic economics, banking and finance', *Review of Islamic Economics*, 8(1): 5–34.

Rutledge, Emilie (2008), *Monetary Union in the Gulf: Prospects for a Single Currency in the Arabian Peninsula*, Abingdon: Routledge, Abingdon.

Vadillo, Umar Ibrahim (2004), *The Return of the Islamic Gold Dinar: A Study of Money in Islamic Law and the Architecture of the Gold Economy*, Kuala Lumpur: Madinah Press.

Wilson, Rodney (2011), 'Approaches to Islamic banking in the Gulf', in Eckart Woertz (ed.), *Gulf Financial Markets*, Gulf Research Centre, Dubai, pp. 221–38.

Wilson, Rodney (2012), *Legal, Regulatory and Governance Issues in Islamic Finance*, Edinburgh: Edinburgh University Press, pp. 17–38.

Chapter 7

Ahmed, Ziauddin and Ziauddin Ahmad (1975), 'The concept of Jizya in early Islam', *Islamic Studies*, 14(4): 293–305.

Algar, Hamid (2001), 'The centennial renewer: Bediüzzaman Said Nursi and the tradition of Tajdid', *Journal of Islamic Studies*, 12(3): 291–311.

Altug, Sumru, Alpay Filiztekin and Şevket Pamuk (2008), 'Sources of long-term economic growth for Turkey, 1880–2005', *European Review of Economic History*, 12(3): 393–430.

Atacan, Fulya (2005), 'Explaining religious politics at the crossroad: AKP-SP', *Turkish Studies*, 6(2): 187–99.

Choudhury, A. (1998), 'The political economy of enterprise, polity and knowledge: a case study with respect to Musiad and Islamic banking and finance in Turkey', *Middle East Business and Economic Review*, 10(1): 87–95.

Cooper, Malcolm (2002), 'The legacy of Atatürk: Turkish political structures and policy-making', *International Affairs*, 78(1): 115–28.

Dagi, Ihsan (2008), 'Turkey's AKP in power', *Journal of Democracy*, 19(3): 25–30.

Göle, Nilüfer (1997), 'Secularism and Islamism in Turkey: the making of elites and counter-elites', *Middle East Journal*, 51(1): 46–58.

Grigoriadis, Ioannis N. and Antonis Kamaras (2008), 'Foreign direct investment in Turkey: historical constraints and the AKP success story', *Middle Eastern Studies*, 44(1): 53–68.

Gürsel, Seyfettin (2005), 'Growth despite deflation: Turkish economy during the Great Depression', *Sixth Congress of the European Historical Economics Society*, Istanbul, pp. 1–33.

Insel, Ahmet (2003), 'The AKP and normalizing democracy in Turkey', *South Atlantic Quarterly*, 102(2): 293–308.

Kandiyoti, Deniz A. (1987), 'Emancipated but unliberated? Reflections on the Turkish case', *Feminist Studies*, 13(2): 317–38.

Karpat, Kemal H. (2001), *The Politicization of Islam: Reconstructing Identity, State, Faith, and Community in the Late Ottoman State*, Oxford: Oxford University Press.

Kocabaş, Arzu (2006), 'Urban conservation in Istanbul: evaluation and re-conceptualisation', *Habitat International*, 30(1): 107–26.

Krespin, Rachel Sharon (2009), 'Fethullah Gülen's grand ambition: Turkey's Islamist danger', *Middle East Quarterly*, 16(1): 55–66.

Mango, Andrew (2011), *Ataturk*, London: Hachette.

Mardin, Şerif (1989), *Religion and Social Change in Modern Turkey: The Case of Bediuzzaman Said Nursi*, New York: State University of New York Press.

Morris, Chris (1998), 'Turkey bans Islamist party', *The Guardian*, 17 January 1998.

Mufti, Malik (1998), 'Daring and caution in Turkish foreign policy', *Middle East Journal*, 52(1): 32–50.

Okumus, H. Saduman (2005), 'Interest-free banking in Turkey: a study of customer satisfaction and bank selection criteria', *Journal of Economic Cooperation among Islamic Countries*, 26(4): 51–86.

Okyar, Osman (1965), 'The concept of *etatism*', *Economic Journal*, 75(297): 98–111.

Öniş, Ziya (2012), 'The triumph of conservative globalism: the political economy of the AKP era', *Turkish Studies*, 13(2): 135–52.

Öniş, Ziya and Şuhnaz Yilmaz (2009), 'Between Europeanization and Euro-Aasianism: foreign policy activism in Turkey during the AKP era', *Turkish Studies*, 10(1): 7–24.

Patton, Marcie J. (2006), 'The economic policies of Turkey's AKP government: rabbits from a hat?', *Middle East Journal*, 60(3): 513–36.

Starr, Martha A. and Rasim Yilmaz (2007), 'Bank runs in emerging-market economies: evidence from Turkey's special finance houses', *Southern Economic Journal*, 73(4): 1112–32.

Stirling, Paul (1958), 'Religious change in republican Turkey', *Middle East Journal*, 12(4): 395–408.

Takim, Abdullah and Ensar Yilmaz (2010), 'Economic policy during Atatürk's era in Turkey', *African Journal of Business Management*, 4(4): 549–54.

Tansel, Aysit and H. Mehmet Taşçi (2004), *Determinants of Unemployment Duration for Men and Women in Turkey*, Discussion Paper Series, No. 1258, Bonn: Forschungsinstitut zur Zukunft der Arbeit (IZA), pp. 1–42.

Thomas, Michel, SJ (1999), 'Muslim – Christian dialogue and cooperation in the thought of Bediuzzaman Said Nursi', *Muslim World*, 89(3/4): 325–35.

Thomas, Michel, SJ (2005), 'Sufism and modernity in the thought of Fethullah Gülen', *Muslim World*, 95(3): 341–58.

Ugur, Mehmet and Dilek Yankaya (2008), 'Policy entrepreneurship, policy opportunism, and EU conditionality: the AKP and TÜSİAD experience in Turkey', *Governance*, 21(4): 581–601.

Yankaya, Dilek (2009), 'The Europeanization of MÜSİAD: political opportunism, economic Europeanization, Islamic Euroscepticism', *European Journal of Turkish Studies and Social Sciences on Contemporary Turkey*, 9, available at: http://ejts.revues.org/3696#quotation.

Yavuz, M. Hakan (1999), 'Towards an Islamic liberalism? The Nurcu movement and Fethullah Gülen', *Middle East Journal*, 53(4): 584–605.

Yılmaz, Kaya (2011), 'Critical examination of the alphabet and language reforms implemented in the early years of the Turkish republic', *Journal of Social Studies Education Research*, 2(1): 59–82.

Yolal, Medet (2010), 'Blooming tulip: a decade of Turkish tourism', *Studia Universitatis Babes Bolyai-Negotia*, 4:15–24.

Chapter 8

Alfoneh, Ali (2008), 'The Revolutionary Guards' role in Iranian politics', *Middle East Quarterly*, 15(4): 3–14.

Al-Sadr, Muhammad Baqir (2000), *Our Economics: Iqtisaduna*, trans., commentary and ed. Kadom Jawad Shubber, London: Books Extra.

Ansari, Ali M. (2007), *Iran under Ahmadinejad: the Politics of Confrontation*, London: Routledge.

Aziz, Talib M. (1993), 'An Islamic perspective of political economy: the views of (late) Muhammad Baqir al-Sadr', *Al-Tawhid Islamic Journal*, 10(1): 1–25.

Aziz, Talib M. (1993), 'The role of Muhammad Baqir al-Sadr in Shii political activism in Iraq from 1958 to 1980', *International Journal of Middle East Studies*, 25(2): 207–22.

Bacha, Obiyathulla Ismath (1996), 'Conventional versus *mudarabah* financing: an agency cost perspective', *International Journal of Economics, Management and Accounting*, 4(1/2): 33–50.

International Monetary Fund (IMF) (2014), Islamic Republic of Iran Article IV Consultation, Country Report 14/93, April, pp. 12–27.

Jahanpour, Farhang (1984), 'Iran: the rise and fall of the Tudeh Party', *The World Today*, 40(4): 152–9.

Khan, Mohsin S. and Abbas Mirakhor (1990), 'Islamic banking: experiences in the Islamic Republic of Iran and in Pakistan', *Economic Development and Cultural Change*, 38(2): 353–75.

Kurzman, Charles (1996), 'Structural opportunity and perceived opportunity in social-movement theory: the Iranian revolution of 1979', *American Sociological Review*, 61(1): 153–70.

Mirsepassi-Ashtiani, Ali and Valentine M. Moghadam (1991), 'The left and political Islam in Iran: a retrospect and prospects', *Radical History Review*, 51(4): 26–62.

Rad, Parviz S. and M. Ahsan (2000), 'Theories of ownership and Islam: a case study of the Islamic Republic of Iran', *Review of Islamic Economics*, 9: 127–44.

Ṣadr, Abū al-Ḥasan Banī (1981), *The Fundamental Principles and Precepts of Islamic Government*, trans. Mohannad R. Ghanoonparvar, Tehran and Lexington, KY: Mazda Publishers.

Saeidi, Ali A. (2004), 'The accountability of para-governmental organizations (bonyads): the case of Iranian foundations', *Iranian Studies*, 37(3): 479–98.

Shanahan, Rodger (2004), 'Shi a political development in Iraq: the case of the Islamic Dawa Party', *Third World Quarterly*, 25(5): 943–54.

Siddiqi, Mohammad Nejatullah (2006), 'Islamic banking and finance in theory and practice: a survey of the state of the art', *Islamic Economic Studies*, 13(2): 1–48.

Thaler, David E., Alireza Nader, Shahram Chubin, Jerrold D. Green, Charlotte Lynch and Frederic Wehre (2010), *Mullahs, Guards, and Bonyads: An Exploration of Iranian Leadership Dynamics*, Santa Monica, CA: Rand Corporation, vol. 878.

Torchia, Andrew (2014), 'Politics, markets complicate Rouhani's rescue of Iran economy', *Financial Times*, Dubai, 1 May.

Wilson, Rodney (1998), 'The contribution of Muhammad Bäqir al-Sadr to contemporary Islamic economic thought', *Journal of Islamic Studies*, 9(1): 46–59.

Wilson, Rodney (2011), 'The Islamic economic doctrine: a comparative study', *International Journal of Islamic and Middle Eastern Finance and Management*, 4(1): 104–6.

Wilson, Rodney (2012), *Legal, Regulatory and Governance Issues in Islamic Finance*, Edinburgh: Edinburgh University Press, pp. 89–102.

Zarrokh, Ehsan (2010), 'Iranian Islamic banking', *European Journal of Law and Economics*, 29(2): 177–93.

Chapter 9

Abed-Kotob, Sana (1995), 'The accommodationists speak: goals and strategies of the Muslim Brotherhood of Egypt', *International Journal of Middle East Studies*, 27(3): 321–39.

Abu-Bader, Suleiman and Aamer S. Abu-Qarn (2003), 'Government expenditures, military spending and economic growth: causality evidence from Egypt, Israel, and Syria', *Journal of Policy Modelling*, 25(6): 567–83.

Aggour, Sara (2014), 'Al-Sisi targeting 7% GDP growth, 8% unemployment by 2017/2018', *Daily News Egypt*, 20 May.

Assaad, Ragui (2008), 'Unemployment and youth insertion in the labour market in Egypt', in Hanaa Kheir-El-Dinn (ed.), *The Egyptian Economy: Current Challenges and Future Prospects*, Cairo: American University in Cairo Press, pp. 133–78.

Bayoumi, Alaa (2012), 'The many faces of Mohamed Morsi', *Al Jazeera*, Doha, 13 December.

El Dahshan, Mohamed (2012), 'Where will the Muslim Brotherhood take Egypt's economy? Egypt's Islamists scramble to develop economic policy staying within the dictates of religion', *YaleGlobal*, 6 February.

Fahim, Kareem (2013), 'Egypt's birth rate rises as population control policies vanish', *New York Times*, 2 May.

Fahmy, Ninette S. (1998), 'The performance of the Muslim brotherhood in the Egyptian syndicates: an alternative formula for reform?', *Middle East Journal*, 52(4): 551–62.

Habibi, Nader (2012), *The Economic Agendas and Expected Economic Policies of Islamists in Egypt and Tunisia*, Middle Eastern Brief No. 67, Waltham, MA: Crowne Centre for Middle Eastern Studies, Brandeis University.

Heineman, Ben W. (2014), 'General Sisi's greatest enemy: the Egyptian economy', *The Atlantic*, New York, 27 March.

Henderson, Joan C. (2008), 'Representations of Islam in official tourism promotion', *Tourism, Culture and Communication*, 8(3): 135–45.

Khalaf, Roula (2013), 'Morsi adviser blames IMF for delaying Egypt $4.8bn loan agreement', *Financial Times*, Dubai, 9 June.

Leiken, Robert S. and Steven Brooke (2007), 'The moderate Muslim brotherhood', *Foreign Affairs*, 86(2): 107–21.

Löfgren, Hans and Moataz el-Said (2001), 'Food subsidies in Egypt: reform options, distribution and welfare', *Food Policy*, 26(1): 65–83.

Mayer, Ann Elizabeth (1985), 'Islamic banking and credit policies in the Sadat era: the social origins of Islamic banking in Egypt', *Arab Law Quarterly*, 1: 32.

Mouawad, Sherin Galal Abdullah (2009), 'The development of Islamic finance: Egypt as a case study', *Journal of Money Laundering Control*, 12(1): 74–87.

Moustafa, Noha (2014), 'Managed devaluation? The Egyptian pound is continuing to lose ground against the dollar and other currencies', *Al-Ahram*, No. 1198, Cairo, 22 May.

Nazemroaya, Mahdi Darius (2013), 'Egypt's constitutional referendum: did President Morsi hijack democracy?', *Global Research*, Cairo.

Omran, Abdel R. and Farzaneh Roudi (1993), 'The Middle East population puzzle', *Population Bulletin*, 48(1): 1–40.

Ramnarayan, Abhinav (2013), 'Egypt plans to issue *sukuk* in early 2014', *Reuters*, Cairo, 23 May.

Rohac, Dalibor (2013), 'Solving Egypt's subsidy problem', *Cato Institute Policy Analysis*, No. 741, Washington DC, 6 November.

Said, Aly Abd al-Monein and Manfred W. Wenner (1982), 'Modern Islamic reform movements: the Muslim Brotherhood in contemporary Egypt', *Middle East Journal*, 36(3): 336–61.

Salevurakis, John William and Sahar Mohamed Abdel-Haleim (2008), 'Bread subsidies in Egypt: choosing social stability or fiscal responsibility', *Review of Radical Political Economics*, 40(1): 35–49.

Treisman, Daniel (2000), 'The causes of corruption: a cross-national study', *Journal of Public Economics*, 76(3): 399–457.

Wiktorowicz, Quintan (2006), 'Anatomy of the Salafi movement', *Studies in Conflict and Terrorism*, 29(3): 207–39.

Wilson, Rodney (2002), 'Arab government responses to Islamic finance: the cases of Egypt and Saudi Arabia', *Mediterranean Politics*, 7(3): 143–63.

Youssef, Abdel-Rahman and Mostafa Hashem (2014), 'The Nour Party's precarious future', *Sada: Middle East Analysis*, 9 May.

Chapter 10

Alshahrani, Saad A. and Ali J. Alsadiq (2004), 'Economic growth and government spending in Saudi Arabia: an empirical investigation', IMF Working Paper, WP/14/3, Washington DC, p. 5.

Al-Suhaimi, Jammaz (2001), 'Consolidation, competition, foreign presence and systemic stability in the Saudi banking industry', Background Paper 128, Bank for International Settlement, Basel.

Ayan, A. H. (2001), 'Halal food with specific reference to Australian exports', *Food Australia*, 53(11): 498–500.

Beblawi, Hazem (1987), 'The rentier state in the Arab world', *Arab Studies Quarterly*, 9(4): 383–98.

Bhuian, Shahid N. (1998), 'An empirical examination of market orientation in Saudi Arabian manufacturing companies', *Journal of Business Research*, 43(1): 13–25.

Bhuian, Shadid N., Eid S. al-Shammari and Omar A. Jefri (1996), 'Organizational commitment, job satisfaction and job characteristics: an empirical study of expatriates in Saudi Arabia', *International Journal of Commerce and Management*, 6(3/4): 57–80.

Bjerke, Bjorn and Abdulrahim al-Meer (1993), 'Culture's consequences: management in Saudi Arabia', *Leadership and Organization Development Journal*, 14(2): 30–5.

Doumato, Eleanor Abdella (1999), 'Women and work in Saudi Arabia: how flexible are Islamic margins?', *Middle East Journal*, 53(4): 568–83.

Doumato, Eleanor Abdella (2003), 'Education in Saudi Arabia: gender, jobs, and the price of religion', in Eleanor Abdella Doumato and Marsha Pripstein Posusney (eds), *Women and Globalization in the Arab Middle East: Gender, Economy, and Society*, Boulder, CO: Lynne Rienner Publishers, pp. 239–58.

Fleischhaker, Cornelius, Martin Hu, Padamja Khandelwal, Jimmy McHugh, Haonan Qu and Niklas Westeiius (2013), 'Saudi Arabia: Selected Issues', IMF, Washington DC, June, pp. 14–22.

Frankel, Jeffrey A. (2006), 'The effect of monetary policy on real commodity prices', Paper No. w12713, National Bureau of Economic Research, Washington DC, pp. 1–41.

Hamdan, Sara (2012), 'Saudi Arabia issues its first sovereign Islamic bond', *New York Times*, 25 January.

Hertog, Steffen (2010), 'Defying the resource curse: explaining successful state-owned enterprises in rentier states', *World Politics*, 62(2): 261–301.

Jaffe, Amy Myers and Steven W. Lewis (2002), 'Beijing's oil diplomacy', *Survival*, 44(1): 115–34.

Kamrava, Mehran (2012), 'The Arab Spring and the Saudi-led counterrevolution', *Orbis*, 56(1): 96–104.

Looney, Robert E. (1990), 'Oil revenues and Dutch disease in Saudi Arabia: differential impacts on sectoral growth', *Canadian Journal of Development Studies/Revue canadienne d'études du développement*, 11(1): 119–33.

Madhi, Salah T. and Armando Barrientos (2003), 'Saudisation and employment in Saudi Arabia', *Career Development International*, 8(2): 70–7.

Miller, Michael B. (2006), 'Pilgrims' progress: the business of the hajj', *Past and Present*, 191(1); 189–228.

Ochsenwald, William (1981), 'Saudi Arabia and the Islamic revival', *International Journal of Middle East Studies*, 13(3): 271–86.

Sarno, Lucio (2000), 'Real exchange rate behaviour in the Middle East: a re-examination', *Economics Letters*, 66(2): 127–36.

Siddiqi, Mohammad Nejatullah (2007), 'Economics of *tawarruq*: how its *mafasid* overwhelm the *masalih*', *Tawarruq* seminar organised by the Harvard Islamic Finance Programme at London School of Economics, London, vol. 1.

Silvey, Rachel (2004), 'Transnational domestication: state power and Indonesian migrant women in Saudi Arabia', *Political Geography*, 23(3): 245–64.

Wilson, Rodney (2006), 'Islam and business', *Thunderbird International Business Review*, 48(1): 109–23.

Chapter 11

Ahmad, Najid, Muhammad Farhat Hayat, Muhammad Luqman and Shafqat Ullah (2012), 'The causal links between foreign direct investment and economic growth in Pakistan', *European Journal of Business and Economics*, 6(1): 20–1.

Ahmed, Habib (2002), 'Financing microenterprises: an analytical study of Islamic microfinance institutions', *Islamic Economic Studies*, 9(2): 27–64.

Alavi, Hamza (1972), 'The state in post-colonial societies: Pakistan and Bangladesh', *New Left Review*, 74(1): 59–81.

Al-Ghafry, Maha, Marwa Saleh and Ziad Kronfol (2012), 'Mental health issues among migrant workers in the Gulf Cooperation Council countries: literature review and case illustrations', Qatar Foundation Annual Research Forum, Doha.

Auwal, Mohammad A. (2010), 'Ending the exploitation of migrant workers in the Gulf', *Fletcher Forum for World Affairs*, 34(2): 87–101.

Brouwer, Roy, Sonia Akter, Luke Brander and Enamul Haque (2007), 'Socioeconomic vulnerability and adaptation to environmental risk: a case study of climate change and flooding in Bangladesh', *Risk Analysis*, 27(2): 313–26.

Burke, Jason (2013), 'Bangladesh factory collapse leaves trail of shattered lives', *The Guardian*, London, 6 June.

Butler, Robert, Lewis Owen and David J. Prior (1988), 'Flash floods, earthquakes and uplift in the Pakistan Himalayas', *Geology Today*, 4(6): 197–201.

Cooray, Arusha (2012), 'The impact of migrant remittances on economic growth: evidence from south Asia', *Review of International Economics*, 20(5): 985–98.

Dale, Angela and Sameera Ahmed (2011), 'Marriage and employment patterns amongst UK-raised Indian, Pakistani, and Bangladeshi women', *Ethnic and Racial Studies*, 34(6): 902–24.

Hardgrave, Robert L. (1993), 'India: the dilemmas of diversity', *Journal of Democracy*, 4(4): 54–68.

Ibrahim, Azeem (2009), *US Aid to Pakistan: US Taxpayers Have Funded Pakistani Corruption*, Cambridge, MA: Belfer Center for Science and International Affairs, John F. Kennedy School of Government, Harvard University, pp. 1–44.

Imai, Katsushi S., Raghav Gaiha, Abdilahi Ali and Nidhi Kaicker (2014), 'Remittances, growth and poverty: new evidence from Asian countries', *Journal of Policy Modelling*, 36(3): 524–38.

Iqbal, Javed, Misbah Nosheen and Ammara Javed (2013), 'The nexus between foreign remittances and inflation: evidence from Pakistan', *Pakistan Journal of Social Sciences*, 33(2): 331–42.

Islam, Nasir (1981), 'Islam and national identity: the case of Pakistan and Bangladesh', *International Journal of Middle East Studies*, 13(1): 55–72.

Jain, Pankaj S. (1996), 'Managing credit for the rural poor: lessons from the Grameen Bank', *World Development*, 24(1): 79–89.

Kudaisya, Gyanesh (1995), 'The demographic upheaval of partition: refugees and agricultural resettlement in India, 1947–67', *Journal of South Asian Studies*, 18(1): 73–94.

Mirza, Hassan and Wilson Prichard (2013), 'The political economy of tax reform in Bangladesh: political settlements, informal institutions and the negotiation of reform', International Centre for Tax and Development Working Paper No. 14, Brighton, pp. 1–42.

Morduch, Jonathan (1999), 'The role of subsidies in microfinance: evidence from the Grameen Bank', *Journal of Development Economics*, 60(1): 229–48.

Rammal, Hussain G. and Lee D. Parker (2013), 'Islamic banking in Pakistan: a history of emergent accountability and regulation', *Accounting History*, 18(1): 5–29.

Riaz, Ali (2004), *God Willing: The Politics of Islamism in Bangladesh*, Lanham, MD: Rowman & Littlefield, pp. 1–36.

Raza, Ali, Urooj Saddique, Umar Farooq, Saqib Awan and Atif Amin (2012), 'Customers' satisfaction towards Islamic banking: Pakistan's perspective', *Arabian Journal of Business and Management Review*, 1(6): 71–9.

Sathar, Zeba, Nigel Crook, Christine Callum and Shahnaz Kazi (1988), 'Women's status and fertility change in Pakistan', *Population and Development Review*, 14(3): 415–32.

Smeaton, Deborah, Maria Hudson, Dragos Radu and Kim Vowden (2010), 'The EHRC triennial review developing the employment evidence base', Policy Studies Institute, London, pp. 151–3.

Wilson, Rodney (2007), 'Making development assistance sustainable through Islamic microfinance', *International Journal of Economics, Management and Accounting*, 15(2): 197–217.

Chapter 12

Abduh, Muhamad and Mohd Azmi Omar (2012), 'Islamic banking and economic growth: the Indonesian experience', *International Journal of Islamic and Middle Eastern Finance and Management*, 5(1): 35–47.

Abdullah, Firdaus Hj. (1997), 'Affirmative action policy in Malaysia: to restructure society, to eradicate poverty', *Ethnic Studies Report*, 15(2): 189–221.

Acharya, Amitav (1997), 'Ideas, identity, and institution-building: from the "ASEAN way" to the "Asia-Pacific way"?', *Pacific Review*, 10(3): 319–46.

Al-Hamarneh, Ala and Christian Steiner (2004), 'Islamic tourism: rethinking the strategies of tourism development in the Arab world after September 11, 2001', *Comparative Studies of South Asia, Africa and the Middle East*, 24(1): 173–82.

Ang, James B. (2008), 'Determinants of foreign direct investment in Malaysia', *Journal of Policy Modelling*, 30(1): 185–9.

Ang, Len and Jon Stratton (1995), 'The Singapore way of multiculturalism: western concepts/Asian cultures', *Sojourn: Journal of Social Issues in Southeast Asia*, 10(1): 65–89.

Anwar, Sajid and Sizhong Sun (2011), 'Financial development, foreign investment and economic growth in Malaysia', *Journal of Asian Economics*, 22(4): 335–42.

Arasaratnam, Sinappah (1969), 'Some notes on the Dutch in Malacca and the Indo-Malayan trade 1641–1670', *Journal of Southeast Asian History*, 10(3): 480–90.

Ariff, Mohamed and Saiful Azhar Rosly (2011), 'Islamic banking in Malaysia: unchartered waters', *Asian Economic Policy Review*, 6(2): 301–19.

Athukorala, Premachandra and Jayant Menon (1995), 'Developing with foreign investment: Malaysia', *Australian Economic Review*, 28(1): 9–22.

Bo, Wu Chong (2005), 'Policy moves for rejuvenating the economy by new Indonesian government and prospects for the future', *Southeast Asian Affairs*, 1: 1–3.

Brown, D. E. (1984), 'Brunei on the morrow of independence', *Asian Survey*, 24(2): 201–8.

Choong, Chee-Keong and Kian-Ping Lim (2009), 'Foreign direct investment, financial development, and economic growth: the case of Malaysia', *Macroeconomics and Finance in Emerging Market Economies*, 2(1): 13–30.

Evers, Hans-Dieter (2003), 'Transition towards a knowledge society: Malaysia and Indonesia in comparative perspective', *Comparative Sociology*, 2: 355–74.

Feith, Herbert (1964), 'President Soekarno, the army and the communists: the triangle changes shape', *Asian Survey*, 4(8): 969–80.

Goodall, Heather (2008), 'Port politics: Indian seamen, Australian unions and Indonesian independence, 1945–47', *Labour History*, 94: 43–68.

Gungwu, Wang (1970), 'Chinese politics in Malaya', *China Quarterly*, 43: 1–30.

Haque, M. Shamsul (2003), 'The role of the state in managing ethnic tensions in Malaysia: a critical discourse', *American Behavioral Scientist*, 47(3): 240–66.

Honna, Jun (1999), 'Military ideology in response to democratic pressure during the late Suharto era: political and institutional contexts', *Indonesia*, 67: 77–126.

Hosen, Nadirsyah (2005), 'Religion and the Indonesian constitution: a recent debate', *Journal of Southeast Asian Studies*, 36(3): 419–40.

Houben, Vincent J. H. (2003), 'Southeast Asia and Islam', *Annals of the American Academy of Political and Social Science*, 588(1): 149–70.

Ibrahim, Anwar (2006), 'Universal values and Muslim democracy', *Journal of Democracy*, 17(3): 5–12.

Ibrahim, Uzaimah, Aishath Muneeza and Rusni Hassan (2012), 'Conflicts facing Islamic banking in Malaysia: dual banking system versus dual legal system', *Australian Journal of Basic and Applied Sciences*, 6(11): 246–51.

Koon, H. E. N. G. (1997), 'The new economic policy and the Chinese community in Peninsular Malaysia', *Developing Economies*, 35(3): 262–92.

Liddle, R. William and Saiful Mujani (2005), 'Indonesia in 2004: the rise of Susilo Bambang Yudhoyono', *Asian Survey*, 45(1): 119–26.

Manan, Wan A. (1999), 'A nation in distress: human rights, authoritarianism, and Asian values in Malaysia', *Journal of Social Issues in Southeast Asia*, 14(2): 359–81.

Ong, Aihwa (1990), 'State versus Islam: Malay families, women's bodies, and the body politic in Malaysia', *American Ethnologist*, 17(2): 258–76.

Purcell, Victor (1947), 'Chinese settlement in Malacca', *Journal of the Malayan Branch of the Royal Asiatic Society*, 20(1): 115–25.

Reid, Anthony (1967), 'Nineteenth century pan-Islam in Indonesia and Malaysia', *Journal of Asian Studies*, 26(2): 267–83.

Robison, Richard and Vedi R. Hadiz (2005), 'Reorganising power in Indonesia: the politics of oligarchy in an age of markets', *Bulletin of Indonesian Economic Studies*, 41(1): 395–6.

Sharma, Subhash C. and Soo Y. Chua (2000), 'ASEAN: economic integration and intra-regional trade', *Applied Economics Letters*, 7(3): 165–9.

Siddique, Sharon and Leo Suryadinata (1981), 'Bumiputra and Pribumi: economic nationalism (Indiginism) in Malaysia and Indonesia', *Pacific Affairs*, 54(4): 662–87.

Siregar, Mulya E. and Nasirwan Ilyas (2000), 'Recent developments in Islamic banking in Indonesia', *Proceedings of the Fifth Harvard University Forum on Islamic Finance: Islamic Finance: Dynamics and Development*, Cambridge, MA: Center for Middle Eastern Studies, Harvard University, pp. 189–96.

Starner, Frances L. (1963), 'Malaysia and the North Borneo territories', *Asian Survey*, 3(11): 519–34.

Thompson, Mark R. (2001), 'Whatever happened to Asian values?', *Journal of Democracy*, 12(4): 154–65.

Vatikiotis, Michael R. J. (1993), *Indonesian Politics under Suharto: Order, Development and Pressure for Change*, London: Routledge, pp. 1–49.

Webber, Douglas (2006), 'A consolidated patrimonial democracy? Democratization in post-Suharto Indonesia', *Democratization*, 13(3): 396–420.

Wilson, Rodney (1998), 'Islam and Malaysia's economic development', *Journal of Islamic Studies*, 9(2): 259–76.

Woo, Wing Thye (2011), 'Understanding the middle-income trap in economic development: the case of Malaysia', World Economy Lecture delivered at the University of Nottingham, Globalization and Economic Policy, pp. 1–12.

Postscript

Burke, Jason (2014), 'The Isis leader's vision of the state is a profoundly contemporary one', *The Observer*, London, 24 August.

Jones, Sam (2014), 'Opaque structure adds to the challenge of defeating ISIS', *Financial Times*, London, 25 August.

INDEX

EU Authorised Representative: Easy Access System Europe Mustamäe tee 5

0, 10621 Tallinn, Estonia gpsr.requests@easproject.com

Printed and bound by CPI Group (UK) Ltd, Croydon, CR0 4YY

16/04/2025

01846988-0001